REPORTAGE PRESS

G000099590

ABOUT THE AUTHOR

OLIVER POOLE first went to Iraq in March 2003 when he crossed the Kuwait border in the back of an American armoured vehicle as the only British daily newspaper reporter 'embedded' with the US Army. Eighteen months later he returned as the *Daily Telegraph*'s newly appointed Iraq correspondent. For two years his home became a hotel room in the middle of Baghdad's 'Red Zone'. He witnessed the bloody impact of car bombs, saw first hand the consequences of the growing sectarian conflict, travelled across Iraq with British and US troops and had his own offices destroyed by a suicide bomber. Finally in November 2006, with the *Telegraph* closing down his office and his Iraqi assistants fleeing the country, he joined the masses escaping Iraq through Baghdad airport.

Born and brought up in London, he was educated at Oxford University. After working for two years at the *South China Morning Post* in Hong Kong, he joined the *Telegraph* Group in 1999 and was appointed West Coast of America correspondent in September 2001. He now lives in Hackney, east London.

His account of the 2003 invasion *Black Knights: On the Bloody Road to Baghdad* was published in November 2003.

Praise for *Black Knights*

'The best reporter's book of the war so far – and it deserves to be one of THE books of the whole Iraqi crisis. The eyewitness accounts of the fighting, the terrible guilt of the soldiers and bystanders at the killing of civilians, the overwhelming confusion, the continuous question of why they are there are exhilarating and chilling' – Robert Fox, *Evening Standard*

"He [Poole] understands the risk of being infected by gung-ho militarism when reporting brutality and stupidity, at the same time tempering this with fellow-feeling for the men on whom his life depends... This is an exhilarating, honest, often scary account of modern war as close-up spectator" – Peter Millar, *Sunday Times*

'A very honest account, devoid of false heroics, and an admirable lesson in how a reporter can share the solidarity of enduring fear and discomfort with troops to whom he owes his survival, but not lose his critical detachment' – Jonathan Steele, *Guardian*

'Poole is a great reporter...possessed of a cool eye, natural sympathy and curiosity, and brisk honesty. He has immortalised them [the Black Knights] in such a true, funny and poignant book' – Patrick Bishop, *Daily Telegraph*

'[Poole's] account of the baptism of fire endured by a US tank company is starkly horrific in places. It is also witty, often laugh-out-loud funny, and spiced with some wonderfully colourful pen-portraits' – *Soldier* magazine

RED ZONE

FIVE BLOODY YEARS
IN BAGHDAD

BY OLIVER POOLE

Oliver Poole

rp

REPORTAGE PRESS

Published by Reportage Press
26 Richmond Way, London W12 8LY United Kingdom
Tel: 0044 (0)7971 461 935
e-mail: info@reportagepress.com
www.reportagepress.com

Copyright © Oliver Poole 2008
All rights reserved. This book is sold subject to the condition that
it shall not, by way of trade or otherwise, be lent, resold, hired out,
or otherwise circulated without the publisher's prior consent in any
form of binding or cover other than that in which it is published
and without a similar condition including this condition being
imposed on a subsequent purchaser. Nor shall this work be
reproduced or stored in an information retrieval system (other than
for purposes of review) without the express permission of the
publisher in writing.
Oliver Poole has asserted his right under the Copyright, Designs
and Patents Act 1988 to be identified as the author of this work

A catalogue record for this book is available from the British
Library.
Hardback: ISBN-13: 978-0-9555729-7-5
Paperback: ISBN-13: 978-0-9558302-5-9
Cover design by Joshua Haymann, Paris.
Printed and bound in Great Britain by Antony Rowe,
Chippenham, Wiltshire, UK
www.antonyrowe.co.uk

*To the memory of Eileen Donald
and the 124 journalists killed so far
during the war in Iraq*

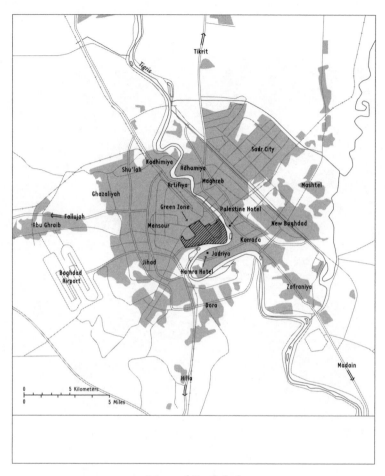

Map of Baghdad

Preface

I recently learned about an internet blog being posted by an Iraqi woman. Its author, Sahar, describes in it how she was woken one morning by the sound of her dog barking. Soldiers were outside and she asked if she could get dressed before they came in, to which they agreed. There were ten of them: three Americans and seven Iraqis. The soldiers began searching her belongings. One of the Americans spotted a cabinet filled with books, many of them in English.

'You read a lot, Ma'am?' the soldier asked.

'Yes, in fact I do,' she answered, speaking in English for the first time.

'What's this?' he said, surprised. 'Heinlein? Asimov? Grisham?'

The American soldier saw a pile of board games and computer CDs. 'You play *Diablo* and *Grand Theft Auto*!' He turned around with a wide grin and for the first time properly looked at her, astonishment in his eyes.

'You can't imagine the look on his face,' Sahar said. 'He was inside a house, with love, a family, like anywhere else. When he looked at me, he didn't see an Iraqi woman in a hijab, he saw a human being.'

For the last few years Baghdad was my home. I was

living there as a foreign correspondent, covering a period when the certainties of life fragmented as a society unravelled. Some of my friends were abducted, others were murdered and a few were simply sent mad from the horror of it all. By the end of my time in Iraq, each morning brought news of the latest mutilated bodies found dumped by the roadside.

Despite the extremity of what was happening to their country, the majority of people I met remained not that different from you or me. They worried for their children; they got stressed about how to pay their bills; they commuted to work; they watched television; they made jokes about their hardships and they tried to maintain good relationships with their spouse and children. Even amid the violence, the normal pattern of life continued. Shops opened, weddings were arranged, students sat exams, babies were born.

This book is, above all else, about human beings. It is about the families in Baghdad who insisted on providing food to a foreign guest even as outside coalition troops and armed gangs fought for control. It is about the US soldiers posted from homes half a world away to a place they were equipped neither to understand nor to help. It is about the British troops sent to do a job for which they never had sufficient numbers. It is, inevitably, also about me: a reporter from London learning the consequences for those on the ground of decisions made by politicians and diplomats in their offices far away in Washington and Whitehall.

I do not seek to explain in detail the intricacies of the policy decisions that shaped the war or the military strategies used during it. Rather my intention is to help people understand more about those anonymous figures – civilian or soldier – shown in news bulletins and newspaper photographs amid the sand, dust and danger of Iraq. The story in these pages is about what it was like to be in such a place, what that did to people and how they reacted. When society breaks down the old rules disappear and each individual becomes free to set their own limits. Many, far too many, used this opportunity as an excuse to explore how low they could go. But not all did. I was in the privileged position of witnessing individuals, many of whom I knew and cared for, deciding that they would not bend to the evil that surrounded them. It was what ultimately made the experience of having lived in Baghdad an unexpectedly inspiring one.

The account that follows is a true story, one motivated by my desire to be an honest witness to the events that occurred. Baghdad was confusing and chaotic, and notes were lost when my office was destroyed by a suicide bomber, but I have tried to make the content of these pages as accurate as possible. Iraq remains a dangerous place and many of those mentioned wish to remain anonymous in case they or their families suffer reprisals as a result of having aided a foreign reporter. I owe them all a debt of gratitude for their assistance and information, and in some cases for having risked their own safety to ensure I was neither kidnapped nor killed. For this and for other reasons, including legal ones, names, some details and occasionally the chronology of events have been changed.

This book is primarily based on what I and my Iraqi interpreters and drivers saw or heard from eyewitnesses that we believed were reliable. The majority of its content comes from the notes I made and the interviews I conducted. While in Iraq I also drew on the articles of other journalists to inform my understanding of what was happening. This book likewise uses the facts and explanations that their hard work and bravery uncovered. I would particularly like to credit the Associated Press, Reuters, Agence France-Presse, the *New York Times*, the *Washington Post*, the *Los Angeles Times*, McClatchy Newspapers, the *Stars and Stripes* and the *Christian Science Monitor*. In addition the book draws on information that appeared in Britain in *The Times*, the *Guardian*, the *Independent* and the *Economist*. For reference I used a number of books, notably *The Assassins' Gate* by George Packer, *Iraq Ablaze* by Zaki Chehab, *The Fall of Baghdad* by Jon Lee Anderson, *State of Denial* by Bob Woodward and *The Longest Night* by Gavin Mortimer, the latter providing much of the detail on London during the Blitz.

At the *Daily Telegraph*, Adrian Blomfield, Anton La Guardia and Jack Fairweather wrote articles that provided indispensable context. I would also like to thank my foreign editor, Alan Philps, for his willingness to send me to Iraq in the first place and his subsequent support in writing this book. The foreign desk team – Alex Spillius, Joe Jenkins, Paul Hill and Patsy Dryden – were always the epitome of professionalism and good humour. Working with them was a privilege that I will not forget.

At Reportage Press, I cannot thank enough Rosie Whitehouse and Charlotte Eagar for believing in this project and guiding it to fruition. The Author's Foundation of the Society of Authors generously provided me with funds that helped create the time to write these pages. My agent, James Gill, consistently provided support and advice.

I would particularly like to express my gratitude to everyone who offered me help in telling this story, particularly Fraser, Miller, Kate White, Norman and my parents, who all went through the manuscripts and provided guidance on improvements. As I start a new chapter in my own life, I would also like to thank my family and friends, including those I have recently met in Penzance, for being there to remind me how much good there is in this world.

Oliver Poole
London
January 2008

1. Genesis

My journey to Iraq started at a pub in Hackney. It was a Saturday night in 2004 and the place was heaving. The barmaids were struggling to keep up with the crush at the bar and some revellers were already drunk enough to start dancing to the jukebox. I was playing pool. Playing well for a change. I was two games in and looking secure in the third. There were a satisfying number of coins lined up on the edge of the table indicating those who would take me on next if my game did not go to pieces. It was near midnight, I had friends around me, and there were enough girls around to hint at possibility. It was a good Saturday night.

I sank a yellow, looked up, saw the people shouting at each other over the cacophony of music and voices, and realised that being there was not going to be enough. I had hoped it would be, had tried to break the habit that for the previous decade sent me back and forth across the world, but I knew at that moment that it was not yet going to happen. All I could think about was not what my next shot would be, who was getting the next round, or even the girl in the corner in her tight black top. It was a conversation that I'd had with my boss the previous day.

He had e-mailed me to come over to his desk and then

asked if I had any concrete plans for the future. I didn't. I had spent the previous two and a half years working in the United States and I had only arrived back in Britain three weeks earlier. I was still trying to find somewhere to live and was dealing with the customs documents that would allow me to retrieve all my belongings from storage. My boss had then asked me whether I fancied going to Baghdad.

I had been there before. I was a journalist and worked as a foreign correspondent for a British newspaper, the *Daily Telegraph*. It was the *Telegraph* that sent me to live in the States. I had arrived in September 2001 a week after the World Trade Center came down. The following months were spent covering the impact of 9/11, criss-crossing the country to ask Americans how their world had changed and their reaction to it. Then, as the drums of war began to beat and Washington marshalled its legions to fight in Iraq, I was assigned to cover a US army company in the 1st Battalion of the 15th US Infantry Regiment, 3rd Infantry Division, which was to be at the forefront of the upcoming invasion force. In March 2003 I crossed the Kuwait border, travelling in the back of one of the unit's armoured vehicles. Seventeen days later I reached Baghdad. It was a bloody and brutal journey. The invasion may have been completed quicker than anyone in the Pentagon or Whitehall dared hope but it was still a merciless experience for those like me who had witnessed the fighting. There were long days advancing under gunfire, mortar attacks, the spectacle of burned cars with corpses hanging out, and then the final push to Baghdad when it seemed that civilians were as likely to be killed as any of Saddam's soldiers.

I was now being asked if I wanted to go back. It was while I was playing pool in Hackney that I realised with utter certainty that I did. I did not actually have much choice. I had to go for the same reason that I had left the States and tried to start afresh in Britain. Even surrounded by people enjoying their Saturday night out, I could not forget the bodies I had witnessed.

I had never seen a corpse before I joined the US troops for their invasion of Iraq. I can remember the first time. It is as clear as if it had just happened. I was in the back of an M88, the armoured pick-up truck that accompanied tanks into combat. We were driving down a road outside Nasariyah, an Iraqi city just north of Kuwait, as the Americans fought to seize a nearby military airstrip in one of the first battles of the war. I was looking out of the back hatch when we rounded a corner and there, by the roadside, were two Iraqis crumpled in a hole in the dirt, their skin crisp and black. A helmet had been fused to the top of one of the dead soldiers' skulls. Lips and eyes could still be made out on what remained of a face, but the eyelids had been burnt clean off, the cornea turned grey by the heat of the explosion that had killed him.

Before we crossed the Kuwait border the American soldiers had been excited at the prospect of putting into effect the skills that they had trained long and hard to master. Tank crews talked about the tickertape parades they expected when they returned to the States, and laughed about which Hollywood actors should play them if a film was made of their coming heroics. By the time we reached Baghdad, no one was joking around. The unit's commanding general had told his men to expect welcome parades from the Iraqis and not to anticipate significant resistance before they reached Saddam's elite units entrenched around Baghdad. What they had received was a very different kind of welcome. From the moment they entered Iraq, US forces were hounded by mortar and sniper fire. Iraqi soldiers cast off their uniforms to attack from the anonymity of crowds of civilians, while members of the Saddam Fedayeen, a paramilitary organisation established to hound the invaders, emerged from sandstorms to fire their rocket-propelled grenades. Those bodies near Nasariyah may have been the first I saw but they certainly were not the last. In Baghdad, at night I heard the screams of the American soldiers as they suffered their nightmares and during the day watched as with ruthless efficiency they hunted down those seeking to kill them.

The Iraqi Ba'ath Party that Saddam led had first emerged in the 1940s as an idealistic organisation committed to working for pan-Arab unity. Its name means renaissance and its founders had hoped that it would bring about a Middle Eastern revival by ending foreign control of its lands, introducing economic modernisation and easing the worst suffering of the poor through a mass of socialist initiatives. After Saddam seized control of Iraq in July 1979 it had not experienced a renaissance. The Ba'ath Party became a body that did not look after Iraq's citizens but oppressed them. Its leadership was purged of any who would not bend to Saddam's will and the security apparatus he created snuffed out opposition with a mixture of intimidation and torture. Saddam dominated the party and through it he dominated the Iraqi people, leading them into a catastrophic war against Iran in the 1980s and then into the

1991 invasion of Kuwait that united almost the whole world against him. Now he had led them to his downfall.

On the 9th April 2003 Saddam fled Baghdad and went into hiding while his state buildings were occupied by US troops and his statues were pulled down across the city. America had invaded with two official aims: to remove the Ba'athist regime and to uncover the weapons of mass destruction that Washington and London believed Saddam was stockpiling. The first of these had been achieved: Iraq's leaders were now either dead or scattered. Few of the American soldiers I was with expected it to be long before the first chemical or biological weapons were uncovered. It was difficult to doubt their existence if you had been wearing chemical weapon protection suits since first crossing the Kuwait border and had spent weeks before the invasion drilling how to don a gas mask in the shortest time possible. The soldiers in my unit had been promised that the weapons of mass destruction were there, believed they had fought to ensure that they were never used, and now presumed that all there was left to do was locate and secure them. This was not expected to take more than a couple of months and so they were talking as if the war was won. In late April 2003, I said my goodbyes and was flown out of Baghdad airport in the hold of a C-130 military transport plane.

Life in the States had been less enjoyable after I returned from Iraq. I found myself feeling lonely. I had friends but it was not home and that was where I felt I needed to be in order to put all I had seen behind me. So I asked to be reassigned to London – moved back to the *Telegraph*'s newsroom in Canary Wharf – where my plan was to start afresh and enjoy the delights of normality.

Back in Britain, however, I still could not forget those bodies. It was not only the sight of them, the ease with which a person's life could be snuffed out, but also the way they reproached me for what I had been thinking in the days before the war started while I was in the Kuwaiti desert waiting for the order to invade. My primary concern had not been whether the war was right or wrong but merely whether it would happen. I was excited and naive and had not considered whether those in positions of power might either have deceived me or could be able to misinterpret the situation in Iraq so badly. What I knew was that I was going to be covering a massive story, be a reporter in the right place at the right time, and that was what I had wanted more than anything else.

The war did not end when those statues of Saddam came down. The weapons of mass destruction were never found and pockets of stubborn resistance emerged as the invading armies became forces of occupation. Rebellion was met by military suppression. Barely a day seemed to pass without reports of the latest victims of the violence. The difficulty in using Western armies to force an Arab country to run on Western precepts was becoming clear. Since I had left Baghdad there had been thousands more bodies; thousands more corpses that would not have looked dissimilar to the ones I had seen lying on the roadside by that army base outside Nasariyah. This was why I wanted to go back. I needed to know if anything worthwhile could result from the deaths I had witnessed; if those lives had been lost for a reason that could ever be justified. Knowing the answer to that would hopefully let me move on in my life and start to forget.

I arrived in Baghdad a month later, a year almost to

the day since I had last been there. I was not due to start my new post until the beginning of the following year but it was considered sensible for me to see the situation on the ground before I started. I flew to Jordan on 25 April 2004, and the next day caught the plane that took me back to Iraq.

The best way into Baghdad was on board Royal Jordanian Airlines. No one I knew in the UK could quite believe that I could simply fly into Baghdad on a commercial jet. However, Jordan's ruling monarch, keen for his country to establish itself as the preferred entry point for the international companies selected to spend the billions of US dollars earmarked by Washington for the reconstruction of Iraq, had instructed its national airline to start running two flights a day.

Some Westerners were still risking the land route, the road from Amman that passed through the Sunni city of Ramadi and on into the Iraqi capital. Even at that relatively early stage of the conflict it was a foolhardy thing to do. Only a fortnight before I arrived in Baghdad a British reporter from *The Times* and his American colleague had had the tyres of their car shot out and been bundled into a waiting car. I was later told that it was the internet that helped secure their freedom. Their abductors googled their names and learned that they really were bona fide reporters rather than spies. They were fortunate to have been captured by Iraqis who were still willing to accept there was a difference.

They were the last reporters I know of who took that road. Within weeks, whatever Washington or London may have claimed, the Sunni heartland was unambiguously in open revolt as people's anger erupted at the affront to their dignity of their loss of sovereignty. The only non-uniformed Westerners still driving the road were the security contractors who ran the convoys that ferried supplies to the American bases spread across the desert of Western Iraq. These were employees of private firms, mostly American and British, hired by the US government to supplement the work being done by its military. Though civilians, most of them were ex-forces and their convoys resembled something out of a *Mad Max* film. The lorries were stripped down for speed, festooned with strapped-on armour, had machine guns pinned to the top, front and back, and had armed men in every cab. They went fast and did all they could to avoid stopping. The primary principle for survival most adopted was to treat anything suspicious as hostile, and if in doubt deploy maximum force. According to the Iraqis, cars that got in their way were fortunate if they received a couple of rounds in the engine chassis rather than through the windscreen.

Travelling into Iraq by plane was a very different experience. The destination may have been Baghdad, but the crew's studious commitment to normal airline custom made me feel I could have been on my way to Brussels rather than to the most dangerous city on earth. Two perfectly made-up South African stewardesses, resplendent in their Royal Jordanian uniforms, used their most dazzling smiles to greet the procession of hacks and security contractors climbing on board. The Fokker F28 we were flying in had blue leather seats and a free magazine to read. Once we were up in the air, a trolley appeared and was wheeled down the aisle to provide drinks. A meal was served.

It was an hour and twenty minutes into the flight when the descent began. Suddenly things were not so routine. The Americans could only guarantee that roughly a square mile around the airport was cleared of those who might want to shoot down an approaching aircraft. It was a tight space to keep a plane in as it dropped towards landing, especially one that wanted to get down fast. Sitting in the window seat, I was pushed against the fuselage as the plane banked steeply and the nose dropped into its sharply turning dive. It was then, as we fell into our corkscrew descent, that the streets of Baghdad emerged in front of me.

It is a view stuck indelibly in my brain. This was the city that, a century after the time of the Prophet Mohammad, had become the centre of the Islamic world, the capital of its governing Caliphate and the setting for Scheherazade and her tales of Ali Baba. It had survived being ransacked by the Mongols in the 13th century, absorbed the Ottomans when they came two hundred years later, and been host to the British when they marched in during the First World War. It was at least 1,200 years old and was lived in by seven million people. It was now to become my home.

No people were visible from that height, only ordered lines of streets and the loop of the Tigris river throwing off reflections in the sunlight as it casually meandered its way south. Rows of buildings disappeared into the shrub desert that marked the city's outer edges. There were the minarets of the mosques, the remnants of Baghdad's ancient defensive wall, the lines of bushes just visible along the largest avenues and the flash of green that marked the city's park with its lake and clusters of eucalyptus trees. Looking down, I could imagine Baghdad the way elderly Iraqis described it as being before Saddam Hussein's grip got too tight; still that sedate place where couples courted in the shade of palm fronds on the banks of the Tigris and friends wiled away afternoons playing backgammon in a tea house off a side road in Karrada. Baghdad looked serene. The shock of that, I think, is what helped make the sight of it so memorable.

As we flew lower the outlines of Saddam's palaces emerged with their ornate domes and ceremonial battlements. I could make out Ba'athist statues: the Monument to the Unknown Soldier, with its raised copper sphere symbolising a shield dropped from the dying grasp of an Iraqi warrior, and the Martyr's Monument, its split blue dome sheltering an eternal flame. The airport appeared in my line of sight, the US transport planes lined up on its runways like a row of grey metallic cigar cases. Around the terminal spread thousands of military tents and barrack blocks, the size of the camp filling the view through my window and providing the first tangible clue as to the scale of the operation being played out there.

The ground was close now, close enough that I could make out the soldiers unlucky enough to have been assigned to the top hatches of the military Humvees on the surrounding roads, yet the plane still seemed to be standing on its wing tip. At the last moment it shuddered as the flaps were lowered to force the final, acutest turn. We levelled out and the wheels touched tarmac.

As we taxied to the terminal I saw a DHL transport plane with scorch marks down one wing, the result of a missile attack that had hit it shortly after take-off five months earlier. We passed the main airport building, its façade still showing the battle damage from the fight to secure it the previous year.

'We've now landed at Baghdad International Airport,' the stewardess said over the Tannoy system. 'I hope you enjoy your stay and will choose to fly with Royal Jordanian again soon.'

Unexpectedly, I did enjoy my stay. Baghdad was on the turn and Western civilians were getting killed (four, in fact, while I was there) but it was still recognisable as a functioning city. I went out to restaurants at night, stayed late at parties, visited shops, drove outside Baghdad and even walked down streets after dark – the simple pleasures of life that within a year were too dangerous to risk. There was still hope, not only among the American and British soldiers and officials, the vast majority of whom seemed to have no doubt they were going to win, but even among many Iraqis, who remained pleased Saddam had gone and were excited about the possibilities the future held.

The intended focus of my visit was a British security firm, Arawn Security Management. This firm and the other civilian military outfits operating in Iraq were controversial because they were the hired guns who had been brought in to do the jobs too menial or too messy for the soldiers stationed in the American-led coalition to take on. Their supporters maintained that their presence was essential because, it was said, there were not enough troops to stabilise Iraq without them. Their critics called them 'mercenaries' and highlighted that they were not directly under the power of a sovereign government and were less tightly controlled by the rules and customs that guided soldiers at war. It was a debate made urgent by the scale of these organisations' contribution to the Americans' reconstruction project. Thirty security companies were in Iraq with twenty thousand people on their books, which made them the second largest force after the Americans, twice as big a presence as the British.

Arawn's personnel met me at the airport. This was fortunate because they knew their business as far as personal protection was concerned and at that point I had no idea what I ought to be doing to try to keep myself alive. They gave me a bullet-proof vest and helmet, sat me in the back of a car with windows made of reinforced glass, and made sure I was flanked by two enormous Fijians, both armed with folding stock AK-47s. The car itself was a navy blue Nissan that had a dent down the side and was in urgent need of a wash. It looked in the same condition as almost every other vehicle in Iraq, which was entirely the point.

As we pulled onto the airport road I learned my first lessons about how to travel around Baghdad, all of which remained as pertinent during my final days in that country almost three years later as they were then on what was almost my first.

The most inescapable of these lessons was that in Iraq no one cared about official traffic rules. This was not a new development. Pile-ups had been a routine occurrence during Saddam's time. The Iraqis' imperative was to try to keep moving forward whatever might be in front. This was done by driving down the wrong side of the street, ignoring traffic signals, going the wrong way around roundabouts and accelerating as fast as possible whenever they found a clear stretch of road. Iraqis were particularly proud of their road anarchy. One later told me that he considered his countrymen the best drivers in the world because no one from anywhere else would be able to navigate Baghdad's streets successfully. He was almost as proud of the fact that he had never bothered to take a driving test but instead bribed the official responsible to obtain the necessary documentation.

The second lesson was that any opportunity to go fast for any distance, which in Baghdad was anything more than 20 mph, happened very rarely. The city was almost always on the verge of total gridlock. This was partly because no one obeyed the rules of the road, making every junction a battle of wills, but it was also because the war was resulting in lanes shut off, bridges bombed and army checkpoints set up where guards would insist on searching passing vehicles for illegal weaponry. More and more streets were closed as the war went on. Within a year I risked spending hours each day stuck in traffic, not going anywhere and with only the hope that my dark hair and the Iraqi clothing I wore to obscure my identity would be enough to stop someone looking through the window and recognising a foreigner.

The third lesson was the most important. This was the never-to-be-broken rule that if an American military patrol drove past, you pulled into the side of the road and stopped. These patrols had signs in English and Arabic strapped to the front of the leading vehicle telling Iraqis they risked experiencing 'lethal force' if they either failed to keep a distance of one hundred yards or did not park and turn their cars away from the passing convoy. As these signs were normally too small for anyone to read at a distance of a hundred yards, and as the people of Iraq had had no prior experience of being in the midst of an occupying force, it was the litany of deaths that the first few months of the war brought which had primarily made sure people understood the urgency of keeping out of the Americans' way.

Steve Myers, a journalist I knew at the *New York Times*, told of a car caught up in the violence of Baghdad during that time. The car had been in the middle of a highway when a truck had driven at an American column, a gun mounted on its back. The US soldiers had directed a hail of bullets at it, sending the truck careering across the central crash barriers and into the stranded car, causing it to burst into flames. A mother and her three children, the youngest an infant, were badly burned. Her husband, their father, was seen lying by the roadside, barely moving.

By 2004, there was usually no mistaking that a patrol approached. The Americans would sound their horns and a GI would be placed half out of the hatch of the front vehicle to blow a whistle and wave everyone out of the way. If a car did not move fast enough then a rifle might jump to his shoulder, the power of that message being the knowledge that he might just use it. When everything was gridlocked, and no vehicle could possibly be a hundred yards from another, the soldiers would dismount and start shouting in English at people to move. The Iraqis, trapped in their cars, would try to look as meek as possible while not understanding a word of what was being said to them. The thrust of the message, however, was clear and, despite it seeming hopeless, space would still be found, even if cars had to drive almost into the front of shops to let it happen.

Everyone did all they could to get the Americans moving again as it was terrifying when a US patrol was anywhere nearby. It was not only that you never knew if they were going to panic and start shooting. Far more worrying was that you did not know if the patrol you were trapped beside was going to be one of those attacked that day. If it was, then you were going to be the one in the wrong place at the wrong time when that road-side bomb went off. I knew an American aid worker who died like that. She drove down a slip road and found herself beside a line of Humvees at the exact moment when the explosion happened. She was so badly burned the authorities had trouble identifying her body.

The drive from the airport with the team from Arawn was the first time I had properly seen Baghdad. When I was last there, during April 2003 when American tanks started to roll through the city, its streets were empty as people stayed inside to avoid the fighting. Occasionally you would see a car making its way slowly down a highway but it was a rarity. The people in those vehicles would be acutely aware of how exposed this made them and the danger which came with it. White handkerchiefs would be held out of windows to signal that they were not out to cause trouble.

Now, a year later, Baghdad was alive once more. The occupation was ongoing but people still needed to work and shop so the streets were bustling. Taxis with their dirty orange-painted bonnets and boots touted for passengers. Youths dragged wonky carts piled high with sacks of grain. A boy led a donkey laden with baskets of wood. At one point we followed a flock of sheep around a roundabout. Restaurants had posters outside showing luridly coloured kebabs. Photograph shops displayed portraits of chubby babies. Cigarettes, fizzy drinks, fruit, rolls of cloth, electrical appliances and cans of petrol were stacked in shop fronts. Shelves were filled with gold-plated bracelets and earrings. There were towers of water bottles, racks overflowed with newspapers and magazines, kitchen equipment spilled out onto pavements.

Baghdad is primarily a concrete city, the box-like buildings resembling above all the Soviet style commonly found in parts of Eastern Europe, though with walls stained a dirty yellow by sand and dust. Saddam's close ties with the Soviet Union had led to thousands of East Germans and Poles coming to Baghdad in the 1970s to build a modern city paid for by Iraq's oil money. A few apartment blocks boast touches reflecting the country's heritage, the occasional Assyrian-style bas-relief incongruously etched onto a wall, but most ornamentation is determinedly twentieth century: typically modernist in style with concrete triangles or zigzag motifs. Balconies consist of intricate designs of connecting rhomboids and doors are inlaid with friezes of ever-diminishing circles.

It was not the buildings, however, which most demanded my attention on that journey, but the people. They were everywhere, filling the pavements and spreading out onto the roads. Most of the women had covered their heads with an Islamic headscarf, called the hijab, but not all of these were coloured black. There were yellow ones, blue ones, cream ones and patterned ones consisting of a mix of purples and reds. Some did not even wear a hijab at all but instead boasted the pleated power jackets and bouffant hairstyles not seen in the West since the 1980s. Most men were dressed in ankle-length robes but jazzier types sported Turkish shirts with long pointed collars and garish stripes. Clusters of children in their school uniforms took over sections of the pavement, the boys in blue shorts and clean white shirts and the girls in long skirts and pleated blouses. Exercise books were clutched to their chests or satchels dragged behind them.

I had read about the money pouring in to finance reconstruction and had expected forests of cranes working to build a new city. Instead there was no sign of any building at all and the poverty of the place was inescapable. It was partly the age of everything: the battered cars, the fading paint on shop signs and the rusting air-conditioning units sticking out of buildings. However, it was also the rubbish that abounded. The streets were thick with it. Even in the car I could smell the filth as it rotted in the heat. Sometimes there would be a break in the lines of houses where a wasteland was piled high with rubbish bags. Almost every ditch was littered with packing cases and plastic bottles. Sewage ran along the edge of pavements where street children hawked confectionery or domestic bric-a-brac.

Not even the damage caused by the war had been repaired. Street lights bent double by tanks lay untouched. There were bullet holes in the walls of buildings. At a street corner, one of the Fijians sitting beside me indicated where the pavement had been destroyed by a bomb that had recently killed a Western businessman. A crater and shattered bricks competed with potholes to mark the spot. We passed the sites targeted by the air bombardment that the US had intended would both shock and awe. The attacks were so precise that the buildings next to them appeared completely undamaged, whilst the targets themselves lay crumpled like a collapsed house of cards, the shattered layers of each floor lying one on top of the other amid the skeleton of a few obstinately unbowed supports.

We drove through a wealthy residential area. It was quieter there, the energy gone and the houses hidden behind high walls. Many boasted intricate hedges with bushes cut into the shape of animals or geometrical designs. We then turned onto an avenue that followed the banks of the Tigris. It was late in the afternoon so the sun had softened and the river was at its most beautiful. A woman was doing her washing. The Fijian on my left pointed her out to me, and then gave a grunt to make clear how filthy he considered the water.

Our objective was a side entrance into the Green Zone, the great fortress in the centre of Baghdad that housed the administrators sent from Washington with instructions to turn Iraq into a Western-style democratic state. They had taken over the buildings that had formed the administrative heart of Ba'athist rule, set up their offices and ringed the site with blast walls and concertina wire to keep out those who wanted to stop them. The checkpoint at the entrance that we approached was manned by half a dozen American soldiers. A tank, its gun barrel pointing down the road towards us, was stationed behind them. As we drew close a soldier raised his palm to tell us to stop and then came over, his hands gripping his rifle, to demand identification. A plastic ID card was shown to him and we were waved through into a parallel world.

At the checkpoint there had been cars queuing as

Iraqis with grievances tried to persuade the troops to let them pass in the hope that they might be able to address their cases personally to one of Iraq's American rulers. Many had files of paper they waved in front of the soldiers' faces. Others were trying to explain in halting English exactly why they deserved compensation for some loss. None of them were getting anywhere. The soldiers, nervous of possible suicide bombers and not enjoying a shift exposed in the centre of Baghdad, kept back the cars with hand signals and the pedestrians with an occasional shove. Inside the Green Zone, however, it was calm and for the first time since I had left the airport I felt safe. The Fijians flicked the safety catches on their Kalashnikovs and the man sitting in the front passenger seat, a Zimbabwean who had not spoken since we started our journey as he scanned the road ahead for dangers, turned around and asked me if I was a fan of cricket.

In the rest of Baghdad cars had looked like they were held together by love and a few pieces of string but in the Green Zone we passed lines of brand new Chevrolet Suburbans, every single one of them presumably brought in specially from the States. I saw a jogger running in a grey army T-shirt and a group of American soldiers wandering to one of the mess halls who were not even wearing helmets. In the shade of a tree a man in slacks was sitting reading a book, seemingly without a care in the world.

The Green Zone's name was a designation set by the military. It means a secured area. A zone that has not been secured, which in Baghdad meant almost every other part of the city, is called the Red Zone. Some reporters did not like the artificial atmosphere of

Baghdad's Green Zone but there was no denying its classification was deserved. Mortar rounds were thrown into it and suicide bombs detonated at its entrances but at no point while I was in Iraq was there a significant breach of its perimeter. Compared to what was happening in the rest of Baghdad, it was secure. Inside the Green Zone I felt protected and it never ceased to amaze me how a semblance of order was maintained however bad things became outside. There were speed bumps and traffic signs. Military police would come up and berate those driving too fast. Lawns were mowed. The lighting worked.

The Green Zone was also big. I quite routinely became lost. You could drive around it for almost an hour and still not see everything. A dozen blocks of central Baghdad had been sealed off to house administrators, diplomats, military commanders, Western security companies and US troops. It had its own helicopter landing pad, a shopping complex, military messes, a hotel, private restaurants, a State Department bar, gyms and even a radio station. The British Army had its own base within it, located in the complex of buildings where Saddam was said to have previously housed his mistresses. They were pleased with that. It was why, the British maintained, they had secured some of the most comfortable accommodation on the entire site.

At the heart of the Green Zone was Saddam's Republican Palace. This was where Iraq's most senior US administrators had set up their headquarters. It also housed Arawn's office and it was therefore to the Republican Palace that we now drove. By its main entrance was a car park in which more than two hundred vehicles must have been stationed. We stopped, climbed out of the car and walked towards what had been the heart of the Ba'athist regime. Stretching up six floors and arched in a quarter-circle, the palace's roof was capped by two forty-foot-high bronze busts of Saddam dressed in a traditional Islamic helmet. The building had been spared during the American bombing campaign as it was thought to hold important documentation. It had not, however, escaped the looting which followed Saddam's defeat. That was so thorough that even some of the palace's heavy gilded doors disappeared.

We walked through the main entrance and into bedlam. There were people everywhere. Some were in full combat gear, others in the bureaucrats' fatigues of blue shirt and tan chinos. American soldiers and marines, Brits, even an Italian soldier, rushed past me. There were Romanian and Polish troops; Australians in their uniform with its incongruous bubbly-shaped camouflage design. Gurkha guards were dressed in tan jackets and floppy-rimmed hats. They had been hired by the private security firm that protected the palace and were desperately trying to maintain a semblance of order.

I was led through the throng and along a particularly ornate passage, up some stairs, across a room where figures stared at laptops and a Coldplay song played through a computer, then into a vast chamber that must have once acted as a reception room. A chandelier hung from the ceiling and a mural covered one wall. It was presumably of Saddam but its subject's face was hidden by rough brush marks of black paint. In one corner a dozen sleeping GIs lay on the floor. I passed a shiny black door behind which, I was told, were the offices of the

Green Zone's most senior official, Ambassador Paul L. Bremer III, and was then led down a stairway. There was a memorial to the victims of 11 September 2001, a sign of how, in people's perception, Iraq had become linked to the events of that day despite the absence of evidence that Saddam was in any way involved. The two towers of the World Trade Center were depicted and above them the words: 'Thank God for the Coalition Forces and Freedom Fighters at Home and Abroad.'

We passed a mess hall in which scores of soldiers with rifles slung over their shoulders lined up to eat. In the larger rooms wooden partitions had been erected to provide temporary offices. Military canvas cots were placed beside desks. People were sleeping while others worked only yards away.

Another door was opened and we stepped outside into the sunlight. We rounded a corner and in front of me was a vast kidney-shaped swimming pool with a multi-level diving platform and a stone cabin that acted as a pool house. The water was perfectly blue. Soldiers in swimming trunks were doing back flips off the high board. Women lazed on recliners in bikinis. It was like walking into a holiday brochure. I was told it was time for a swim. There was clearly to be no work that day.

'You should've been here last Thursday,' one of the Arawn guys, an Australian called Mike, said to me. 'At ten at night there must've been four hundred people here, dancing and swimming, when two mortars came over. Everyone stopped, and then someone shouted, "It didn't hit me. Party on!"'

2. The Hands of Victory

The next day I received the Green Zone tourist treatment. Two of Arawn's employees were assigned to show me around, the Australian Mike and a Glaswegian former marine called Danny who had a handlebar moustache and a delight in finding fault with the English. They revelled in the opportunity to take time from their daily routine to see what entertainment was on offer.

We started with breakfast at the site's Burger King, a restaurant which operated out of a converted lorry and had been sent to Iraq to supply soldiers who were hungry for home. We then visited the 130-foot Hands of Victory triumphal arches dedicated by Saddam in 1990 to mark his 'victory' over Iran. Shaped like two pairs of crossed swords, they were surrounded by five thousand Iranian helmets taken from the battlefields of the Iran–Iraq war, most set into the ground for Iraqi troops to walk over as a symbol of their foes' humiliation. Many still showed the hole made by the bullet that had killed their original owners. A group of Iraqi guards let us climb inside the arches after we gave them $10 to bend the no trespassing rules. They then charged another $5 to take a photograph of us looking out from the top.

In the afternoon we visited the palace where Saddam's

son Uday had lived, a building which had three lions housed in the back garden in an iron cage covered by wire mesh. Uday – reputed to have turned into a full-blown psychopath after a failed assassination attempt left him impotent – was widely believed to have enjoyed throwing his enemies into the cage to see them torn apart. Some Iraqis claimed that the largest lion used to have a gold chain around its neck and prisoners were told that if they could remove it, and get out alive, they would be set free.

The lions did not look particularly forbidding when I saw them. In fact they looked more tragic than terrifying. I could see shoulder bones through their emaciated flesh as they sat looking dispirited in the shade of an over-hanging tree. A South African vet turned up with a dead donkey for their dinner and he threw it into the cage. That succeeded in rousing them and they went at the carcass with notable fervour.

The vet told us it was his job to look after the animals left at Baghdad zoo and, as no one else knew how to care for them, Uday's pets had fallen under his remit. The lions had apparently suffered terribly in the first weeks of the war when, with Baghdad in chaos, they had not been fed and had almost died from malnutrition. Plans were being drawn up to have them released into the wild in Africa. In the meantime the vet provided their daily meal and tran-quillised them when the cage needed to be cleaned. No human bones had yet been found, he assured us.

The vet's time in Iraq had not left him impressed with the average American soldier. He recounted how he had lost one of the lions housed at the zoo after a pair of bullish GIs decided to pay a visit. One stuck his hand through the railings and a lion had fastened its jaws around it. He only got free after his buddy shot the animal through the skull with his pistol. US High Command had apparently declared the zoo out of bounds when another group of soldiers threw a dog over the fence to watch the lions hunt down and eat it.

That evening we visited Mike and Danny's favourite restaurant in the Green Zone. It was a Chinese place, established amid the shell of a looted Ba'athist villa, some of its windows still broken and most of its rooms empty or covered in dirt and litter. There was a courtyard in front on which stood groups of plastic chairs and a few tables. To try to brighten up the place a line of red paper lanterns had been hung off a piece of rope to one side, but their colour had faded almost to white from the daytime sun and as a result they looked more forlorn than cheerful.

A solitary waitress took orders dressed in jeans and a Disney T-shirt. I could not see why Mike and Danny were so keen on it, although there was an intriguing smell of exotic spices and sizzling meat coming from the kitchen. The food was tasty enough, particularly the beef in oyster sauce, but it was when they began talking about a Chinese masseuse plying her trade in one of the restaurant's back rooms that I thought I might finally have cracked the secret of its appeal. Neither would go into details about what sort of service she offered so I could not determine if she was simply a masseuse or if this was a money-making venture selling extras to the Green Zone's sex-starved security industry. Either way she was clearly one of the main attractions and all those I met that night were insistent about what a kind person she was, which only deepened the mystery as to her true profession.

From their time in the forces, Mike and Danny knew half a dozen of the other contractors eating there and they introduced me to them. They were a motley bunch with their tattoos, penchant for shaved heads and the obligatory pistols strapped around their waists. It took them time to stop viewing me with a mixture of distaste and mistrust, but when they did they delighted in recounting horror stories involving some of the smaller security companies working in Iraq. I learnt that many contractors were required by their employers to drive around in bullet-proof 4x4s. Instead of being made safer by these vehicles' armour, their size and modernity made them stand out amid the rusting saloons that filled Baghdad's streets, a conspicuousness which invited the attention of every jihadist in the area. As a result, those riding in them often concluded that it was prudent to take shots at any car that got too close just in case those in it might be out to kill them.

Although all Mike and Danny's friends had a military pedigree, I learnt that this was not obligatory for those undertaking their line of work in Baghdad. There were firms that they respected, and consequently worked for, but the more amateurish outfits would apparently take on almost anyone willing to brave Iraq's dangers. It was because they could pay these employees less, I was told, making their bids more competitive when contracts were put out for tender. This was deflating wages in the industry, which might partly have explained their rancour. Mike and Danny knew of contractors whose only previous experience in security work was as night watchmen at office blocks in the States. An Italian security contractor who had been kidnapped and then murdered earlier that month had as his qualifications merely that he was a military reservist who liked doing martial arts in his spare time.

These were the kind of people, I was told, operating in Baghdad with their guns and nervous trigger fingers. They were working on site security, guarding convoys, delivering supplies or protecting visiting businessmen. As employees of military security firms, none were under Central Military Command therefore and neither could be court-martialled nor bound by the Geneva Convention. Under a law issued by Iraq's American administrators those working on government contracts could not be tried for murder if they killed someone. It sounded as if a new Wild West was being created.

Although Arawn operated in the same questionable legal sphere, it was one of the more reputable organisations. It was a security firm that sought to mirror the practices of the British military with comparable methods and required standards of conduct. There were rules of engagement and an emphasis on discipline. Its employees had served in the Army, many in elite regiments or the special forces, so such behaviour came naturally to them, indeed made them feel at home. No one was hired unless someone in the company could provide a personal recommendation as to their suitability, which helped promote a camaraderie of purpose. Most were now in their late thirties or forties, experienced heads back for one last big payday, only too aware that they were as reliant on the professionalism of others in the organisation as on their own if they were to stay alive.

That was probably why the company had invited me to spend time with them. The owners knew its employees were not trigger-happy cowboys and wanted to get that message across, presumably in the hope that if there was a backlash against the private military companies working in Baghdad they might avoid being discredited by the behaviour of others. Graham, the cricket-loving Zimbabwean who had driven with me from the airport, even argued that they were better suited for the job to be done in Iraq than the young men in the military. 'We're better trained,' he told me. 'We're older and we've got families at home we want to get back to.' Or, as one of his colleagues bluntly put it, they would not panic when things turned nasty. 'Old warriors like us already know that war doesn't bring flowers but death and bullets, and that you'll lose good friends.'

Despite the repeated reminders from those I met at Arawn about how controlled and professional they were, it was nevertheless clear they were enjoying themselves in Iraq. While primarily attracted by the £650-a-day paycheques, most of them could not believe their luck that the war had come along to save them from lives that had seemed humdrum compared to their time in the military. Mike had been stuck organising security at the Athens Olympics when the call came from a former colleague suggesting he join the company. Danny had been unable to reintegrate into civilian life and had left Scotland to live barefoot in an Aboriginal village in northern Australia. Others had been glorified drivers for rich businessmen in the UK or reduced to being hired hands to keep the paparazzi away from pop stars.

They were now allowed to be soldiers once more and had new war stories to prove it. Mike and Danny described with joy how over Christmas they were guarding government offices in Hilla, a city south of Baghdad located near the ruins of ancient Babylon. They were attacked along one side of the complex's perimeter. Mortars had come in and the night had been illuminated by muzzle flashes as they fought for forty minutes to hold the ground while waiting for the nearest foreign troops, a Polish contingent, to arrive and drive their attackers away.

One of their favourite stories was about an incident shortly after that firefight. A taxi had drawn up outside their base in Hilla and a 23-year-old Swedish backpacker dressed in a T-shirt and sunglasses stepped out, asking if anyone knew where the ruins of Babylon were. She had apparently crossed the Turkish border into Kurdistan and come down to see the sights. They stuck her on the next military plane out of the country. 'Silly cow,' was Mike's view. 'Good tits though,' was Danny's.

Spring 2004 was the era of the Coalition Provisional Authority (or the CPA as everyone called it), the governing body designated by the United Nations, but established by the Americans, which from April 2003 to June 2004 ran Iraq like a colonial administration. It was staffed primarily by foreigners, controlled all aspects of the state and had been given the responsibility of building a new Iraq. This would be a country, the White House said, that would be secular and modern, a beacon of democracy in the Middle East.

Later it became clear that the likelihood of the CPA having ever been able to turn this aspiration into reality had been greatly reduced by the fact it had largely been made up of the wrong people doing the wrong things at the wrong time. Point-scoring between the US Defence and State Departments meant that the Pentagon, which

President Bush made responsible for the CPA, chose to exclude the experienced Iraqi hands in the State Department from the reconstruction process. Donald Rumsfeld, the Secretary of Defence, thought Colin Powell, the Secretary of State, too liberal so sought to limit his influence over Iraq by preventing his people from having involvement in it. Political ideology was as important as practical experience in determining who the Pentagon sent to Baghdad. Republican Party-supporting youths fresh out of Harvard Business School were hired to help establish a new country. A 25-year-old was overseeing the creation of a stock market and another the same age was helping write the interim constitution while filling out his law school application.

At the CPA's head was Paul Bremer, a man who had never been to Iraq prior to his appointment and gave every indication of wanting to have as little meaningful contact as possible with Iraqis while there. Looking like an American celebrity divorce lawyer with his white teeth, tailored suits and carefully combed hair, he would be helicoptered around the country for photo opportunities at a newly built school or hospital before returning as quickly as he could to the security of the Green Zone. His intent seemed to be to change as much as possible in a short period of time in order to shock Iraq into becoming the modern, Western-leaning state the White House demanded. Iraq was being taken apart so it could be rebuilt to American specifications. Laws were changed and legal procedure overhauled. State-owned businesses were privatised, Ba'athist institutions closed down and tariffs slashed.

Two decisions Bremer made in the first few weeks after his appointment in May 2003 proved to be the most momentous in determining Iraq's future because they contributed in particular to creating the Sunni insurgency that emerged to resist the American occupation. It was Bremer who issued the proclamation that disbanded the Iraqi army, thereby sending thousands of trained troops to their homes with guns but no pensions, and who initiated the de-Ba'athification process that removed hundreds of senior and middle-level Ba'ath party members from government jobs, many of them civil servants and school teachers, even though a significant number had been party members solely for career advancement rather than ideological conviction.

Sunnis were the Iraqis most affected by these decisions because of the nature of Saddam's state. Saddam did not trust the Shia, particular after the Shia in southern Iraq launched an uprising against his rule following Iraq's defeat in the 1991 Gulf War, so often excluded them from government posts. Sunnis and Shia are both Muslims but separate sects within Islam. Although there are rarely outward indications to distinguish between them, their doctrinal differences date back to the death of the Prophet Mohammad in AD 632 and the conflicting viewpoints as to who should have been his successor as leader of the Muslim community. Mohammad had never stated clearly who should lead the movement after he died and this led to a disagreement that has divided the sects ever since. The Sunnis say that the Prophet's successor was best selected by popular consensus from amongst his closest companions. The Shia maintain that Mohammad wanted his successor to be his cousin and son-in-law, Ali ibn Abi Talib, and that the community's leadership should subsequently have remained within the Prophet's bloodline.

31

It was one of Mohammad's companions, Abu Bakr, rather than one of his relatives who received the leadership after the Prophet's death. According to the Shia, it was a decision Ali acquiesced to because he did not want to split the faithful. It was only after the assassination of the third person to hold the post, Uthman Ibn Affan, in AD 656 that Ali was finally elected leader of the Islamic community, a position known as the Caliph. This resulted in civil war and Ali's death five years later, while praying at a mosque, from a poison-coated sword. Ali's supporters at first pledged loyalty to his son, Hasan, but those who had organised his assassination bribed many of them to change sides, leaving Hasan's army in disarray. He was forced to sue for peace and step down from the Caliphate. In return for his acquiescence, the new Caliph, Muawiya, promised that his successor would be chosen by council.

Shortly before Muawiya died, however, he made his supporters swear allegiance to his son, Yazid, thereby breaking the key condition of the peace treaty. Another of Ali's sons, Husain, refused to accept Muawiya's deceit. With 72 men, many of them Mohammad's closest relatives, he marched to what is now the city of Karbala, sixty miles south-west of Baghdad, where, on 9 October 680, he was met by Yazid, who had with him several thousand soldiers. Husain and almost all his companions were killed in the subsequent fighting. It was a battle that ensured the Sunnis secured the Caliphate but it was a day that also shaped the future of Shia Islam. It became one of the most significant events in their history, one that was subsequently given an increasingly romantic and spiritual dimension and which made the concepts of suffering and martyrdom central to the sect's sense of identity. The Battle of Karbala is still commemorated each year by Shia in the festival of Ashura when believers mourn the sacrifice of Husain and his followers. The battle came to define the Shia's belief that what had been rightfully theirs was unfairly taken from them and ensured that a history of bloodshed and revenge would forever afterwards colour Islam's doctrinal schism.

Saddam was a Sunni and consequently preferred Sunni Arabs to hold Iraq's most important posts, especially if they were from his own tribe. Consequently Sunnis predominated in both Iraq's military and government and were proportionally worst affected by Bremer's disbandment of the army and his introduction of de-Ba'athification. As a result many Sunnis concluded that they would have no place in the new Iraqi state unless they fought to get one.

On my third day in Baghdad I saw the workings of the CPA first hand when Mike and Danny handed me over to its officials, who were to brief me on the improvements being made to Iraq. I spent a morning in Saddam's Republican Palace as a succession of chino-wearing figures sought to demonstrate that America would not only win in Iraq but that it was already succeeding. Lists of schools and hospitals being built were rattled off. Great store was set on the recent currency change in which Saddam-era notes, resplendent with his image, had been replaced by a new currency featuring Iraq's archaeological monuments. Baghdad's intermittent electricity supply should be viewed as a positive development, I was told, as it was partly due to the vast number of electrical goods the average Iraqi could now buy.

It was explained that the CPA was putting in place the foundations for a modern society, one with legislation that would prevent discrimination in the workplace and a new national curriculum that would ensure Iraq produced the world's next generation of great scientists. A public awareness scheme was planned that would save Iraqi lives by encouraging people to give up smoking. I attended a PowerPoint presentation which detailed how Iraq's new army would be ready for operation by the end of the year. Ambitious plans had been drawn up to reform the tax system. The number of insurgents being killed was cited as an indication of progress. Every official I met that morning seemed to have computer print-outs, complete with coloured graphs and pages of figures, which proved how effectively their area of responsibility was being implemented. It was very corporate and, in its own way, impressive. There was no denying that, whatever their other faults, those working in the CPA had seemingly boundless energy and commitment to its cause.

On my fourth night in Iraq, at the end of my stay with Arawn, Mike and Danny took me back to the Chinese restaurant for a farewell dinner. It was a Saturday night and the place was heaving, every table and chair taken. Mike, who was as Australian as they come, made sure I got stuck into the beers, and made clear that he would have considered it impolite if I hadn't.

Everyone I talked to was confident that the Americans would succeed in Iraq. A number of the security contractors were even buying up Iraqi banknotes in the expectation that the country's exchange rate would soon soar when the war was won. There were some I met who complained about the arrogance of the American troops they dealt with. Those who had served in Northern Ireland were not particularly happy to be lectured on the evils of terrorism by a people whose countrymen had partly funded the Irish terrorists who used to take pot shots at them and their mates. However, they all appeared to believe victory was inevitable. There was an apparent truism they seemed to trust absolutely: the US was simply too powerful for any other outcome to be possible.

It was home, not politics, that dominated conversation that night. I talked to a security contractor from Devon about how his wife would not let him sleep in the main part of the house on his first day back on leave in order to give him time to let the Baghdad stress flow out of him.

'When I came back from exercise or a posting abroad while in the Army I'd be so wound up that if she disturbed me in the night, while I was sleeping, I would grab her. I mean grab her roughly. It was an automatic thing – fight or flight – but it unsettled her. So now she sets up a camp bed in the garage and makes me sleep on that when I arrive home.'

There was a contractor who claimed to have been a bare-knuckle fighter before he joined the military. He said that he had been born a gypsy and had spent his childhood moving around Britain, often living in Wales. His father had been a force to be reckoned with in the gypsy bare-knuckle fighting world and his son had followed in his footsteps. He had the squashed nose and disjointed facial features that indicated there might be truth in what he was saying.

While in the Army he had been accepted by the SAS and had spent considerable time on covert operations in Northern Ireland. After he had been in the regiment for a few years, his father became ill with cancer and asked his son to visit him on leave as he had something to tell him. His father wanted to reveal the story of how his family had ended up gypsies. They had apparently originally come from Northern Ireland, his father born to a family of committed nationalists. He got caught up in the Republican cause and joined the IRA. What exactly he had done for them was not made clear but it was enough for the police to learn who he was and to begin searching for him. He had fled to mainland Britain and adopted the life of a gypsy to avoid discovery.

'It's a funny old world, isn't it,' the contractor said to me. 'There was I hunting down these fellas as part of the British Army when apparently there's a statue of my grandfather in a village in Ireland put up because of his great fighting skills against the British. It hails him as the great nationalist hero!'

At a corner table was an American, marked out as a CPA official by his pink polo shirt and carefully parted hair. He did not have stories about bare-knuckle fighting or having a secret terrorist as a father. He was, in fact, from a preppie family in Idaho. Unlike the others he preferred to talk politics as there was something he wanted to say about what was going to happen next in Iraq.

'The worst is over,' he predicted while enjoying his chicken fried rice and a cold bottle of Carlsberg. His job was to run democracy awareness courses for the Iraqi people, a task he fulfilled by staging workshops at government offices across the country during which the principles of the rule of law, fair elections and the impor-tance of an independent judiciary were outlined. In this role had seen a lot more of the country than most of those in the Green Zone, many of whom had barely even seen Baghdad.

'The people I've met understand they've been given a turning point, an opportunity that won't come again, and they want to grasp it,' he told me. 'The hard work's been done now, the foundations for a new Iraq set up.

'What we need to do is hand power over to the Iraqis as soon as possible so that it doesn't look as if we are occupying the country. That'll take the wind out of the insurgency. I am sure of it. The Iraqis can get on with putting all our plans into action. People will look back and not believe what's been achieved so quickly.'

I said I hoped he was right, that the violence would soon end, and we clinked beer bottles in agreement.

It was perhaps not unexpected that those who ran the occupation were confident of the war's ultimate success. My biggest surprise during that visit to Iraq came at the end of my stay with Arawn when I was dropped off at the building in the Red Zone where the *Telegraph* and a number of other newspapers and TV companies had set up their offices. The news from Iraq that I had read in the UK had been primarily about bombings and military casualties. I was expecting the atmosphere among Westerners in the Red Zone to be that of a wake. Instead, among the journalists, it was as much party time as it had been at my local pub in Hackney or by the pool at Saddam's palace.

Most of the press pack, the *Daily Telegraph* included, had based themselves at the Hamra, a hotel in the quiet residential area of Jadiriyah on the opposite side of the Tigris from the Green Zone. It became the iconic reporter's hotel of the Iraq war, the place to which new arrivals rushed from the airport and where the war's old hands lived. Part of its popularity was based on the fact that the perimeter blast wall that protected it stretched beyond the hotel itself to include the half block of buildings that surrounded it. These included two or three hostels, which provided cheap rooms for freelancers and therefore increased the range of reporters able to stay in the compound, and also a couple of restaurants, one of which occasionally had a guitar player at weekends. It does not sound much but, by Baghdad standards, this was a wealth of entertainment of Las Vegas proportions. Even during the darkest days of the war, in the later parts of 2005 and for all of 2006, it meant I still had a choice as to where to eat dinner, even if I was by then normally too exhausted and strung out to do anything but order room service and slump in front of the television. A handful of the larger media organisations, such as the *Washington Post* and *Time* magazine, had hired villas within the compound, renting the buildings from their owners who gratefully took the thousands of dollars a month offered and relocated to Syria or Jordan. This added even more places to visit for anyone in search of distraction.

At the compound's centre was the Hamra hotel itself. It was a former Ba'athist-run place built in a Frank Lloyd Wright style made up of two towers that were by far the tallest in this neighbourhood of Baghdad. From the balconies on the tenth floor of the main tower there were panoramic views of the city in its grimy glory and many of the largest palaces and government buildings could be clearly made out. The hotel was not, however, particularly comfortable. The decor had not been refurbished since the building was constructed in the 1970s and, in the main café, diners sat on red plastic seats at white tables under strip lighting. The lifts routinely broke, stranding people mid-floor as the hotel's in-house engineers struggled to get them operating again. The air-conditioning was so archaic that in the summer months it was best to leave a cold bath overnight and, when it was impossible to sleep, jump in it to cool down.

The Hamra was nevertheless preferred by most Westerners to the other major hotel used by journalists, the Palestine, an 18-storey structure located a few miles north of the Hamra by Firdos Square, as the rooms were not as dark and dreary. At the Palestine, walls were painted brown and the carpets coloured off-grey. At the Hamra the walls were at least whitewashed and the flooring either tan carpet or, in the entrance hall, grey marble. There was also normally one coloured picture in each room, usually a rip-off of some French impressionist, and a balcony to sit on for those seeking fresh air. The Hamra also had a better swimming pool, which was without a doubt its best feature. The 25-yard-long pool with its expanse of refreshing water dominated the courtyard that separated the Hamra's two towers, providing a central point for those staying at the hotel to congregate and relax.

In the first weeks after Saddam fell, an American TV network, NBC, chose the Hamra as the site at which to house its news crews. An editing suite was built and a studio constructed on the roof for its journalists to monopolise. Their presence required the channel to install a contingent of security guards who immediately started making the site safer. It was they who had supervised the construction of the blast walls that surrounded the hotel's perimeter. They also ensured that the procedure of arriving at the hotel was a unique one. At the main entrance your car would be funnelled into a narrow space by tapering lines of concrete blocks. Half a dozen Iraqi guards would surround you, Kalashnikovs in hand, and insist on searching the vehicle and inspecting all those within it. A line of metal spikes was placed across the tarmac to burst the tyres of anyone who tried to avoid stopping. Only when the signal was given that the car was clean would the spikes be pulled aside to permit you to drive forward, threading through a collection of stone blocks and sand-filled plastic barriers put in place to further slow down potential suicide bombers, until you drew up by the entrance to the hotel itself. Its front door, a sheet of black-tinted glass reached by climbing sixteen gently-sloping steps, was framed by a metal detector. Everyone was required to pass through it, and any new arrivals given one last pat-down, before you could, finally, step inside. It was a lengthy process but the procedures established by NBC's security detail meant the Hamra felt reasonably safe for everyone else who subsequently latched onto it, which was perhaps the most important reason of all for its popularity.

It is hard now to remember what staying at the Hamra was like in the spring of 2004 as it eventually became such a gruelling place to live, somewhere in which the handful of reporters still willing to be based in Baghdad dwelled amid power cuts, repetitive food, terror of what was going on outside and rampant insomnia. Things were very different when I first stayed there. So many people were at the hotel it took me days to learn who they all were. The US papers were out in force; not only the big ones but also the smaller city papers such as the

Boston Globe and the *San Francisco Chronicle*. There was *Newsweek*, *Voice of America*, a bevy of freelancers, half a dozen journalists from the smaller news wires, a couple of French reporters and all the British broadsheets. Even *Rolling Stone* had someone on assignment in Baghdad, though her job seemed to be to cover what the press pack was doing rather than what was actually happening in the war. On my first evening, I was invited to a salsa-dancing night. The dancing proved a bit of a damp squib but there was still alcohol and food, and after midnight everyone stripped off and leaped into the hotel's swimming pool.

The *Telegraph*'s office was in the hotel's second tower, a smaller building of five floors located on the far side of the pool from the main entrance. The paper had a suite on the third floor. It consisted of my bedroom, an office for me to work in, and a main room with a kitchen table at which we conducted interviews. Opposite it was a TV, which was almost always on, usually tuned to the Arab news station al-Jazeera so that we could know what the rest of the Arab world was learning about the situation in Iraq.

Two Iraqis worked for the paper, both of whom became my closest companions during the next few years. Abu Omar was the driver. He ferried the correspondent around in his black BMW, sun-shades stuck to the back-seat windows to try to obscure any Westerner sitting inside. He was 42 years old and had been a car mechanic before he realised that the fall of Saddam and his ability to speak English offered an opportunity to earn better money by working with the journalists now descending on his home city. One day in the autumn of 2003, he had turned up at the Hamra on the off chance that anyone might need a driver. The *Telegraph* had a vacancy as their previous driver had proved too hot-headed for comfort, always insisting on demonstrating his bravery by driving towards danger rather than doing his best to avoid it. Abu Omar was hired for a day's trial and had been with the *Telegraph* ever since.

When I first met Abu Omar I was wary of him. He looked like the stereotypical Iraqi of Western imagination with his waxed-down black hair, bristling moustache, preference for mirrored sunglasses and a black leather jacket that hung almost to his knees. Yet this authoritarian image hid a kind and generous spirit. Whenever we had lunch he would pile food onto my plate to ensure I was eating properly and would indicate that it would be a personal insult if any was left unfinished. He was an excellent driver, unflappable when things got dangerous, and constantly proved able to extricate us from potential trouble before it escalated into something serious. In the back window of his car he had a fluffy toy camel that he had bought years earlier on a visit to Jordan.

The mainstay of the office was our translator, Ahmed. It was he who made sure that all the necessary equipment and office supplies were present and who organised and translated any interviews. He had been working for the *Telegraph* since the first week after Saddam's regime fell. The correspondent in Baghdad at the time had been looking for a translator and Ahmed was a friend of one of the Iraqi staff already working for a North American news network. She knew Ahmed's English was excellent so had suggested that the *Telegraph* invite him for an interview. A job offer followed. As the hotel where he previously worked as a tourist guide had been closed down and placed under American military control, Ahmed accepted.

When I first met Ahmed he was enthused by the work and excited by the unfamiliar world of journalism. He was 33, which was more or less the same age as me, and lean by Iraqi standards with closely cut hair, which he brushed back, and dark eyes that dominated his round face. He liked to look his best – his ironed shirt tucked into the jeans and his black leather shoes freshly polished – and enjoyed showing off his latest mobile phone or discussing which car he would like one day to buy. At times he could almost be domineering, not least when dealing with Iraqis less educated than himself, but he was not arrogant. Ahmed did not lack confidence – when he walked he strode – but it was tempered by a cheerful optimism and a humility born of his conviction that all people were equal in the eyes of God.

I liked him from the moment he introduced himself. It was in the café on the ground floor of the Hamra hotel. I had been eating breakfast when he came over and started dissecting the merits of the English football team with not only insight but wit. He had particularly strong views on why David Beckham should avoid wearing a sarong if he wanted to remain a top player that revolved around Beckham's nickname of Goldenballs. He told me stories of his time working for the *Telegraph*. The paper had already lost one Iraqi member of staff, a driver killed during the American bombardment of Baghdad at the start of the war, and Ahmed had endured his own terrifying experiences with the company. There had been the moment when his car was stopped by bandits and he was forced to convince them it was not the behaviour of a good Muslim to kill the British correspondent in the back seat. He had been on patrol with an American unit and also driven into the heart of Fallujah to facilitate an interview. He had a way, rare among the Iraqis I met, of being willing to make a joke of the dangers he had experienced without minding the loss of face that came with admitting his fear. That was something I warmed to and admired.

During the first days after I arrived at the Hamra, I must have done some work. Looking through the archives on the *Telegraph*'s internet site there is even evidence of it: articles with my by-line about gunfights in eastern Baghdad and growing unrest in southern Iraq. I cannot, however, remember anything about researching or writing them. Indeed the Baghdad outside the Hamra's perimeter walls remains in my memory of that time as an indistinct blur of slow-moving traffic and road after road of dirt-encrusted buildings. What sticks out from that period is life in the Hamra itself and the socialising that went on there. There were so many people to meet, all with their exciting stories from their lives as foreign correspondents and the war zones they had visited. When dusk fell and final deadlines passed, people would gather on the patio surrounding the hotel's pool to eat and drink long into the night.

There was always something to gossip about: the British correspondent who had accidentally been shot the previous week when a bullet had ricocheted off a pavement and embedded itself in his bottom (an entry point which meant his war wound prompted more laughter than sympathy), or the US photographic agency rumoured to be selling bags of marijuana from its office. One evening, a week after my arrival, two mortars were fired close by and the flash of the discharge shot over where we sat. Everyone rushed for the protection of the nearest doorway, but a few minutes later, when everything was quiet again, we were back in our seats, laughing at how frightening and unexpected it had been.

It was not only at the Hamra that reporters seemed to be making the most of the amusements on offer. I spent one evening at the BBC compound, an old Baghdad building near the French embassy, where one of their Western security guards was preoccupied with demonstrating his culinary skills by cooking everyone dinner. On Saturdays the American news channels took turns to throw parties at the various secure hotel complexes that they had moved into across the city. Bins were filled with ice and beer while barbecues churned out spare ribs and steak. Often people got so drunk they lost track of time and their Iraqi drivers would head home to their families. Once a British reporter gave me a lift to a party being held at the Sheraton, a place that had not been officially linked to the hotel chain since Saddam seized control of the building during the 1991 Gulf War. When it was time to leave we found that his ride back to the Hamra had long gone. The solution was to hail a taxi. We navigated our way through the streets in broken Arabic, our driver looking terrified the whole way at the prospect that someone might realise he had foreigners in the back of his cab.

A week later, following a reception in the Green Zone at the British embassy, a group of us emerged through the main entrance into the city at large only to find our cars had again disappeared, their Iraqi drivers too sensible to sit around after sunset by such an inviting target. This was a problem because once it was dark people were allowed out of the entrances to the Green Zone but not back in. Luckily two Iraqi police vehicles were stationed at the checkpoint. The officers in them took pity on us and offered to give us a lift. Sitting in the back of their trucks, we sped through Baghdad with the lights on and the sirens wailing.

It was not as if there were no dangers then. Two Polish reporters were in fact killed a week after I landed in Baghdad when their car was ambushed. The contractors working for Arawn never risked going out without their flak jackets and weaponry. The journalists I met, however, seemed determined to prove they were neither scared nor willing to let the hazards impinge upon their ability to do their job and I took my lead from them. Nights out in restaurants were routine. I went shopping to buy Iraqi-style clothing and drove across the country – up to Kirkuk, down to Kufa – with only my driver and translator for company. Some reporters took their bravado to limits recognised even then as ridiculous. One night two of them left the Green Zone after an evening spent socialising only to find their drivers gone and this time no helpful police around to save them. Their response was to climb into one of the surrounding houses, abandoned by its owners due to its proximity to Baghdad's most popular target, and fall asleep on the floor. They woke at dawn to find themselves the centre of attention for a gaggle of curious street children.

In Iraq it was never possible to escape reality for long, as I was to learn again and again during my time there. Even on that first post-invasion trip when, more than at any other point, I was intoxicated by the excitement and audacity of being in Baghdad, honesty still forced itself upon me; the power of events guiding me towards what was actually happening rather than what I had hoped or presumed.

Abu Ghraib taught me the most valuable lesson. Even before the scandal became public many Western journalists in Iraq had heard rumours about what was taking place in that former Ba'athist prison commandeered by the US military to house its detainees. Whilst researching other stories, Iraqis would come forward with tales of American troops mistreating a friend's imprisoned husband or son by beating them or depriving them of food and sleep. These claims were difficult to verify as the press had no access to Abu Ghraib. So in the absence of cast iron proof most reporters had considered these stories to probably be untrue. It is important to appreciate why as it illustrates the personal challenge those reporting in Iraq faced in interpreting what was happening there. It was not hard to conceive that the US might be out of its depth, culturally arrogant or plain incompetent. It was possible to believe that America's armed forces contained people willing to be methodically cruel. However, it was a very different matter to accept that the US military could either sanction such behaviour or have such poor supervision as to let them get away with it, particularly for the reporters in Iraq for whom the United States was their home.

Even many Iraqis could not believe it. A significant number still hoped that the US might be what it said it was, particularly among those working for the international media, who due to the nature of their employment were usually more predisposed to believe in the good intentions of the West. Nearly all the translators and drivers I met working for the press at the Hamra told me in the first few days after I arrived there that the Iraqis repeating such stories were troublemakers, their claims lies that should be ignored.

It was always difficult to sort fact from fiction in Iraq as a lot of Iraqis did love propagating conspiracy theories. Rumours abounded. Every week I heard unconfirmed tales of American helicopters being shot down, CIA agents killed or Jews being spotted near the spot where a bomb later went off. 'Everybody knows it is true,' I would be told, a mantra that quickly became depressingly familiar.

Hearsay was a particular problem for the British in the south who consistently found their efforts to win over hearts and minds stymied by the latest rumour put out against them. When bird flu was identified north of Basra, intelligence officers reported imams preaching that the British had been spotted throwing dead chickens out of helicopters. When a plague of badger-like animals started harassing local livestock, this too was blamed on the British who were said to have released these previously unseen creatures despite the head of the local veterinary hospital insisting, repeatedly and publicly, that they had been in Iraq for decades and were simply now moving south in greater numbers.

Abu Ghraib, however, was not like that. What was happening there was very real. Behind its walls the moral justification for what the Americans were doing in Iraq was being eroded. It was a turning point in the conflict, one that created an image that redefined the world's view of the United States, and the event that taught me that in the war in Iraq there would be no side that was clear-cut good or bad.

It is hard even now to believe what took place there. The testimony that was to come out after the scandal became public is still scarcely credible. Detainees were sodomised with batons, phosphoric acid was poured on wounds, people were urinated on, women made to expose their breasts and prisoners forced to have intercourse with each other. Men being pulled across the floor by ropes tied to their penises. Guards would have sex in front of their charges. When the official investigation into what happened finally ended, the American officer in charge of the prison was cleared of having had any knowledge of what took place. She admitted, however, that 90 per cent of the people being held there were probably innocent.

After the story broke – an event that was testimony to the power of photographic proof – the Iraqis who had doubted the rumours were notably quiet. I did not hear many Iraqis subsequently question if rumours of American brutality were mere exaggeration. Nor did I doubt that the stories I heard might hold an element of truth.

I joined two other reporters for a visit to the prison's perimeter. Our intention was to interview the families who had gathered there in the hope that their relatives might be among the detainees released that day. The facility was huge, stretching across 280 acres with four kilometres of walls and twenty-four guard towers. Most of the waiting Iraqis surrounded a metal gate, protected by lines of concrete blast walls and Hesco barriers, that was the prison's main entrance. There must have been more than a thousand of them. Seeing the arrival of Western reporters, scores crushed around us: angry, emotional and desperate to tell their stories.

Soon I was in the centre of a crowd six deep; a throng of figures trying to grab my attention so they could describe their particular plight. Faces were contorted by urgency; hands caked in dirt shook my shoulder; voices rose louder and louder as they struggled to be heard. I frantically scribbled what they told me in my notebook, struggling to keep up with Ahmed's explanation, desperate to focus on doing my job to hold back the sense of claustrophobia that such a mass of humanity was stirring within me.

To listen to them was to be introduced to a different world. US officials and officers I met described meticulously planned military operations, strategies for reconstruction and ordered steps leading to the introduction of democracy. That was the Iraq they lived in. Now I was allowing myself to learn about the Iraq that the Iraqis lived in. It was not a place where people were worrying about dying from cigarette smoke. This Iraq was one where crime was rising, not least because Saddam in one of his final acts as president had ordered the country's prisons emptied. It was a place where US soldiers would apparently break into houses and grab people purely on the say-so of an informant with a grudge, and where people were frightened to go outside in case they ran into a military patrol, as they never knew when the Americans might start shooting.

A man, his white robes stained by the mud churned up by the crowd, started shouting at me. 'He is furious,' Ahmed explained. 'American soldiers keep conducting searches of houses after dark and it means they are seeing women in their nightclothes.' As a result women were sleeping fully clothed just in case the troops came, and

Iraqi husbands were desperate to gain revenge for such an unforgivable insult. No US soldier or official had mentioned this to me. I do not know if they even realised it was a problem.

There were too many people, their tales too raw. I pushed my way towards the road. A woman, her face lined by sun and suffering, stood in my path. She refused to let me go any further until I listened to what she had to say. She had heard nothing from her husband, I learnt, since he had been taken from his home by US troops four months ago. Now she wanted me to write about him so that the Americans would feel guilty and release him. It seemed a faint hope but, in sympathy, I had re-started my note taking when the prison's main gate unexpectedly opened and a prisoner stepped out. He was dressed in a dirty blue shirt, his hair matted. Seeing the mob in front, he looked terrified. Bodies now rushed to surround him. Iraqis were demanding to know if he had seen any of their relatives and were asking what was happening to people inside. The woman with the missing husband lost interest in me and pushed closer to the freed man. I followed in her wake.

The released prisoner was too scared to speak, looking back at the US troops manning the gate behind him. 'Nothing,' he answered finally. 'It is good, they treat us well.' He spotted members of his family and reached towards them. They surrounded him and led him to their car. Iraqis ran beside it, still calling out questions as it drove away along the highway.

I was standing beside the woman who had been seeking my aid and I got my translator to ask her what she thought about what the freed prisoner had said. 'He is too scared to say the truth because otherwise the

Americans will come again and take him,' she answered dismissively. 'He would say anything to make sure they do not come for him again. When the time comes, God willing, for my husband to be released, he will be the same.'

The gulf between the American and Iraqi world was illustrated every afternoon in the self-assurance exhibited during the press conferences held by Brigadier General Mark Kimmitt, the US military's official spokesman. He would list the major events of the day and the latest abuses enacted by the insurgency. Graphs and tables would demonstrate the progress being made. Reporters would tell him what they were seeing outside on the streets and argue that the situation could not be as unequivocal as he was claiming. In response Kimmitt would often use tales from his family life to add emotional impact to his answers as he sought to establish that life in Iraq was improving.

Once he was told by an Iraqi journalist that the low-flying US helicopters criss-crossing Baghdad were scaring children. Kimmitt responded that he had spent most of his life on military bases and his wife had worked as a teacher on them. When her pupils were upset by the sound coming from the artillery or tank ranges, she calmed them down by telling them what they could hear were the 'sounds of freedom'. That was what the Iraqis should do, Kimmitt said: tell their children growing up in the middle of a war that it was the 'sounds of freedom' that were frightening them.

The full range of his rhetoric was on show in press conferences dedicated to the situation in the increasingly out-of-control cities of Fallujah and Najaf. Fallujah was a city of around 450,000 people located in Anbar province, a region in western Iraq that was predominately Sunni. It had originally avoided damage during the 2003 US invasion as the Iraqi troops stationed there had abandoned their positions, taking their rifles with them as they melted into the local population, but had subsequently become a centre of resistance to the US occupation. The locals turned against the occupiers when American troops fired on a crowd that had gathered to demand the reopening of a secondary school, after rocks and, the US said, gunshots were directed against the watching soldiers. Sunni extremist groups exploited this discontent to entrench themselves and make Fallujah their command base. At the end of March 2004, a month before my return to Iraq, four American contractors working for the private military company Blackwater had been ambushed. Their bodies were set on fire and dragged through the streets before being hung from a bridge. The Americans responded by massing troops outside the city, effectively placing it in a state of siege. An assault was planned and an air bombardment launched. Then, in early April, the attack on the city was aborted amid concern at the number of civilians being killed. American forces remained in outlying districts, where they were now being attacked by Sunni fighters.

Kimmitt said there had been 'numerous engagements' in which Iraqis had used children as shields. He looked particularly grave at that point. It was an expression not that dissimilar, I imagined, to the one his wife would have adopted to chastise a naughty child in her class. 'We were disappointed by the quality of our adversary,' Kimmitt explained. 'We were shocked by their breaking of the custom of war.'

Then he spoke about Najaf, a city south-west of Baghdad where it was the Shia who had taken control, primarily the Mahdi Army followers of the radical cleric Moqtada al-Sadr. There too the Americans had responded by massing troops outside the city. The situation was complicated by the fact that the tomb of Imam Ali ibn Abi Talib, the Prophet Mohammad's cousin and son-in-law who was revered by the Shia, was located in Najaf. Any damage to the mosque in which it was housed risked alienating Iraq's entire Shia population, thereby prompting a more widespread revolt.

Kimmitt was quick to emphasise the 'extraordinary care we take to protect civilians'. To illustrate this he described the action taken against a Mahdi Army mortar team firing at a US patrol in Najaf from the adjacent town of Kufa. The two cities bordered each other and the Mahdi Army were operating freely in both. A picture of the area where the mortar team had been based was put on an overhead screen. It was a military aerial photograph, black and white and divided into quadrants. It showed a stretch of wasteland surrounded on three sides by houses. A small arrow pointed to where the mortar team was located. A second photograph was brought up of the same scene taken a few minutes later. Where the mortar team had been there was now only a crater.

'We dropped a five-hundred-pound bomb,' Kimmitt said. 'We calculated that due to the location of the mortar team away from direct housing it was safe to do so without causing damage to the surrounding buildings or people.'

I knew Ahmed had cousins who lived in the outskirts of Kufa and I asked him if it might be possible to visit them. He agreed and we went to see what had happened from the Iraqis' viewpoint rather than that of their American rulers when the bomb described by Kimmitt dropped.

Kufa, like Najaf, had been under the authority of Moqtada al-Sadr and his supporters for a month. Sadr, a fanatical Iraqi cleric who preached that the American occupation should be resisted, had created a militia called the Mahdi Army. It had originally been limited in size to a few hundred of his supporters in a Shia area of Baghdad but it had grown steadily throughout the second half of 2003 and the first months of 2004 to become a force that numbered in the thousands, its members recognisable through the black shirts they normally wore as identification. Units were now based across the cities of southern Iraq, the predominately Shia area of the country. Those in the Mahdi Army were primarily drawn from the poorer elements of Iraqi society, largely attracted to it by Sadr's message of a more equitable and just Iraq ruled according to the teachings of the Prophet Mohammed rather than to the agenda of foreign invaders. They were also the Iraqis who often most needed the food and clothing regularly given to the Mahdi Army's members.

On 4 April 2004 the Spanish–Salvadoran base in Najaf, the only coalition presence in the area, was attacked by a contingent of militiamen as part of a co-ordinated Shia uprising across central and southern Iraq. The coalition soldiers in Najaf had panicked and demanded to be pulled out, which had led to elements of an American armoured cavalry regiment being dispatched with orders to re-establish control.

The cemetery in Najaf is the largest in the Muslim world as its proximity to Imam Ali's tomb meant Shia aspired to be buried there. In late May 2004 it became a battleground after Mahdi Army fighters entrenched themselves within it and US tanks and soldiers fought to clear them from its network of tombs and mausoleums. When I was in Kufa a few weeks earlier, however, an uneasy calm still held. There were almost no cars on the streets, and most shops were closed but the real fighting had yet to start. The US forces remained camped outside the city while their commanders sought to determine what to do next. An occasional probe was being launched but the only permanent American presence in Najaf was an Abrams tank stationed outside the mayor's office. The mayor who had originally fled the city but returned on the orders of the CPA. Inside the tank, soldiers were said to be playing cards while listening to the ping of bullets hitting the side of their vehicle.

Kufa is a small city of around 110,000 people, its centre dominated by the same Soviet-style apartment blocks and office buildings that defined Baghdad. Our objective was a building in the suburbs, an area where the apartment blocks had been replaced by houses and the roads were lined by concrete flower boxes that each boasted an array of multi-coloured blooms. We turned off a main street and drove down a side road. A battered metal gate was opened and we pulled into a small court-yard outside a two-storey house. It was a typical Iraqi townhouse: a building set back from the street surrounded by a walled garden, creating its own sense of sanctuary. The walls were painted a dark red, making the green leaves of the alder trees planted to provide shade from the summer sun look particularly vibrant.

Ahmed's relative covered his heart with his right hand as he greeted me, an Iraqi gesture of respect to an honoured guest, despite the fact that my presence in his home was putting his and his family's lives at risk. He appeared far older than the 56 years I had been told he was, a grey beard covering his chin and his face gaunt with the skin pulled tight over his cheekbones. I later learnt that he was already suffering from the cancer that killed him the following year. He beckoned me into the main room, an area twenty feet square, and indicated I should sit on one of the cushions that ringed the floor. These were the room's main decoration: a weave of red, green and blue. The walls were bare and a black felt sofa was the only other piece of furniture in sight.

My host and Ahmed sat down either side of me. Two women came in, their faces veiled, and placed pots holding a mixture of chicken, rice and pickles on the floor in front of us. The women disappeared behind a cloth that hung over the door into the kitchen. I did not see them again. A young man, our host's cousin, joined us. He was wearing a T-shirt with a picture of a beach shaded by palm trees. We ate with our hands and the men talked in Arabic.

The conversation became more heated and I asked Ahmed what it was they were saying. It was about the Americans, Ahmed told me. Our host was asking why they were so foolish. Why were they building up a force to retake Najaf and Kufa and patrolling within the cities? Did they not understand that most Shia would feel it an honour to die to protect the holy tomb of Imam Ali? The best way to resolve the present problems was to sit down and talk about it. It was the only way to do so without causing grave and lasting resentment. The religious leaders could control Sadr if they were given time. Our host was sure of that and his cousin nodded agreement.

Apparently it was an indisputable fact that foreigners fighting in one of Iraq's holiest cities could only be a recipe for disaster. Our host was particularly insistent that the Americans were radicalising people by driving around its perimeter in their tanks. All it was doing was encouraging more Iraqi teenagers to come to Najaf and Kufa with their guns and dreams of martyrdom. He and his cousin really resented these teenagers, the Mahdi Army rank and file, who had come into their city and were telling their elders where they could drive and what they could do. They grudgingly respected their bravado in taking on the Americans but disliked their rudeness and enthusiasm for violence. Worse, everyone was losing money as the continuing disorder led to businesses being closed. This was a particular concern. It was not safe to work and, until the Americans left the city, neither could see any end to the disruption.

'Their nerves are very tight,' Ahmed explained. 'The Americans can be very useless and may cause great trouble. The things that can happen in life now are unbelievable.'

After we had finished eating we went to look at the crater. The house was about seven hundred yards from where the bomb had dropped. Our host, his hand constantly fiddling with prayer beads, described how his home had shaken 'like an earthquake' when it struck and, before we left, pointed to the cracks in the ceiling and on one of the support pillars that had been caused by the blast.

As we walked down an alleyway he pointed out a garden wall that had collapsed and then a pile of rubble that had been an outside toilet. A woman had apparently died there when the roof caved in as the bomb went off.

About half a dozen people had also been injured, he said, mostly cuts and bruises due to falling bricks and tiles. One person had been badly hurt: an old lady who had broken her hip when she fell over from the shock of it.

We found the crater in the middle of a field of mud and beaten-down grass located on the edge of the city. The hole was at least twenty feet deep and its sides tapered to the bottom in a near-perfect cone. There was little else to look at, the field spreading for at least three hundred yards in every direction, and so we were staring into it when I heard a cry go up. People on a road at the far side of the field were shouting in Arabic and the sound quickly spread as it was repeated by others closer to us and passed on into the surrounding streets. My companions looked startled. I had no idea what was being said or what was happening.

'The Americans are coming,' Ahmed explained.

People were running for sanctuary and we joined them. They grinned at us, their eyes wide, some even laughing, all sharing the same false euphoria caused by the adrenalin flooding through their bodies.

Behind us, at the opposite end of the field, I could now see the Americans. It was a patrol, a line of Humvees with a tank leading the way, its gun barrel clearly identifiable. The smoke-glass windows gave the vehicles an other-worldly appearance and the machine guns fixed to the top were being arced from side to side. It was a sight that only added greater speed to my step. We ran back up the alleyway and through our host's front gate. Doors were locked and shutters closed. We stood in the gloom and looked at each other. I got Ahmed to ask the old man why we had run so fast.

'If they see people they might kill them,' he told me.

No further words were said as the vehicles drew closer and rumbled along the road outside. We stood in silence, concentrating, until not a sound of them could be heard and we knew that the danger had passed.

3. Baghdad

A year later I could tell the time of day in Baghdad by the nature of the explosions. I was living there full time by then and it had quickly become a familiar routine. The early mornings were the busiest as roadside bombs buried during the night were set off by the first patrols. It would be a fresh dawn introduced by a dull pop, a finger of smoke rising into the still subdued sky and the knowledge, even as I waited for the kettle to boil, that someone was already having a really bad day.

The suicide bombers liked to strike in the mid-morning. I could often hear the blast in my room in the Hamra, sometimes even feel the vibrations, and I would rush up onto the hotel's flat roof to try to pinpoint its location. If it was close, I would then head out to see the extent of the damage. I hated those trips. The Iraqi police were always jumpy and the traffic terrible as it snarled back from the strike point. It could take half an hour to move a mile. When I got there it was a push through the crowds, trying to avoid the American soldiers telling people to get back, and then the bomb site itself, depressing in its predictability: a crater in the ground, burned-out cars, smears of blood on the pavement, a carpet of shattered glass. The Iraqis were already practised at getting the bodies away but sometimes there might still be a shape lying under a sheet, a hand or foot – the skin like burned paper – poking out one side. To look or not to look? I looked, of course, and one more body was added to the memory bank.

When the bombings started being organised in pairs – one to cause the initial damage, the second to kill the people who rushed to help – I stopped going because I never knew when the second bomb might go off. To be honest, it was a relief. It had always seemed a dangerous and potentially pointless exercise but it was something I had felt compelled to do in order to mark the event as significant, not simply another day's demonstration of normality. Now I would merely climb onto the roof, look at the size of the smoke cloud and ponder how big the bomb must have been. Then back downstairs to see if anything was on the television about it.

Afternoons were favoured by the mortar teams. A few rounds thrown into the Green Zone at tea time to make sure no one was too relaxed. Then, after sunset, came the machine gun fire. Most military operations and extrajudicial killings occurred at night. There would be the controlled phat-phat-phat of the disciplined bursts from American M-16s or the torrent of flat pings that marked the splurges from Iraqi Kalashnikovs. Neither would go on long. Ten seconds, twenty seconds maximum. I never knew why it was taking place or exactly where. It was only sound, a jarring out there in the darkness.

Not every day brought them all, but by 2005 almost every day brought some, the Baghdad clock marking time with its particular tick.

Support for Iraq's national football team bridged the country's sectarian and ethnic divides. The side's glory period had been the 1980s, when Iraq qualified for the 1986 World Cup, but in 1994 Saddam's son Uday took charge of the squad. His motivational techniques had involved punishing missed practices with prison time and losses with a flogging or a bath of raw sewage. Some of the best players fled abroad and Iraq plummeted down the world rankings. Following the overthrow of Saddam, exiled players were available once again for selection and consequently football now offered Iraqis not only a chance for distraction but even sometimes for celebration. When their side beat North Korea in late 2003, an American TV network broke into its regular coverage with a news flash that Baghdad was in revolt as the city filled with machine-gun fire. The gunfire was, in fact, jubilant Iraqis hailing the victory in the traditional manner by taking out the family Kalashnikov and firing it into the air in celebration.

The *Daily Telegraph*'s driver, Abu Omar, invited me to his home to watch a game against Saudi Arabia, the best team in the Middle East. It was being played in Amman, the stadium in Baghdad still not having recovered from when it was used as a base by the Americans and its pitch as a parking lot for their tanks. The match was a big deal, the talk of that day, though expectations were such that no one seemed to be checking their stocks of celebratory ammunition in advance.

I loved Abu Omar's house. It was the one place that I always felt it safe to visit, a family home where his four children did normal family things. The eldest daughter dutifully helped her mother keep house while secretly chatting to boys via instant messenger on the family computer. The rebellious one, a boy in his mid-teens, used to torment his parents by telling them he wanted to join the police, a particularly dangerous career in war-torn Iraq, while the youngest, a little girl of only four, liked to dress up as a princess and perform cartwheels across the carpet in the front room.

The family had been marshalled by Abu Omar in front of the television to ensure they did not miss a minute of the match, all but his eldest boy who had been dispatched onto the roof to move the aerial to see if he could get rid of at least some of the static. He was a thin, pale youth who suffered from the anaemia common amongst Iraqis since Saddam's time. That, however, was not considered reason enough to allow him to abrogate his responsibilities as the eldest child in the family.

Abu Omar's younger sister, Asmaa, who worked for a Western oil company and spoke perfect English, was also visiting to watch the game. Stubbornly unveiled, adamant she would not submit to an arranged marriage and realistic that she had no chance now of fulfilling her dream of moving to Europe, she was damning of the chances of the Iraqi team.

'Where we strive, they bribe,' she said of the Saudis. 'We have suffered enough disappointment not to expect good fortune.'

Bowls of food were placed on the floor and as we ate I was told the latest family gossip. They laughed as they recounted the misfortune of a brother-in-law who had been taken hostage by criminals the previous February and, on his release for a $40,000 ransom, thought it prudent to leave the capital for the then tranquillity of Fallujah just in time for it to be besieged by the Americans. Cups of black tea came with the kick-off. Abu

Omar's wife and two daughters squealed with excitement as the Iraqi team pushed forward. 'He's a great player,' it was reported of midfielder Haitham Khadim. 'He plays in Oman.'

The match started badly. The eldest son resolved the worst of the static problem in time for the Saudis' goal to be viewed clearly – and to be judged offside by those watching, if not the referee.

'You see,' Asmaa said.

Before half-time the Iraqi team got a goal through a Sunni player and in the second half they dominated, leaving the Saudis to hack at their ankles in frustration. A Shia player scored, and then in the 90th minute a Kurd; making it a victory secured by the three key elements of Iraq's population.

Abu Omar roared with approval and we danced around his four-year-old daughter, who shook with excitement at all the attention. He ran to get the family's AK-47 and everyone stood respectfully in the garden as the head of the household emptied a full magazine. 'See! We still have our pride,' he announced.

For thirty minutes there was a cacophony of shooting across the city. 'Iraq, Iraq, Iraq,' the family chanted, while taking care not to step out from under the protection of the veranda in case they were struck by a falling bullet.

Abu Omar was not the only driver I used. Occasionally, during particularly busy periods, the *Telegraph* sent two correspondents to Baghdad, while at other times Abu Omar was ill or had family responsibilities that kept him from work. I would then have to find a substitute; my preferred choice, at least at first, was Khaled. I met

Khaled when I arrived in Baghdad for my visit in April 2004. He was fat, his stomach pushing against his shirt so that the buttons could barely contain the rolls of flesh, aged somewhere in his mid-40s, though he did not like to specify, and had an ebullience that it was impossible not to warm to.

Whenever he drove me he would talk of two things. The first was his obsession with women wearing jilbaab, the loose-fitting ankle-length Islamic robes favoured by the more devout. He would suddenly slow down and give out a deep sigh as some black flowing sheet walked past us. 'Did you see the body on that?' he would ask.

Under his tutelage I did develop an eye for it. I realised that not all jilbaab were the same, that some were tapered and closer cut than others. The real trick, as he laboriously explained, was to see how they fell when their wearers were walking. The ones moving fast were letting the wind mould their clothing to their bodies. 'Better than naked,' he would say appreciatively.

His second favoured subject was how wonderful the Americans were and his delight in their invasion of his country. He spoke of America as a place of infinite possibility, where dreams could and did become reality, and he looked forward to what the US would now do for Iraq.

'The United States is the most rich and civilised country in the world,' he told me. 'Its people can do anything they set their minds to. They put people on the moon. What problem can Iraq be for a country like that?' So enthused was he that he hoped that one day Iraq would become America's 51st state.

By 2005, when I started working full time in Iraq, Khaled was primarily employed by a photographic agency. He loved it. He would drive the photographers to cover the stories of the day and come back with tales of the professionalism of the American soldiers they encountered. These were people who you could still trust, he assured me, even after what had happened at Abu Ghraib.

In mid-2006 he was coming out of his local mosque when a man with a bomb wrapped around his chest walked into the entrance. Khaled was miraculously unharmed despite the forecourt around him being left littered with bodies. His shirt was covered with blood and human parts. His wife washed it but he could never accept that it was clean.

He was only seen in the Hamra complex a few times after that. I met him once in the foyer and he laughed and then cried in a two-minute conversation. Ahmed, my translator, told me that his family no longer knew how to cope with him. Khaled was acting in the most extraordinary way. He had started to drink and no longer prayed. He was buying everything he could get his hands on and sitting up late at night playing the latest computer games. He was refusing to look after his relatives, no longer financially assisting his cousins. He had abandoned the communal bonds to the extended family that Iraqis hold most dear and was focusing exclusively on himself. He was, in fact, acting like the Westerners he idealised. By then he had also, of course, gone mad.

I started as the *Telegraph*'s Iraq correspondent in January 2005, my brief to report on the events happening across that country and the people in it. The Baghdad I flew into was very different from the one of the previous spring. I had returned briefly for a stint in October, the month Ken Bigley, a kidnapped British civil engineer, was murdered, and so knew things were getting no better. However, nothing could have prepared me for quite how bad conditions had become.

Almost no Western journalist now drove outside the city because it was considered too dangerous. Visits to restaurants were avoided and those to shops only undertaken when absolutely necessary. The spate of kidnappings of Westerners, which had so dominated the previous months' news agenda, and the horrific nature of the subsequent deaths, had left everyone feeling distinctly nervous. Many of the hostages were people with no direct link to the military or the occupation but who had been seized anyway. Being Western was clearly enough in itself to make you a target, even if you were married to an Iraqi and were a dedicated aid worker who had spent most of your life helping Iraqi children, as in the case of Margaret Hassan. She had been head of the Iraqi branch of CARE International, was taken from her home in the autumn of 2004 and killed four weeks later.

Behaviour among the press corps changed accordingly. The time of the war tourist was over. Everyone now knew that when they felt hunted it was not mere paranoia: there were people out there wanting to get them. It was a sobering revelation and one that inevitably hindered your ability to report effectively. However, that was not the main concern any more. The greatest priority was to avoid becoming that figure in an orange jumpsuit being beheaded.

If a car followed me around a corner I wondered who was inside. If a vehicle stopped suddenly on the road in front it could be the first stage of a planned ambush. My whole feeling towards the city changed. Baghdad looked remarkably the same. The rows of apartment blocks still had washing drying on their balconies and the streets still remained filled with people hustling for the money they needed to support their families. However, I was now no longer looking at it solely to improve the depth of my articles; I was looking to catch a warning that something might be about to go terribly wrong.

Organising interviews became a logistical nightmare because no one wanted to tip anyone off as to their movements. Reporters would routinely not even tell an organisation they were coming and would instead simply turn up in the hope that those who they wanted to see were there. Most newspaper journalists adopted the 'twenty-minute rule' that meant they did not stay in an unsecured place for any longer than that time. The theory was that this was how long it would take potential kidnappers to learn of your whereabouts and organise themselves. Using this rule, I would go to a location, find whatever details I could in the minutes available, and then on to the next place to try to learn what there had previously been no opportunity to uncover. In this piecemeal way I was hopefully acquiring some idea of the whole picture. In fact I knew I was only being left with fragments.

For the TV channels, the nature of whose work made them far more visible, the challenge was even greater and any trip into the city could take days to organise. One American station's procedure was first to send out a team to scout the area. Guards would then be placed in the surrounding buildings to scan for trouble. When the reporter and cameraman finally emerged there would be bodyguards surrounding them. At that same moment a car would be dispatched to drive around the block. The time it took this car to return to where the segment was being filmed was dependent on traffic but when it did return, whether it had taken five minutes or fifteen, it was the signal to pack up and move out. That was what the company's security advisers had judged to be the minimum time in which it was practically possible for anyone hostile to get close enough to pose a threat.

Although these precautionary steps were unquestionably extreme, few doubted their necessity. We had our own regular reminders of that. Despite the care everyone was now taking, there were still incidents when reporters with whom I socialised in the Hamra became the news themselves when they were the ones attacked or abducted.

The kidnap cases that involved the people I knew best – Rory Carroll from the *Guardian* and Jill Carroll, no relation, from the *Christian Science Monitor* – ended safely for both of them, although Jill's translator was murdered during her abduction and she was held for more than two months before finally being released. The stories surrounding their kidnappings, however, only reinforced the need for constant alertness as both were taken while covering stories they had believed were safe.

Jill was kidnapped after arranging an interview at the offices of the leader of one of the main Sunni political parties, a national figure who was demanding to be given a senior role in the cabinet. She ended up in the hands of Al-Qa'eda in Iraq, held in a series of the organisation's safe houses as her captors moved around Iraq to evade searching US forces. Even now no-one knows how it leaked that she was to conduct the interview. She had been careful to ensure as few people as possible knew her plans and her expected time of arrival. The information was limited to a handful of her Iraqi employees and the politician's key aides. Nevertheless armed men had surrounded her car outside the Sunni leader's office, taken her captive and shot her translator, Allan Enwiya.

Allan's body was left on the street as his killers drove away with their prize. He had never intended to become a media translator and used to run a record shop in Baghdad's A'arasat district that was renowned as having the best selection of Western music in Baghdad. 'Everything from Abba to Marilyn Manson,' he would say proudly. That dream had died in 2004 when he started receiving death threats for stocking non-Islamic music and a hand grenade was tossed through the shop window. He had only been working with Jill because he needed the money. Now he was dead, leaving a widow and two young children.

Rory was a friend. We had got to know each other well as there were only a couple of British newspaper reporters in Baghdad on a regular basis and his office in the Hamra was on the floor below mine. He had arranged to watch the first session of Saddam Hussein's trial, which was being broadcast on local TV, with victims of his regime. It was the kind of story idea many reporters came up with that day. However, Rory's interview had been arranged through the Baghdad representative of Moqtada al-Sadr, the radical Shia cleric. This was an official Rory had dealt with many times before but who this time was working to a different agenda. When Rory and his translator arrived at the house of the family the Sadr official had assigned to them they found armed men inside. When they tried to leave they were boxed in by three vehicles – one of them a police 4x4 – before they had driven twenty yards. His driver was struck on the head with a cosh and three bullets were fired into his translator's car, which had been following behind.

Rory was released two days later, but only after the full extent of the plot to take him had been exposed by the negotiators orchestrating his release. An Iraqi army special forces team raided the house from which he had been taken and arrested its owner and two of his sons. The Iraqis interrogated them – I don't know how but it was very effective – and they revealed that the police car involved in the abduction was part of the special protection team assigned to the Minister of Transport, a leading Sadr supporter. His intent, apparently, was to kidnap Rory so that he could be used as a bargaining chip to try to secure the release of two Mahdi Army leaders arrested by the British in Basra.

Arrest warrants were drawn up for the minister and his bodyguards. Hundreds of troops were sent to surround the main Sadr office in north-east Baghdad. They were only an hour from hitting it when the call came that the Sadrists were going to let Rory go as long as no one was charged with his abduction. Rory was safe, but it seemed as if anyone, even the police and government ministers, was willing to use Western reporters in their power games.

In order to operate in such an environment I clearly had to act with the utmost precision to have any hope of safety. Attention to detail became paramount. Nothing was allowed that might differentiate me from normal Iraqis. Flak jackets and helmets were avoided as being far too conspicuous. To blend in I began to wear Iraqi clothes and only used equipment – whether a watch or a mobile phone – that could be bought in Baghdad. My wardrobe consisted of brown and green-striped shirts and a selection of stonewashed jeans. Two more staff members were hired, joining my driver, Abu Omar, and my translator, Ahmed, as the *Telegraph*'s Iraqi team. They were Marwan, a security guard, and Sajad, who was to drive a second car.

Marwan was a reassuring presence, calm and steady, who belied the sallow dark bags under his eyes with a constant alertness. He had military experience as a former member of the Iraqi army's most elite element, the Republican Guard, and had fought in the Iran–Iraq war. He was also Ahmed's older brother and I trusted that family duty would lead him to do what was necessary in order to protect us. His job was to travel in the back-up car, keep a watchful eye on the road around us and surprise any attackers by rushing to our aid if anything went wrong. It was a task he seemed to take to with remarkable equanimity despite the fact that if anything had happened he would almost certainly have been killed whilst giving us time to flee.

Sajad was a friend of Abu Omar, who vouched for his trustworthiness and bravery. He had been a taxi driver before he started working for me, a particularly dangerous job in occupied Iraq where most people tried to avoid making unnecessary journeys let alone spend all day cruising the streets looking for fares. Escaping that life meant he was delighted with his new, better-paid job despite its potential dangers. He was in his early forties, as was Marwan, and Ahmed quickly nicknamed him the 'giant rooster' as Sajad did somewhat resemble a chicken.

Days spent behind the wheel had given his back a permanent arch, his head popped up straight from his hunched body and a shock of greying hair sprouted in an uncontrollable quiff.

Sajad's task was to drive the second car, which was to trail us discreetly while Ahmed, who was in the front car with me, and Marwan discussed any problems they had spotted via walkie-talkies. The theory behind having a second vehicle was that extra sets of eyes would enable greater forewarning of potential dangers. Moreover, if something happened, Sajad was expected to drive towards the danger and help rescue us. If I was being followed he was meant to put his car between me and my potential attackers and, if things got really bad, supposedly force them off the road. I always trusted he would do what was required as, like many Iraqis, he clearly took his pledges of loyalty seriously. He also had Marwan sat beside him to make sure he did not hesitate when needed.

At the start of 2005 the Western media organisations in Iraq banded together to secure advice and training from a group of security contractors. Two of them were to be based at the Hamra, which most commonly proved to be a team consisting of a former member of the SAS and an ex-Royal Marine who had joined the SBS. I got to know both of them well. They were always supportive, never questioning why someone like myself with no combat training was trying to operate in such a place. They did not go out onto the streets with us but instead helped me through the steps that marked my own militarisation.

In a series of training sessions they instructed my team and me on how to move around without drawing undue attention, how to respond if shot at, and what to do in every situation from a breakdown to a car crash (a likely event on Baghdad's chaotic roads and one for which the solution was apparently to thrust cash into the hands of the driver of the other vehicle before a crowd lynched you). Car doors offered no protection from gunfire, we were told. Even a wall would not necessarily stop a bullet if it was fired from a high velocity rifle. Mortars could kill a person standing a hundred yards away. Armoured vests might stop a bullet but they would not prevent ribs getting broken as the Kevlar plate was pushed into your chest.

We went through combat medical training: how to keep a pierced lung inflated by strapping a credit card across the entry wound, what not to do if someone's skin had been burned off, the danger of internal bleeding from bones smashed in a bomb blast, and the best way to tourniquet a shattered arm while using only one hand and your teeth. Then, in the summer, my newspaper decided to follow other media groups and carry a weapon in the back-up car. We bought a semi-automatic pistol, a Browning 9mm, from our security advisers and they took us to the shooting range at the interior ministry. Shell blockages, target selection and the techniques of firing from positions of cover were outlined and practised.

It was a big step deciding that it was time to carry a weapon. Where those of us in the Baghdad press corps had once simply been journalists, we now risked resembling leaders of our own militias. Everyone had their own security procedures, our two-car system being simply the method our budget stretched to, and by 2005 most of us were armed. My team, with Marwan and his pistol, were minor league. The larger American papers had dozens of guards and the TV stations small armies.

While I was the *Telegraph*'s Iraq correspondent I never heard of any media organisation that started shooting, though they would probably have kept it pretty quiet if they had. The closest call appeared to have been when reporters from a US television station were unlucky enough to have been driving past the Palestine at the exact moment when the hotel was hit by a cement mixer filled with explosives and came under sustained machine gun fire. A massive gun battle erupted as its guards shot back at their attackers. The American TV crew was caught in the middle. Their security detail was certainly on the look-out for targets as they sought to get away as quickly as possible. If we had been in the same situation we would have been killed. The correspondent's armoured saloon had bullet marks down one side. I was pretty jealous of their budgets when I saw that. The *Telegraph* was never going to be able to afford a similar level of protection.

This escalation in our security precautions nevertheless left me with mixed feelings. I could not quite accept that a media company might have to kill someone, nor was I sure how carrying guns would help if, like Rory Carroll, we found ourselves surrounded by three vehicles with nowhere to go. As far as I could see it risked only making matters worse if we started going pop-pop-pop with our semi-automatic glorified peashooter. The bottom line, however, was that my newspaper approved of the pistol and my team had made it pretty clear they were unwilling to go out without it. So I hid behind that knowledge and tried not to think too hard about what its presence might turn us into.

The truth, moreover, was that the pistol did make me feel more secure, despite my misgivings. It provided an emotional sense of security if nothing else. I knew that whatever happened I did not want to be the next person shown on the internet being beheaded. That pistol might have brought false hope but it seemed too much to go out with nothing to rely on for protection but the Iraqi-style shirt on my back.

I had been a journalist for a decade by the time I started my job in Iraq. Ten years in which I had learnt my trade, completed my apprenticeship at a local paper in Yorkshire, worked in Hong Kong during the years that straddled the 1997 handover to China, and then fought my way onto the national papers in London. I had secured a job at the *Telegraph*, become one of their foreign correspondents when they posted me to the States and filed for them from countries across the world. I knew how to construct a story, what information was needed, who you had to talk to and how you ordered your quotes to lure the reader in. Journalism is a craft, certainly not an art. You learn the techniques and drill them until they become automatic so that against a deadline events can be put into the required style and set out in a way that is comprehensible to the reader.

Ten years' practice was not enough for Iraq. Twenty years probably would not have been. The situation defied easy packaging and clear conclusions. Facts, facts, facts, editors had drilled into me. Double, triple-check your facts, and then put them in an order that ensures they provide answers. In Iraq there were few facts and far more questions to which no one had answers. Due to the limitations imposed by the dangers we faced, few reporters had a comprehensive understanding of what was going on beyond the concrete palisades that ringed the Hamra.

This lack of understanding did not mean that there was no value in us being there. You only had to hear what was being claimed in Washington and London, let alone by the officials in the Green Zone, to know that it was essential the media publicised even the limited information it could gain. I still believe that now. I am proud that the work done by all the journalists working in Baghdad helped make clear to the world what was really going on in that city. However, it did not stop my efforts seeming depressingly inadequate whenever I let myself think of the hundreds of unreported stories unfolding each day: the myriad of personal tragedies never told, the individual triumphs that would fail to be recognised.

Most of the Iraqis I met were unable to understand much more than I could, which was in its own way reassuring. They would routinely tell me that they did not comprehend how such a thing could have happened to their country and clutched at explanations that might rationalise what had occurred. Maybe it was because the Americans intended to create chaos in order to destroy Iraq for ever, I would be told, or possibly it was God's judgement on the worst moral excesses of Saddam's secular regime. For some the foreign Wahhabi coming into Iraq to impose their brand of ultra-conservative Islam were to blame, for others – and this was a real favourite – it was in some unspecified way all the fault of Iran.

Only America's senior officers and officials seemed unwilling to admit to the possibility that they did not know exactly what was going on. I would come across the odd clued-up officer out in the field who really understood his area of operations and could explain, in detail and with insight, the problems he faced. In the official briefings by the top brass, however, everything was always on course and they still had their flipcharts and PowerPoint presentations to prove it.

One time I did come across a senior American who was willing to acknowledge the extent of his ignorance. I was on a trip to the north-western town of Tal Afar where I stayed with the local US unit stationed there. Their commander was Colonel H. R. McMaster and he was the smartest American officer I had ever met. Shaven haired and bulging with muscles, he looked like the archetypal hard-nosed soldier. In fact, he had been a military history professor at West Point and had a PhD from the University of North Carolina where he wrote a thesis about the mistakes made in the Vietnam War. In the first Gulf War he had headed a tank troop that had taken on units of Republican Guard that vastly outnumbered his own and destroyed them all without losing a single soldier. It was an achievement that earned him not only the Silver Star but a hero's write-up by Tom Clancy in his 1994 book *Armored Cav*. When I met McMaster in his office in the old Iraqi barracks that his unit's camp were built around, he batted away the broad policy question I had flung at him as being impossible to answer.

'Anyone who claims to understand what's happening in Iraq doesn't understand it,' he said.

He was an officer who had successfully done his job, had that year taken Tal Afar and restored it from being a place where freshly severed heads were placed in the centre of road junctions to one that bore some semblance of civilisation. Not that it lasted. After his tour ended it took only three months for his successor to lose control and for the town to once again become a rat run for the suicide bombers making their way towards Mosul.

In our compound, with its blast walls and electricity generators, we were living the good life by Baghdad standards. In the city at large conditions were deteriorating rapidly. This realisation was inescapable, however confused the overall situation might have been. Everyone you talked to, everything you saw, testified to it.

It is hard to conceive the state that Baghdad was being reduced to. Try to imagine that it was where you had grown up and lived. Think what fundamentals you would take for granted and the presumptions on which you had built your life. Then imagine them being stripped away one by one, what you would be left with and what such a situation would do to you.

It was not only the war but the general lawlessness that made Baghdad so dangerous. People could not go outside without fear of becoming the victim of a violent robbery. There was still no effective police force and criminals were taking full advantage of the vacuum. The health ministry was advising doctors to start carrying weapons for their protection because thieves were pretending to be patients to seize drugs and equipment. Gangs preyed on the roads into and out of the capital. The *Telegraph* had been a victim when a colleague on a trip to Basra had found the road in front blocked by a lorry and armed men emerging from a car behind. That time he, his driver and his translator had been lucky. It was only their possessions and the car, not their lives, that were taken.

It was rare to hear of resolutions so bloodless. An Iraqi friend of mine, a receptionist in one of the city's hotels, had his son kidnapped as he emerged from a mobile phone shop in central Baghdad. He paid the ransom and was sitting in the main room of his house when he heard a car stop and someone run to the front door. There was a burst of gunfire. He opened the door to have his son collapse into his arms. The boy died there and then as his family tried, and failed, to stem the bleeding.

The basic necessities for life were eroding. Saddam, as part of his system of state control, had instigated a rationing system to ensure every Iraqi received basic food items on a regular basis. By 2005 the country's new rulers were unable to guarantee supply. The system for sugar and baby formula collapsed, forcing many to go without. By the spring, electricity in the capital was limited to eight hours per day and rarely came on for more than two hours at a time. Output averaged only 850 megawatts, compared with 2,500 megawatts before the war started. Partly it was because of the looting that had followed the collapse of the Ba'athist regime but it was also because the network was a target for those opposing the occupation. They knew that maximising people's discomfort helped turn them against the country's new rulers. Sewage processing plants were another favoured objective. The attacks against them resulted in pipes overflowing and sewage being reported on almost half of Baghdad's streets. Sadr City, the vast Shia slum in east Baghdad, was consequently in the grip of a hepatitis epidemic. In the height of the summer the water plants were hit, cutting off supply to two million homes. The temperature was above 40°C as I watched people queue at emergency water pipes to fill their jerry cans and buckets.

I used to ask Ahmed to translate the city's talk radio

shows. They provided insights into everyday life that the security situation made it so hard to glean. From my office on the third floor of the Hamra I could see Baghdad stretching around me: the stacks of flats with their box-like windows, the roofs covered with their jumble of cables, abandoned furniture and bent television aerials; the streets with their rusting cars pumping out the cheap petrol fumes whose odour imbued the city, and the occasional palm tree bringing a burst of life to the city's otherwise beige exterior. As we listened to the radio I would sit looking at it, hearing the voices coming to me from out there.

I liked Radio Tigris the best as it was usually the liveliest. In the summer of 2005 a programme debated where people could sleep to escape the oppressive heat. I still have the notes I jotted down:

Air-conditioning? None working as the electricity not reliable enough. Children crying because so tired. Very exhausting for the parents.

Woman concerned about danger of sleeping outside on the roof. A popular solution apparently. Has heard of people being hit by falling bullets and shrapnel. That a big worry.

'We heard one night an American plane bombing nearby,' another woman says. Had been on the roof of her home at the time trying to keep cool. 'What should we do when that happens?'

A caller complaining that the five families living in their block of flats could not all fit on the roof and those forced to sleep in the garden were plagued by rats that appeared to be 'bigger than cats'.

An architect, Abu Rhadi, 'This city was once the most beautiful in the Middle East. People would walk by the river at dusk and the restaurants were filled with laughter. Now our life is this.'

That summer I visited a US army unit in Kirkuk, a city in the north of the country which marked the boundary between Iraq's Arab and Kurd populations and was therefore among the country's least stable cities. It was one of Iraq's oldest settlements, a place lived in continuously for 5,000 years. At its heart was an ancient citadel, first built in the 9th century BC, which was ringed by 72 towers. It stood on a 130-foot high mound, dominating the modern buildings that surrounded it.

I arrived at Kirkuk General Hospital just as it started taking in the injured from a suicide bombing. At least thirty had been killed and more than fifty injured, a number of them from bullet wounds inflicted in the aftermath of the blast when local police panicked and started shooting in every direction.

The hospital had been built by the British in 1946 and it had barely been improved since. Brown paint was peeling off the walls and the ceilings were black with dirt. As patients were rolled in on metal trolleys they left trails of blood on the floor of the entrance hall.

In the central ward a dozen beds had already been filled. The skin on the face of one of the wounded had been peeled back and hung in flaps. Blood oozed through bandages on the leg of another, his chest pepper-marked by stones lifted off the street and flung into his body in the blast. A man stood over a bed where a figure lay unconscious. He was holding one end of a tube, the other end of which had been stuck into the patient's nose. He was methodically placing his end next to a ventilation machine to inflate the injured man's lungs, and then moving it away to let them fall. The hospital did not have the valve to enable it to be connected properly.

An Iraqi doctor, a striking man with a strong nose and powerful chin, emerged from surgery and pulled off his plastic gloves. He was one of only three working there. His face crumbled. 'We have no resuscitation devices and no intravenous fluid. We do not have enough equipment and what we do have is twenty years out of date,' he said. 'We cannot save most of these people.'

When they learned of the explosion, the Americans had sent doctors to the hospital to help. Though they had brought their own medicines with them, they were despairing about the level of hygiene. Used needles were being flushed down toilets, blood was left to congeal on floors and there were no antiseptic wipes. It had been one of the US medics, Captain James Schroeder, who had ferried me to the hospital from the base at which I was staying. He was one of those Americans I found throughout the US military, someone who had come out filled with excitement and optimism about how he was going to be doing good by making Iraq better. Now he was faced with this.

'They do their best,' he said of the Iraqi doctors. 'But you can see the reality of this place.' He was called to treat a police officer whom I had seen brought in. His leg had almost doubled in size from the bleeding from a fracture in his hip.

Outside, the ambulances ferrying in the wounded were little more than transit vans equipped with first aid kits and extra bandages. Cars joined them in dropping off the injured. On the ground lay four bodies covered by white sheets. A woman in a black hijab was standing beside them weeping silently.

I sat on a low brick wall and waited for my lift back.

Half an hour later Captain Schroeder sat down beside me. He normally had the demeanour of the High School jock he once was, all white teeth and clean features. Now sweat and dirt marked lines down his face and there were red stains on his uniform. I asked him how his patient was. 'He died,' he said. 'Too much blood loss by the time he got here.'

4. USA

When I visited Iraq in April 2004 American forces had placed Fallujah in a state of siege after four security contractors were ambushed, killed and their burned bodies paraded through the streets. US High Command promised the city would be pacified but plans for an assault were aborted amid concern about the number of Iraqi civilians at risk of being killed. A compromise was reached in which a local Iraqi security force was given the responsibility of stabilising the city. Over the summer of 2004 this unit dissolved and handed over its American-provided weaponry to the extremists. In November, the US military attacked. For nine days its troops battled their way through Fallujah's streets until the city had been wrestled back under American control.

Three months later, in February 2005, the marines who had taken Fallujah were preparing to go home. They had been in Iraq for a year, a year in which they had been involved in the American military's most intense house-to-house fighting since Vietnam, had killed around 1,500 of their enemy and seen a hundred of their own die with a further thousand wounded. These men were the self-styled 'Devil Dogs', troops who proudly had as their motto that there was 'no greater friend; no worse enemy'. Soon they would be back at their base in Southern California, able to enjoy days on the beach, trips to Tijuana and races up Highway 5 to the delights of Los Angeles. First, however, the United States government wanted to influence exactly what would be coming home. Before being allowed on their flight back to the States, the soldiers were being required to undergo therapy. The sessions were given the military-sounding mame of 'Warrior Transition' but what they resembled was a segment from *The Oprah Winfrey Show*. It was time to share.

In February 2005 I was allowed to attend one of these sessions in Camp Fallujah, the marine barracks on the outskirts of the city. It was being held in an auditorium in the Saddam-era military base that the US troops had adopted. Rows of seats upholstered in blue cloth formed a semi-circle facing a raised stage. Normally a TV tuned to ESPN was placed on it, enabling the marines to keep up with the sports news from back home. On this occasion, however, it hosted the unit's senior officers and regimental chaplain, who were warning their charges of the new fights to come, this time ones in their everyday lives.

'Go slow when reconnecting with your children,' the men were told. 'Don't be surprised by the nightmares. Tolerate bad traffic. Don't expect wives or girlfriends to have been transformed into the sexual Houdinis you fantasised about while apart. Feel good about yourselves and what you achieved in battle.'

One of the senior officers stepped forward. 'Iraq is changin' and it all started here in Fallujah,' he said. 'Freedom started in Fallujah. Freedom from fear. Freedom you brought to this place. Everyone is proud of you. Your nation is proud of you. You're the heroes of Fallujah and that will be with you for the rest of your lives.

'When you hear veterans from the D-Day landings they talk about how it was a seminal day in their lives, the formative event of their lives. I submit to you that Fallujah will be a seminal event in your lives, somethin' that is uniquely yours. There can be good things from that, but there can also be bad. The images are seared on your mind. We can't make them go away: the burned bodies, the pieces of humans or the effect of a roadside bomb. Be aware, the battle of Fallujah may go on inside you.'

There were nearly a hundred men present. Their guns lay on the floor in front of those sitting and were slung around the shoulders of those who stood. They all listened intently.

'What good are you goin' to take from here?' asked the chaplain, who despite his job title had the physique and presence of a boxer.

It took a while for an answer. 'To appreciate the smaller things in life,' a voice said.

'Like what?' the chaplain responded.

'Beer!' This got a laugh from everyone, the chaplain included.

'The sense of havin' served my country,' said someone.

'The fact we fought them here so they can't take it to our homes,' proposed another.

The chaplain asked, 'What of the negatives?'

The answers came quicker this time. 'Loss of comrades,' said one Hispanic serviceman. 'Not all of us are here.'

The chaplain nodded. 'They laid down their lives for a cause greater than themselves.'

'Dogs eating corpses,' a voice called out.

'That's right,' said the chaplain. 'I saw a dog comin' from the chest cavity of a man, its face drippin' with blood. That was pretty bad. I've got dogs and I don't think I'm quite goin' to look at them the same way again.'

A marine said, 'The smell of it. When you're barbecuin' on a Saturday morning in your back yard, I'm not looking forward to that.'

'The suffering of the women and children,' another offered.

There was a lot of agreement about that one. 'I know there is not a man here who wouldn't choose to put down their life for a child,' the chaplain said.

'Getting shot at,' came the next response.

'That's goin' to change you fundamentally as a human being,' the chaplain said. 'You need to talk about that stuff but be careful who you talk to. People can't understand what it's like here. They may look at you like you're crazy. This isn't good dinner conversation.'

'What do you do if someone talks shit to you in a bar about the war in Iraq?' he asked.

A marine shouted out, 'I'm goin' to crack them over the head with a bottle of beer.'

That got a lot of laughs too.

The next day their commander took me on a tour of the city. Mike Shupp was like someone out of every war film you have ever seen. He was the trusty tough guy: a strong handshake, straight talking, broad, and emotionally powerful. There was a story about why he should no longer have been in Fallujah which made him seem only more impressive. He had been in Iraq for five months when his wife developed cancer and he was flown home as she underwent chemotherapy. It was terrible to watch, he admitted, but she beat it. He had been given compassionate leave from the rest of his tour so he could help her recuperate. Then a rocket came through the roof of his old HQ in Camp Fallujah and took out his successor, and he was called back to Iraq to lead his men.

Colonel Shupp was one of those people who were rarely quiet. The words flowed from his mouth so fast that even with shorthand I could barely get them down. He was proud. He had fulfilled his assigned task. In fact he had hopefully won the war. Two years into the fight, Fallujah had fallen and Iraq could now start moving towards peace. That was what he believed. He was going home with the conviction that his had been a job well done.

'Look at our accomplishments here,' he said. 'The insurgents wanted Fallujah as a safe haven. We took it from them. My men didn't let me down. They were exhausted and tired but they looked after each other and won. After the battle an old woman came up to me and kissed my hand. She said, "Thank God for you people." It was incredible.'

Although I had read the reports and seen the photographs, I was not ready for the level of destruction I saw as Shupp took me into Fallujah itself. We drove down the main street in a convoy of Humvees and it seemed as if there was not one building that had been left without pitting from shell fragments or machine-gun fire. At the first corner a house had simply disappeared, reduced to a pile of sharp pebbles and dust. Half-way down the next block was a mosque, its dome shattered and the minaret lying in ruins. Doorways still showed the white crosses that had marked buildings as cleared of insurgents. Rubble covered the pavements and street lights lay across intersections. The Humvees had to swerve every few minutes in order to avoid craters in the tarmac.

We turned right at a corner and in front of us was what remained of an apartment block, the windows blown out and three four-foot wide holes running in a diagonal down the side wall where American missiles had struck. Beside it lay the remnants of clothing, a purple blouse and a pair of black cotton trousers the most identifiable, scattered by the force of the blasts. There was another corner and this time we turned left onto a side road. The breeze-block walls of the surrounding buildings had crumbled across the dirt-covered street. Broken wires hung from telephone poles and, ahead of us, a goat was foraging amid the piles of debris and rubbish.

It was February, the end of Iraq's brief but unpleasant rainy season, and craters had become pools. A truck was parked outside a house. Its owner was one of the families drifting back into the city after having originally joined the rush to escape before the showdown between the Americans and Sunni gunmen began. Some of their possessions lay in the back under a black tarpaulin. A figure stood in the doorway to the house, looking dejected as others walked past her to see what else might have survived.

Access to the city was limited by checkpoints, every entrance having been blocked. At the one we passed through on the way back to camp marines were methodically searching every vehicle going into the city, causing a queue to snake back a hundred yards from the barriers. The Americans had taken Fallujah once and were damned if anyone was going to have to do it again. No weapons would get back in if they could avoid it.

A group of marines were taking photographs as final

mementoes. They gathered in front of the checkpoint with the city behind them. 'Smile and say Fallujah,' the serviceman taking their picture shouted.

Colonel Shupp was still talking, now about the reception he expected when he arrived back home. 'I think the people back in the States appreciate what we've done,' he said. 'There may be a difference of opinion about the war in Iraq but there is no difference of opinion about the military. These men will be goin' back as veritable war heroes.

'They deserve it. They were the most heroic people I ever saw. They are the next greatest generation. They're goin' to go back and be the next leaders of our country. They showed a passion here no one can imagine. These are truly amazin' people.'

In the base, marines were lining up outside the camp post office with boxes of kit they wanted sent to the States. These were the physical reminders of the seminal event of their lives. It was a slow queue as everything had to be laboriously approved, checked and weighed. Three marines from San Diego were playing cards and talking about their Warrior Transition while they waited. They had seen *Rambo*, I learned, so they knew what war could do to the psyche.

'It was like being in a movie, it felt unreal,' one, Ivan Getierrez, said of the fighting. He was 21 years old, a skinny little thing with ears far too big for his head. 'Everything was just being played out. There were bombs, explosions, bullets – I was in the zone doing what I had trained for. It was like being in a trance going through it.

'Then I woke up. I'd lost two good friends. I think about why it was them and not me. Most nights I think about that. Go figure.'

His fellow card players really did not want to get into it. Instead they kept studying the hands they had been dealt to ensure there was no way I could attract their attention and ask what it was they might be feeling.

Due to the deteriorating security situation, by 2005 the US military provided almost the only way to get out of Baghdad and into the rest of Iraq. My translator, Ahmed, and the rest of my Iraqi team were always pleased when I did because, in my absence, they did not have to risk coming into the office and could work the phones from their homes, e-mailing me with the information I needed to write my articles. It was a better life for them than having to share a car with a foreigner or waiting to see who might attack the Hamra complex.

Joining up with the American forces was a relatively simple procedure. I would send an e-mail request to the central press office in the Green Zone and they would pass it on to the unit in the area I wished to visit. Nine times out of ten the request was approved. There were far fewer reporters around by then and some of the units would only get a couple, if any, coming to visit them during their entire year in the field. They did not like that. It made them feel that what they were doing was being forgotten – or, worse, was unimportant. Often a visiting journalist, even a Brit like me, would bring a welcome sense of validation.

Getting approval to go somewhere and actually getting there were two separate things, however. I spent days sitting by helicopter landing pads trying to travel from one place to another. It was like an extreme form of hitchhiking. A helicopter would come and I would get as far as I could, then I would wait for the next one that might take me a little bit closer. Occasionally I found myself on a helicopter doing the whole trip in one leg. That was when I knew Sod's Law would leave me grounded halfway by a sand storm, or knocked off the manifest by a sudden influx of soldiers with orders to get somewhere fast.

Sometimes the contortions I went through to get out of or back to Baghdad became ridiculous. Once, while stuck by an airstrip in a base west of Ramadi, I was utterly fed up after having spent four days waiting in a world of transit tents and portaloos, with nowhere to wash and only the semi-tepid contents of self-heating ration packs for food. In the end I boarded the first flight possible, a plane going to Kuwait. Once there, and after considerable effort, I finally got on another flight that was heading to Baghdad via a stop in Qatar. Three countries and seven days for a trip that would have been a six-hour drive in safer days.

When I could get a lift from a helicopter there would be the race to climb in as I pulled my bag onto my back and piled into the side while the gunner urged me to go faster because the pilot had no plans to stop for long. Then the vertical lift-off to weave across the skies of Iraq. One time, going from Kurdistan to Tikrit, we spent the whole journey never more than a hundred feet off the ground – down the sides of valleys, skimming across the desert, rising up to cross electricity lines, scattering goats. Everyone on board had their cameras out for that trip.

The hairiest journeys were always the ones into the Green Zone itself, especially if I found myself on the British shuttle that ferried people to it from Baghdad airport after a stay with the Army down south. On most helicopter trips the pilots had done the route so often they felt it to be almost routine. The British pilots, however, were often out of their normal area of operations and on maximum alert. As a result they knew how to make you feel scared. The automatic defence system would be set to such a high level of receptivity that a sudden reflection of sunlight off water could be enough to trigger the anti-attack flares. They were usually set off at least once every journey. When the flares started firing the pilot would twist and bank so that I would fall against my harness, the passengers who had never done the ride before would look pasty-faced with fear and I would be left desperately wondering if it was just a misfire or if this really was an attack. Only a couple of times did I hear gunfire on these trips, and who knows if we were being fired at or if it was simply the muzak of Baghdad. Nevertheless, on those occasions, the helicopter turned all the way over onto its side as the pilot sought to get out of trouble and I was as pasty-faced as everyone else.

Anbar province was the heart of the Sunni insurgency. It is home to the cities of Fallujah and Ramadi and there was not a settlement in it that did not have its local youths keen to cause as much damage as they could to American forces.

One time in June 2005 I travelled through Anbar along a road north-west of the city of Hit. I was at the back of a six-vehicle US convoy, in a Humvee that made up part of the guard detail for a military investigator who had been dispatched to determine how an Iraqi civilian was killed.

The case was one of those confused stories I often heard in Iraq. The marines had been raiding a house. The oldest son was shot dead. The marines said he had come at them from the main bedroom with a gun. His family said the marines had shot him in cold blood and then produced a gun to put beside him. It became a serious problem for the military when it emerged that the dead Iraqi was related to a senior local politician, hence the investigation. I could not see how, amid the chaos and deceits of Iraq, anyone would be able to get to the bottom of it, let alone the Marine Corps judge advocate the US authorities had sent.

In mid-summer, Humvees were never the most comfortable way to get anywhere. Due to the number of roadside bombs, most vehicles had been fitted with as much armour plate as they could take. This was obviously good in one way but Humvees had not been designed to carry such a weight. The overstretched engine left little power for the air-conditioning system. It was hot in there in your helmet and body armour.

One of the four marines in my vehicle, Private Casey, had just returned from two weeks home leave in California. He was a gangly youth, too tall and at the same time not wide enough for his uniform. His parents lived near the liberal haven of Santa Cruz and he was recounting how the local students had treated him while he had been there.

'They're rich kid hippies,' he said of the Santa Cruz student scene. 'You'll see them sittin' on the sidewalk with their fake dreads. They knew who I was and were giving me shit. I was at this party and this guy was not holdin' back, saying, "What are you doing goin' over there killin' babies and droppin' bombs?" So I told him I was an infantryman so I don't drop bombs and I saw everyone I killed. But he wouldn't get the message.'

One of his colleagues, Corporal Philip Lathrop, wanted to know why he had not beaten him up.

'I did,' Robinson assured him.

Their commander, a bullish staff sergeant called Dan Thompson, was particularly pleased that he had a Brit on board. He was sitting beside the driver and turned round to tell me so. 'It makes me glad that America and Britain are such staunch allies,' he said. 'Not like the French. We heaped a lot of bodies on the beaches in Normandy and they seem to forget that.'

It was a long drive, at least two hours there and two hours back, and there was little to see to break the boredom. Away from the section of the Euphrates river that curls though Anbar, the landscape was a repeating expanse of arid desert broken only by the occasional sand-bank or boulder. In my Humvee, a machine-gunner had been placed looking out of the top hatch to watch for any sign of roadside bombs. For the rest of us the thing to do, it seemed, was talk.

'What I like about President Bush,' Thompson said, 'is he's a man of principle. He says what he believes and does it. I really believe that by being in Iraq we're fighting here so we don't have to fight these people back home. I know some people don't believe that, but I really do.

'The rest of the world doesn't understand what we are up against. What Spain did after that bomb went off on their train, pulling out of Iraq like that, that showed me the rest of the world wasn't willing to step up to it. People like to talk of Clinton's time but he didn't have to face any great threat. 9/11 happened because Clinton took his eye off the ball.'

He took a sip of tepid water. 'I'd actually left the army but rejoined when 9/11 happened. It would've been similar to having trained for the Olympic Games and not being able to race.'

The engine started overheating and the air-con had to be turned down even further. Robinson looked across at me and shook his head. 'It's like a fuckin' sauna in here,' he said. The driver was talking about his father's ranch in Oklahoma and his uncle's ranch in Montana. They were apparently where he would rather be.

An Iraqi car lay on its side by the road. It was a blackened wreck surrounded by scorch marks. Two corpses lay around it. One had been blown completely in half, its arms stuck out by rigor mortis, so that it looked like an Action Man toy pulled apart at the waist and then discarded. The other had had its head blown off. It lay facing the tarmac, the blackened hole at the top of the neck targeting us as we drove passed. No one else on board seemed to see them, the conversation continuing as if I had imagined the entire scene.

The radio warned of suspicious vehicles parked on the road ahead. There was a lorry and, opposite it, a white car with its bonnet open. As we passed them Thompson rolled down the window and pointed his grenade launcher at the car. An Iraqi, who had been working on the engine, stood up, staring at us with a mixture of terror and bemusement.

We were entering the outer edges of habitation now. There were electricity pylons lying on the desert where they had fallen, others bent at the base so their wires trailed along the ground. Then we reached the Euphrates, the water so blue after the grey of the dust and sand. A thin band of green vegetation was visible around its edges and white horses raced along the water's surface.

The village of the Iraqi whose death was being investigated was like all the others in Anbar: concrete boxes clustered in the middle of nothingness. I was led to a house and sat on a red plastic chair by the front entrance as the marines talked to the family inside. A score of troops had been positioned on the surrounding roads to stop any surprises.

I looked through the window. There was a lot of talking going on. The Americans adopted serious expressions. A woman dressed from head to foot in black robes started crying and shaking her arms at them. A group of Iraqi men appeared from a back-room and also started gesticulating. The American soldiers watched the new arrivals wearily. I was told to stay where I was when I asked a US soldier if I could get closer to hear what was being said. The woman opened the door and placed a grey T-shirt at my feet. It was covered in dried blood, spreading in ever lighter rings from a small burn hole at its centre. Her whole body was shaking. The American troops told their judge advocate it was time to leave.

As we walked back to the Humvees I asked if anyone now had a better understanding about how the Iraqi had been killed in the raid. They didn't, or at least not one they wanted to share. So what would happen? 'Give them money to shut 'em up,' I was told, though by one of the soldiers rather than the military investigator.

My Humvee crew were drinking Red Bulls as I got in. This time, as we made our way along the road, all of them spotted the dead bodies.

'Did you see that!' Lathrop shouted. 'That's half a

person. Can we go back so I can take a picture? That was pretty cool. Go on. Just quickly, one picture, that's all.'

'We really blew that shit up,' Thompson observed. 'They shouldn't have tried to bury a roadside bomb. They got what they deserved.'

Whatever my reason for visiting the Americans, it was nonetheless a good break from Baghdad. Such was the reality of Iraq that operating in the capital was the opposite of normal reporting. Usually journalists sought out the dramatic. In Baghdad that was the last thing anyone wanted to come across. The consequences could be far too severe. A good day was a quiet one. Being with the Americans meant they were in charge of my security. I could simply concentrate on doing my job. There was something therapeutic and relaxing in that.

The US's smaller bases – FOBs, forward operating bases, they were called – were relatively austere. Most had been set up in old Ba'athist buildings or army barracks to which little was added but protective barriers and watchtowers. These were intended as temporary camps, sites to be occupied only until the Iraqi army was ready to take control of them.

The larger US bases may have been covered in the same ubiquitous sand and dust but they had a far greater sense of permanence and, as a result, far more effort had been made to ensure they held as many familiar comforts as possible. The US government liked to ensure its troops did not suffer too much deprivation in the field. I routinely saw American soldiers cooking themselves hot dogs, playing ball or enjoying the latest series of *Lost*; everyday activities which created an impression of unexpectedly normal people that was hard to reconcile with the knowledge of the brutality that was their day job.

In the Hamra, I lived off poor-quality kebabs. In US mess halls there were typically rib-eye steaks, burgers, tortillas, salad bars, fridges boasting twenty different kinds of soft drink, chocolate cookies and even Ben and Jerry's ice cream stands. Camps routinely had recreation centres which offered special dance nights boasting evenings of hip-hop, salsa or country and western music. Some bases had cinemas. Never have I heard an audience laugh as long or as loudly as a group of marines did while watching Brad Pitt beat up Angelina Jolie in *Mr and Mrs Smith*.

Al-Assad, the main airbase in Anbar province, was one of the US's biggest camps and consequently one of its best equipped. It spread over more than five square miles and had two bus routes in it. Red 'Stop' signs, the ubiquitous furniture of American streets, had been placed at its road junctions and US mailboxes installed. Subway, a coffee shop and a pizza parlour were open for business, their counters manned by nervous, if friendly, Indian contract workers from west Bengal. The base had its own football pitch and swimming pool. Its recreation room was kitted out with PlayStations and Xboxes. There were pool tables and a basketball court. On 4 July, pig carcasses were flown in and roasted. Screens were set up so the troops could watch the Super Bowl. The camp even had its own Hertz car rental office providing 4x4s with bullet-proof windows for those wanting to cross camp in something more comfortable than a military Humvee.

It was not only material comforts that the US sought to provide for its servicemen in the midst of a war zone on the other side of the world. A military survey had shown that the soldiers' greatest concern was not being killed or injured but the breakdown of relationships. Divorce, rather than death, was what they meant when they talked about the 'big D'. So America's armed forces had done what they could to help those in the field maintain contact with their families. International calls were subsidised and, most significantly, almost every serviceman had access to a free internet terminal.

Never before had soldiers fighting abroad been so connected to home. This was not an environment where letters were sent with sensitive information blacked out by censors. People were instant-messaging their friends and loved ones directly. They could e-mail, set up internet sites, post pictures, use all the wonders of the multimedia age. The internet was so popular that by the end of 2005 there were 200 blogs being updated regularly by active servicemen in Iraq.

This inevitably created its own problems for the military. A national guardsman was demoted after writing on his blog that his company commander was a 'glory seeker' and his battalion sergeant major an 'inhuman monster'. The Pentagon finally had to ban access to YouTube after there were complaints about the number of gory videos being uploaded onto it from Iraq. However, the internet permitted an unprecedented level of awareness in the States of what the troops were experiencing and the problems they faced. Anyone, for example, wanting to know how their friend Elizabeth Le Bel, a 24-year-old sergeant on her first combat posting, was doing needed only to check the latest missive on her blog. One of them even came from the computer at a military hospital hours after the vehicle she was in had been hit by a roadside bomb. 'I started to scream bloody murder, and one of the other females on the convoy came over, grabbed my hand and started to calm me down,' she wrote. 'She held on to me, allowing me to place my leg on her shoulder as it was hanging free. I learned that the driver [of my vehicle] had not made it through, and that is a very tough thing for me. Thankfully, it was quick, I am told.' It must have been a challenging read for those who had known her in better times.

I often wondered how this level of connectivity affected family and friends back in the States. It certainly must have made the worry that something bad had happened more immediate. When a soldier was killed the first thing his base did was shut down its internet connection until the bereaved family had been notified. Wives were no longer waiting for a figure in dress uniform to come knocking on their front door. They were panicking the moment they discovered there was no one replying to their e-mails.

I visited a camp where a battalion had managed to find a local contractor who could set up WiFi in their barracks. The soldiers barely talked to each other at night as they sat in their cubicles browsing pornography or engaging in cybersex with women back in the States.

On another trip I sat next to a gunnery sergeant in the military internet café at a base in al-Qaim. This was one of the most isolated places in Iraq, a camp located right on the Syrian border, where, during the summer of 2005, the Americans routinely fought al-Qa'eda supporters wanting to cross into Iraq's heartland. It was a battle zone in which one of the American FOBs was so exposed, and so routinely attacked, that those stationed in it had burrowed their barracks underground, covering the tops with reinforced concrete as protection from the mortar fire.

The gunnery sergeant had just come back from a night-time operation. Caked in sand and grime, he was talking to his wife on instant messenger. It was snowing in their home town and she could not find the shovel to clear the yard. He was patiently explaining to her exactly where it was hung in the garage. I asked him if he minded being bothered with such domestic inconveniences. 'Not at all,' he told me. 'Means I don't have to worry there's a problem back home that she's strugglin' to cope with.'

Once, when in Kirkuk, I saw a soldier in his base's internet room bow his head and start praying. Looking at his computer screen I realised that he was communicating with his wife via webcam. She was praying too. He later told me that, as long as operations allowed it, they would pray together at the same time each day for his safe return home.

It was while I was with the US forces invading Iraq in the early days of the war that I first understood what American soldiers are trained to deliver when it is demanded of them. It has coloured my attitude to the military ever since. Not necessarily for better or for worse, it is simply that you cannot look at anyone in uniform the same way after witnessing what they do for a living.

It was on Thursday, 3 April 2003, the day the US army took Baghdad airport and for the first time positioned its forces on the outskirts of the city, that I learnt what this involved. I was travelling with a US tank company, part of the mass of soldiers spreading across Iraq. The previous night our camp had been located on the edge of the Euphrates valley, a place where the roads were bordered by three-foot-high grass and clumps of palm trees flourished beside meandering streams. We had now been told to move towards the capital and into the debris of the fighting that had gone on ahead of us.

I was in the back of an M113, an armoured van that acted as the unit's mobile control centre, and as we made our way forward I looked down into a line of foxholes dug by the Iraqi forces and saw the dead lying in them. There was what must have been a small truck, now just twisted metal sheets. An Iraqi tank had been hit so hard that it had been scattered in a circle fifty yards wide. In an orchard was a dead member of the Iraqi army's most elite unit, the Republican Guard. He was lying on his back amid the rotting fruit, his helmet having rolled down a slope and come to a stop at the roadside.

The shooting started at mid-morning, ten to ten to be precise. It began as a salvo in the distance and then spread until it surrounded us on all sides and there was no escape from the constant sound of combat. Many of the Iraqi soldiers were hidden in foxholes. Others were perched on the roofs of buildings. Cars and pick-up trucks drove up side roads to fire off a round before trying to escape. Banks of missiles were attached to the backs of trucks. Men who had been hit half a dozen times still crawled towards their weapons to have one last shot. Soldiers in the path of American tanks stood their ground to fire their machine guns. The air above was filled with the twisting trails of rocket-propelled grenades and missiles.

I hid at the bottom of the vehicle. I could see nothing; the fighting was merely noise. There was no space in my brain for anything but the necessity of picking up every sound that might explain what was happening on the other side of the metal walls in which I was encased. Above me towered an American soldier who was half in and half out the back hatch. He loaded, aimed, fired, loaded, aimed, fired his grenade launcher. His left leg was twitching. At one point he reached down and cut free a box of extra ammunition. He stared at me with vacant eyes as he filled his pockets with so many shells that they spilled out and rolled around his feet.

The gun casings from the .50-caliber fixed at the front fell through the cockpit in a metal waterfall that bounced off the floor around me. I reached down and picked one up. It was burning hot to the touch.

The machine gunner leaned down to light a cigarette. 'You havin' fun yet?' he asked.

It took four hours to reach the outskirts of Baghdad, but when we did the shooting that had surrounded us stopped as suddenly as it had begun. We parked in a small field beside a street sign pointing towards the international airport a few miles to our west. I pulled open the back hatch and stepped out onto the dark green grass, its blades wide as table knives, and looked at the men around me. Soldiers were climbing from their vehicles, and they too stood staring at each other. Smoke was rising everywhere.

A tall black soldier was walking towards me. His name was Sergeant Scott. I had never seen him before and I never saw him again. 'When do we know when this all ends?' he said. 'When do we know when it's all over? How much longer can this go on? There's been a whole load of killing.'

A group of soldiers had gathered nearby. 'I put five rounds, perfectly placed, in the centre of his chest,' one was saying. 'But he wouldn't go down. I could see him still reaching to try to load another rocket-propelled grenade and I changed my machine gun to three-round bursts and sent two into his throat and one right through his forehead.'

'There was a guy at a big fuckin' machine gun and I was pepperin' his bunker with rounds. First Sergeant saw him too and fired off a grenade. It exploded and I saw this arm fly out and roll through the air. The blast blew up all this dirt. It was so hard it felt like shrapnel and I thought I'd been hit. I reached for my face and found there was no blood so I just got straight back into it.'

The driver of the M113 in which I had made that journey was sitting in the cockpit smoking a cigarette. His face was shiny with sweat. 'Did you see it?' he asked me. 'There were dead people everywhere. When I see that many dead bodies it's time to go home.'

He was not one of those who re-enlisted when his time was up. He is a postman now, driving a van along a route in Atlanta.

During the Vietnam War, GIs who had done well, or who had done something so bad it was felt they should get away from the combat zone for a few days, were sent to China Beach. It was a stretch of sand facing the Bay of Danang where, between the swimming and surfing, soldiers and marines were encouraged to put the war behind them and party. That they did with a passion. The booze flowed, the vice girls laboured and the smell of marijuana drifted on the breeze. At night the bars that had sprung up along the shoreline played Jimi Hendrix and the Rolling Stones.

There was nowhere in Iraq that was considered safe enough for US troops to go for rest and recuperation. In this war the four-day mini-break from fear was an air force base in Qatar. By 2005 everyone who had served four months in Iraq was eligible for one visit per tour. Troops flew in around the clock, C-130s depositing their uniformed cargo, and buses ferried the new arrivals to the self-styled welcome centre. There it was quickly made clear what kind of stay could be expected.

Sex was strictly banned and any trips off base prohibited except as part of an organised tour. Alcohol was limited to three beers a night, a limit that would be monitored via a computer logging system that required military IDs to be swiped with each purchase. The only stimulant available in plentiful supply would be chocolate and cans of Coca-Cola.

There was no Jimi Hendrix here, not even any White Stripes. Instead the song that greeted the new arrivals as they walked into the welcome centre was Mariah Carey's 'Hero'.

The Americans had spent a lot of money on the recreation complex. The events on offer included horseshoe-throwing competitions, the occasional comedian, volleyball games and a chess tournament. There was a giant gym, swimming pool, pizza restaurant and burger bars. DVD screens and a mini-cinema filled the main building and pastel-coloured sofas had been provided for this generation's warriors to rest on.

The centrepiece of the facility was its computer-games room. At work these soldiers were expected to kill and maim. As relaxation they were offered a chance to spend time in the modern American teenager's fantasy living room complete with beanbags, Xboxes and unlimited amounts of snack food. GIs could while away the hours in pretend combat while a male Filipino attendant provided sweets and drinks on demand, bringing them straight to their tables so they did not even have to step away from the consoles.

Anything more daring was strictly off-limits. When a two-week tour of installations in Iraq and Kuwait by a scantily clad female group, the Purrrfect Angels, was staged in 2004, one female officer reported it as sexually offensive and the person who organised it was reprimanded.

The older soldiers primarily spent their time talking to their wives and children on the free telephones. The young ones mostly decided the best distraction was the pool, which was where I found them when I visited the base in the spring of 2005. The few female GIs present had clustered in a group at one end while the boys stared hungrily at them.

'It's like a correctional facility,' I heard one soldier say as a group discussed their officially sanctioned release from danger.

'There is just enough beer that it's a tease.'

'How do we get out of here and find some action?'

'I miss being back on base. At least it's not boring there.'

'This is a severely limited hunting ground. What're you to do for pussy?'

In the gym dozens of soldiers silently pumped weights while staring at the provocative music videos being played on the television screens around them.

At night the military police came out in force and patrolled the paths between the accommodation tents. There were two nightclubs. In them soldiers showed off their hip-hop moves, men mostly having to dance with men, each seeking to prove their skills as they padded out the time they took drinking their lagers. The fundamentalist Christians and the recovering alcoholics were petitioned to spread their three-strong allocation wide.

One of the camp officials showed me around. She told me it was necessary to have strict rules to ensure that soldiers acted in line with the contemporary moral values of the Pentagon and the base's Arab hosts. What did she think was the best thing the camp offered? 'Sleep,' she said. 'These soldiers can have some time away from their operation zones and catch up on sleep. That'll help them the most when they get back.'

I noticed that extra lighting was being put up in the lanes that divided the rows of tents. I asked her what it was for. It was apparently to aid safety at night by ensuring everywhere was suitably well lit. I had heard stories of female soldiers being sexually abused and fights breaking out as rival units squared up to each other. She was not at liberty to talk about that. The rules were there to ensure everyone's safety, she said.

In the beauty centre there was a massage parlour, but it was not the vice den the words would have implied to those American soldiers who fought in the paddy fields of South-east Asia. It was run by the military and a sign on the door stated, 'All male patrons are required to wear briefs during the entirety of their session.'

A sniper based in Samarra was seen getting his nails manicured. Apparently he did not want them to interfere with the smoothness of his trigger finger. He had considered getting his toes done at the same time but decided against it as he had extremely ticklish feet.

The memory of the Vietnam War cast its shadow over Iraq. It was why in briefings US High Command would bristle at the word quagmire. It was why American commanders liked talking about post-war Germany or Japan but never about Saigon. It was why no one would accept any parallels to that earlier conflict even as they followed the same policies of building up a local, hastily trained army and bolstering a corrupt and hated government.

The American soldiers doing the fighting had grown up hearing about that war. It was the one many of their fathers and uncles had fought in. It was why they watched so carefully what was happening in America in case they were not going to receive the homecoming promised. It was why there was not a camp I went to that did not have its messages of support from people in the US on prominent display. American schools, business associations, women's organisations and welfare groups would routinely send banners pledging their gratitude to the troops stationed in Iraq. They were hung in mess halls and by briefing rooms to make sure the soldiers knew their efforts were being appreciated and they had not been forgotten.

As a teenager I had also watched films and read books about Vietnam, drawn to its twisted glamour and exoticism. I had once half expected, maybe even hoped, to find in Iraq an American army of rebels and soul-loving African-Americans. The reality was as far from that as you could possibly imagine for this American army was no Vietnam draft.

In Iraq, the US soldiers I met were usually in impassioned awe of their weaponry and in love with what it could do for them. Air strikes or artillery barrages would be accompanied by whooping and excited discussions about the size of the blast and how they really 'blew that shit up'. They were often unthinkingly patriotic and convinced nowhere in the world could compare with the U S of A, certainly not Iraq where, I would be told, the people did not even care enough about their nation to pick up garbage from the streets. They were as nervous as anyone would be at the prospect of being blown up and gave me the impression that they would kill anyone their officers instructed them to. Though they had their faults it did not mean they were undisciplined, at least in most cases, or doubted the ethos of their country and corps. They were people had signed up to be soldiers and had trained for it. This was a professional army and, nearly every time I saw it in action, it acted as such. It may not have always been right, but it was usually ordered.

The servicemen in the American military normally shared the deep moral certainties that form Middle America. I saw soldiers visibly emotional and angry at witnessing the level of destitution the country had been reduced to by Saddam and the war. Units in Kurdish areas were particularly affected by what the civilians around them had endured. Most soldiers gave every impression of genuinely feeling for the plight of the ordinary Iraqis, or at least of having persuaded themselves that they did. Nor were they hesitant about telling me as much. It was rare to come across an American of

any rank who did not volunteer that one of their fundamental motivations was to help the Iraqis and give
them that most precious and mythologised of American
gifts: freedom.

Few can guilt-trip as well as a US soldier trying to
make you feel bad about doubting their ability to achieve
what they have set out to – or, worse, their right to interfere. This was often what used to aggravate me the most
and was what I had least expected to find. Most soldiers
I met, particularly in the first years of the conflict when
doubts in ultimate success had yet to set in, held strongly
to the belief that the sacrifices and dangers they endured
were worth it if they were making people's lives better.
The sincerity that came with this belief could at times be
overwhelming, its forthrightness making it only harder to
take, for this was not how it seemed to me that the war
was being playing out beyond the razor wire that marked
the edge of their bases.

The Iraqis I talked to nearly all had their story of when
they or one of their family members had American
soldiers turn over their homes for no good reason. I had
seen for myself, when I was with the troops advancing on
Baghdad, the difficulty the Americans had in determining
innocents from combatants in the heat of battle, particularly as those they fought often wore civilian clothes.
The soldiers had admitted as much, worried after the
fighting had finished whether they had chosen right
or accidentally killed non-combatants. In April 2003 I
heard a sergeant describe to one of his friends, a soldier
called Trey Black, what happened when his vehicle had
come under fire from all sides and he had started
firing back. He feared he had hit two people who had

merely been trying to hide after finding themselves caught in the crossfire.

'I saw the tops of their heads behind a berm and I shot them,' he said.

'That's why you've got to wait and see them shoot at you,' Black answered. 'You're here to die, boy.'

'But that's the thing,' the sergeant said. 'I'm not.'

My trip to Kufa in 2004 had made me realise that US air strikes were not as clinical as those organising them wanted to believe. Barely a month went by without accusations from Iraqis somewhere in the country that civilians had been killed during a military operation. It was nearly always impossible to know for certain whether these reports were true, but there were so many of them that it was inconceivable that none were. To me there was no question that the operations the American High Command so loved to celebrate resulted in their troops assaulting streets and fields where at least some of those hit had never held a weapon in anger.

Nonetheless I believed the American soldiers when they talked about the intent of their actions, if not their consequences. They were too American in character; too committed to that American conviction that they were the 'good guys' who did the right things. Moreover many were religious, which only added to the urgency of their need to believe that they were acting on the side of righteousness. The soldiers who made up the US military in Iraq were primarily drawn from poor white families from the American south and first-generation Hispanics. Both were instinctively God-fearing. It was what made it so confusing spending time with them, that contradiction again between how the soldiers would behave when

I met them and what they did for their work. When I interviewed them they talked of body counts and the destructive impact of various types of weaponry. When I spoke to them in private, God and Jesus were the figures they were most likely to name-check. Amid the girlie posters stuck to the walls above their sleeping cots would be crucifixes or a prayer to be recited before sleeping.

I once attended a service held by a Southern Baptist, the Reverend Raymond Folsom, for a unit stationed in the midst of the desert. The altar was a cardboard box resting on the back of a Humvee over which a green cloth had been placed along with a cup and a crucifix, their silver plating dulled by exposure to the elements. Another box covered with a camouflage mat stood in front of the chaplain as a lectern. Many of the assembled soldiers clutched their own Bibles, some embossed with gold.

Reverend Folsom cried out praise to Jesus and called on God's protection in times of danger. He told stories of Old Testament prophets who had lived in Mesopotamia. 'Pray, as many times Israel won its battles because they prayed,' he said, 'because it's God who wins battles, whatever your technology. Pray.'

One of the soldiers called for a prayer for his family. Another that he might one day find his own 'special lady'. Reverend Folsom led a rendition of 'Amazing Grace'. An Apache helicopter flew overhead as the congregation was exhorted to raise their voices to offer the final verse as a prayer to God: ''Tis grace hath brought me safe thus far, and grace will lead me home.' The next week he had already planned that the hymn would be 'Onward Christian Soldiers'.

Forty-five per cent of Americans believe that God created the world some time in the last 10,000 years and 59 per cent believe in the message of the Book of Revelation. Seventeen per cent go as far as to say they believe the end of the world will happen within their lifetime. This meant that in the American military there were inevitably some whose passion to be righteous involved more than the satisfaction of religious certainty. Among the soldiers fighting in Iraq there were Christians who viewed what was happening in religious, rather than solely political or military, terms.

I saw an awful lot of soldiers reading the books of Tim LaHaye. Almost totally unknown in Europe, this former Southern Baptist minister is a literary phenomenon in America. His 16-book *Left Behind* series has sold 65 million copies and topped the *New York Times* bestseller list four times. The books are good old-fashioned action adventure stories but their thrust is wholly theological, based on the Book of Revelation and St Paul's Epistle to the Thessalonians. Inspired by pre-millenialism, they teach that conditions are going to get a lot worse before they get better. They say that disasters and wars are good things, signs that the Second Coming is approaching, and that when the day comes Christ will descend from heaven and summon all the true believers, who will instantly disappear in an event known in Christian eschatology as the Rapture. Left behind will be the unbelievers: not only atheists and non-Christians, but Roman Catholics, Lutherans and the rest.

Largely as a result of his literary success, LaHaye was named ahead of Billy Graham as the most influential Christian leader in the US in the past 25 years by the

Institute for the Study of American Evangelicals. The ninth book in the series, which came out in 2001, was the biggest-selling book of the year, ousting John Grisham from the top spot for the first time in more than half a decade. He had met George Bush, and proudly says that the President made clear he was a fan.

In the first of his *Left Behind* books, LaHaye's beliefs were given a particularly dramatic setting. The moment of the Rapture comes just as Rayford Steele, the flawed hero whose journey through the series is one towards salvation, is piloting a commercial craft across the Atlantic to Heathrow. People suddenly disappear from his plane leaving behind their clothes in their seats and an atmosphere of total panic. Steele turns the plane around and when he descends to land in Chicago smoke is rising across the city. Cars, their drivers having suddenly disappeared, crash. A plane, whose pilot was amongst God's chosen, plummets into the ground, killing all on board. People are left terror-stricken as loved ones vanish before their eyes.

In line with LaHaye's religious teachings, what follows in its sequels is seven years of catastrophes before Christ reappears and defeats the Antichrist in a final battle between good and evil, thereby establishing his rule in peace for a thousand years.

I met LaHaye once, shortly after I got back to America from covering the initial invasion of Iraq. I was not expecting the smiling septuagenarian with dyed brown hair who met me at his condo by a golf course in Palm Springs. He was utterly charming and hospitable but it was still one of my more unusual interviews. He had a particularly detailed view of heaven and was keen to reassure me that, although single at the time, I would not be left alone after the Rapture if I embraced God because there would probably be singles groups there.

'If you're alive, your body will be transformed, as it's a corruptible body that needs to be made incorruptible for heaven,' he told me. 'Remember when Jesus rose from the dead? He still looked the same and could eat food, but he could walk through walls. He had an incorruptible body. Scripture says that we will be like Jesus. He was 33 so we assume that everyone will be transformed to their appearance at that age.

'The thousand years of the Millennium Kingdom will be magnificent. We know from the Bible that there'll be trees that each month will grow a different fruit. It will be familiar to this world, but more perfect. Sheep will still be sheep. Grass will be grass. But they will be perfect. What happens after that, none of us can imagine.'

He continued, 'I've had such a fun life serving the Lord so I trust Him completely that I'll be happy doing so for a thousand years. We've been told that we will be able to travel at the speed of thought. Personally, I plan to go planetary exploring.'

He was particularly interested in what was happening at that moment in the Middle East because it was a location at the centre of his literary series. In it the Antichrist is the head of the United Nations, and runs troops called Peacekeepers. His base is orientated around the site of ancient Babylon, which happens to be located only a short distance south-east of Baghdad. There is an awful lot of fighting by God's army across Mesopotamia in LaHaye's books. It must have been an interesting plot twist to have come across for his readers in the American military.

'We're living in very scary times,' LaHaye told me. 'I've studied the signs and I can tell you that our generation has more reason to believe that Christ will return in our life-time than any generation in the history of the Church.'

It was shortly before Easter 2005 that I first realised such beliefs were not unknown among the American troops fighting in Iraq. I was in a US convoy, thirty or forty lorries along with some Humvees and a few Bradley tanks added for protection, on the motorway that heads west out of Baghdad and across the border towards Damascus. For safety reasons convoys like this only travelled at night. That evening the moon was on the wane, so I could not make out much around me, and stars covered the sky.

The road was filled with American vehicles taking men, equipment and supplies to the US bases spread across Iraq's western provinces. We were not, however, going anywhere fast. The radio was reporting that mortars had been raining down somewhere in front and the convoy I was in was waiting for the backlog of cars and trucks to clear. Or maybe we were waiting for the helicopters with their thermo-imaging to come from a nearby strip and check there was no one out there in the darkness still waiting to attack us. The soldiers I was with were not quite sure.

It had already proved to be a particularly difficult journey as the only room available for me was in the back of one of the trucks and it was not a good spot. In a couple of months' time the US would decide journalists could no longer travel this way, the roads having become so dangerous that the military authorities would normally only permit us to be ferried by helicopter. The truck had no roof, and only a two-foot-high wall of armour plating around the sides to provide any form of protection. Two soldiers were in the back with me. One was at the far end, the other right beside me, both of us pressed as close to the shelter of the cab as we could get. We lay on our backs to give the armoured plating the maximum chance of saving us if anything nasty happened.

The soldier next to me, a staff sergeant, was nervous, as was I because it was never good to be stuck in one place for too long if you were in a US military vehicle. He started talking about the war to distract himself from his fears. I could not really see him in the gloom, and anyway I was looking straight up into the edge of the Milky Way, but I could hear him clearly. He had an explanation for what was happening in Iraq and the part he was playing in it that he was keen to share.

'Do you read the Bible?' he asked me.

I would nearly always answer 'yes' to this question because it could make some Americans unsettled if you were not religious.

'Well,' he said, 'in the Bible it says there must be a final battle between good and evil in Mesopotamia. It'll be a time when the Antichrist must be defeated but a time when the fightin' will be so bloody that the rivers will run red with blood. Maybe that is now. Maybe I'm one of those soldiers summoned to fight that battle.'

At the start of 2006 I spent as long as I could jumping from one US base to another. Things were getting very bad in Baghdad and my team's ability to ensure our security felt in doubt, not least because a recent attack on the Hamra hotel where I lived had left us unsettled. I had no desire to be anywhere near the hotel complex and consequently ended up spending almost five weeks away from Baghdad with the American forces. The war was approaching the start of its third year and a number of US troops were already on their second tours, some on their third, most of which had lasted at least a year and some of which had stretched to fourteen months or more. The soldiers knew things were not getting any better because they had seen the situation deteriorate with their own eyes. There was still a general commitment to the mission, to being professional, and a refusal to accept defeat, but it was becoming clear that some of the old certainty was beginning to erode.

It was during that time away from Baghdad that I visited the American camp by Haditha, the town where it was later alleged one of the worst war crimes of the conflict was committed. Only a few weeks before my arrival a unit of marines is said to have methodically gunned down men, women and children, although when I was there this was not yet known. The coming months would bring similar cases from around Iraq: claims that prisoners had been set free so they could be shot while supposedly trying to escape or that drunken US soldiers had raped a 12-year-old girl. It was as if a cancer was growing in the weakest parts of America's exhausted army.

I was only in the camp by Haditha for a few days. The soldiers did not want me to be there and made sure I was on the first convoy out. It was long enough, however, to realise that it was nothing like any base I had visited before.

Haditha is one of Iraq's bad places, a run-down town of ninety thousand people in western Anbar province where the buildings were often merely corrugated shacks and the roads little more than sandy pathways. From the first day the Americans arrived its people had demonstrated their commitment to killing as many of them as possible. Their intransigence, and Haditha's isolation and proximity to the Syrian border, had made the town a perfect point for Iraq's Sunni extremists to congregate. By May 2005 al-Qa'eda ruled it in an alliance with one of the most brutal home-grown insurgent groups, Ansar al-Sunna. Together they decided who lived or died, who got paid, what people wore, what they watched and what they listened to. The right-hand lane on all roads through the town was reserved for their vehicles. All women had to wear headscarves. Pop music and Western films were banned.

Law and order were in their hands. A headmaster who was accused of adultery was whipped with cables 190 times. Two men who robbed a shop were pinned to the ground and had their arms broken with rocks. So many alleged American agents were executed on Haqlania Bridge, the main entrance to the town, that it was renamed by locals the Agents' Bridge and then the Agents' Fridge, in evocation of a mortuary. Severed heads were lined up along the railings that bordered one side.

The American camp was located a half-mile outside Haditha in a hydroelectric dam that spanned the Euphrates. It was the largest such facility in Iraq and one that provided electricity for most of the surrounding region. During the invasion there was concern that the dam might be blown up to disrupt the approaching US troops. A Special Forces unit was dispatched to hold it. For a fortnight there was fearsome fighting until the advancing force finally reached the spot and those attacking the dam abandoned their assaults to adopt guerrilla tactics.

An American deployment had been there ever since.

These troops did not like to go out much, and when they did they usually went in numbers, launching raids backed by armour and aircraft. During these sallies there would be a relative calm and then the Americans would go back to their base, the extremists would move back into Haditha from the surrounding countryside, and things would continue as before. American movements would be disrupted by roadside bombs and snipers, and the occasional mortar or rocket would be fired towards the dam to show who was really in charge.

Even though I knew nothing of the allegations about the marines' recent massacre – that story would not break for another month – it was clear from the moment I arrived that the American troops stationed by Haditha had gone feral. Their main link with the outside world was the convoys that came up from the US camp at al-Assad and they did not arrive very often. The marines, trapped in their slice of territory, had largely been able to determine their own limits and institutional discipline gave every impression of approaching breakdown.

This was not one of those American camps with its coffee shops and polite soldiers who whiled away their rest hours playing computer games or talking about girls back home. This was a place where marines had abandoned their official living quarters to set up their own encampments with signs ordering outsiders to keep out. The daily routine was punctured by the dam's emergency alarm as its antiquated and crumbling machinery risked total collapse.

The dam was made of the same yellow-stained concrete that almost every building in Iraq was etched from. It was at least one hundred and fifty yards long and rose three hundred yards into the air on the downstream side. At its ends were two accommodation blocks, each a series of warren-like floors. Both had at least a dozen different levels and it was in these that the American troops lived, occupying the rooms that had previously acted as offices for the facility's Iraqi engineers. Inside, the grinding noise of the dam's equipment made hearing difficult. The whole place stank of rotten eggs, apparently a by-product of the grease used to keep the turbines running. Lighting provided only a half-gloom. The lifts were smashed.

The washrooms were at the top of the dam and the main lavatories at its base. With around eight hundred steps between them, some did not bother to use the official facilities. Small camps had been built around the dam's entrances. One night I went into one of them looking for a cigarette lighter. A Portakabin had been appropriated and its entrance surrounded by a wooden fence against which were piled empty cans of food, water bottles and tattered magazines. A fire had been lit and a marine, his head covered by a black balaclava against the evening chill, was pulling apart planks of wood with his dirt-encrusted hands in order to feed it. The place stank of urine and smoke. On the door to the cabin was a picture of a skull and crossbones. I knocked on it and pushed the door open. Inside four figures illuminated by the light of a battery-powered lantern were playing cards. Rugs were wrapped around them. Half the room was filled with rubbish. Pictures of half-naked women covered the walls. No one volunteered their lighter.

Unlike in every other stint with American forces, at Haditha I was not allowed to interview a senior officer properly. The only soldiers willing to speak at length were those from a small Azerbaijani contingent whose role was to marshal into and out of the facility the band of Iraqi engineers who kept the dam's machinery going. The US troops liked the Azerbaijanis. 'They have looser rules of engagement,' one said admiringly in a rare conversation.

The camp commandant had a giant poster on the wall behind his desk. It was a cartoon of a terrified-looking Arab in a tribal headdress being stared down by a scowling President Bush. 'You can tell those fuckers with the laundry on their heads that it's washday,' the slogan said.

I busied myself researching who these people were. The battalion had undergone three tours in Iraq in two and a half years. On their last tour more than thirty had died, most when the unit was in the vanguard of the attack on Fallujah. They had been Colonel Shupp's people, among his heroes of Fallujah – his new 'greatest generation' – that he had told me about when I visited Camp Fallujah the previous year while the Warrior Transition sessions were being conducted. These men had left a few weeks before my stay at the camp with the same promises that the worst was now over and that they had done their bit to ensure the war was won. Then they were sent to Haditha after only seven months away.

Six marines had died in three days during August. In nearby Parwana, fourteen died shortly afterwards in the most deadly roadside bomb attack of the war so far. The day before my arrival one soldier had shot himself in the head with his M-16. No one would discuss with me what had happened.

There was only one American civilian at the dam, an engineer sent out five months earlier by the US government to work with the Iraqis to keep the facility operational. His was a difficult task. Each time there was a power cut the turbines stopped working, the water against the dam started to build up, and if the engineers could not get the generators started in time the dam's wall would burst. The American engineer's job was not helped by the marines viewing his Iraqi workers as potential saboteurs and therefore doing what they could to limit their access.

He was easy to spot, the only Westerner for fifty miles who was not in military fatigues. He was dressed instead in an old red sweatshirt and grease-streaked jeans as if he were at home getting ready to work on a car in his garage. I latched on to him for company. He talked to me with just as much relief. The troops he was quartered with terrified him, so much so that he would not let his name be quoted for fear of reprisal.

On the afternoon I met him we stood with a couple of his Iraqi workers as they fished in the lake by the dam's upstream side with hooks tied to pieces of string. There were so many fish in the water beneath us that they thrashed around on top of each other to reach the bait being offered. My new companion was discussing what he had learned, his sandy hair falling forward as he looked at the water below, leaning on an iron rail that marked the dam's edge; beside him, the Iraqis worked their lines.

'Nobody knows back in the States what it is like here. They just can't get it unless they've seen it,' he said in his Georgian drawl. 'I'm a patriot and I thought everythin' was goin' to be so different. This dam's dangerous but the marines don't listen. When I first got here they were sleepin' in the main turbine room and playin' football by the turbines. You can't do that. If those turbines break this dam comes down. I talked to the commander about it and he didn't care. "We kill people," he said, "I don't know anything about that kind of thing."'

He stared down at the fish. 'These guys,' he said indicating the Iraqis. 'These are the folk I have found I can most easily relate to. These seem the most normal folk here, even though I come from a world away. They're the ones who I consider to be brave. Six of them have been killed in Haditha just for workin' here, shot in their homes or taken by the killers and plain disappeared. But they still keep comin' back as they believe in their responsibility to keep the dam working. That I can relate to. That's my world.

'Marines: they're destructive people and these ones real so. I have seen what they do and how they do it. When I get back I'm going to make sure people know what it's really like. All marines are good at killin'. However, the ones here, they like it.'

The next morning I was gone. A convoy of Humvees was going south and the camp commandant made sure I was on it, taken away from the place where the supposed next greatest generation had become as barbarised as the arena in which it fought.

The stepped pyramid at the site of the ancient city of Ur is 4,000 years old. It was built at a time when Ur housed dynasties that ruled Mesopotamia for centuries, a capital for kings and queens who forged and expanded vast empires. It existed long before the rise of the Egyptian, Greek or Roman civilisations. It was at Ur that the wheel was invented and the first mathematical system developed.

Abraham was reputedly born there, the first known poetry written and the epic *Gilgamesh* originally told.

The pyramid survived as Ur crumbled and was consumed by sand. It stood as civilisations rose and fell, wars and drought came and went, and still it stood, in the first years of the twenty-first century, dominating, through its great size, even the structures that the latest world power to come to Mesopotamia had built beside it.

The monument was now located within the outer perimeter fence of an American base. Saddam had built a military facility where Ur once spread, complete with its own barracks, runways and fuel dumps. When the Americans invaded, they expanded it and turned it into their most important base in southern Iraq. From the first days of the war, a parade of freight planes used the runway at Ur to bring in the men and equipment needed to feed the conflict.

For light relief the soldiers liked to climb the pyramid. Dozens were ferried out each day. An Iraqi guide, the grandson of a worker who had helped examine the site with British archaeologists in the 1930s, explained what they were seeing and told them about the span of Iraq's history. Parts of Ur had been excavated, the tops of the buildings uncovered so that in places the lines of streets could be made out. Royal tombs built beside the stepped pyramid could be climbed into, their floors covered with loose stones and broken pottery and the walls bearing traces of Sumerian writing.

There were three full minibuses making the trip to the site when I went there at the start of 2006. The soldiers in them looked absurdly young, and I felt correspondingly old. They rushed up the pyramid, some at the front racing to see who could be first to the plateau at the top. By the time I got there it was already covered in American uniforms. Our guide told us that when the monument was built ceremonies had been held at that spot in homage to Nanna, goddess of the moon, the city's symbolic protector.

Surrounding us was squalid scrubland, clumps of crippled bushes providing the main distraction from dirt-covered fields. It was shortly before midday and the sunlight was so bright it had raised a haze which blurred the landscape and reduced the horizon to a shimmer. Only the base and its array of weaponry looked crisp and clear. There were thousands of tents and Portakabins, hundreds of tanks, trucks and Humvees. Artillery guns and anti-rocket missile racks stood in rows. Toy-sized soldiers could be spotted moving around, rushing from building to building with their matchstick-thin rifles strapped to their backs. Two helicopters buzzed like insects overhead. It was a panorama of contemporary power and intent.

A fat, grey transport plane was making its approach. When its wheels touched the tarmac one of the soldiers produced an American flag from his rucksack. He had brought it with him to be the backdrop for a re-enlistment ceremony that was to be staged on the pyramid that day. As the Stars and Stripes fell open it was caught by the wind. The soldier held it high, his shoulders set, while those around him cheered and whistled.

5. Choice

My translator, Ahmed, had once been a tourist guide showing foreigners the historic sights of Iraq. He was now the guide who led me through the dangers of Baghdad and showed me the sights that signalled the destruction of the life he had previously known.

He understood, as did I, that if we were stopped and identified by the wrong people he risked being killed as a collaborator just as much as I risked being seized as a foreigner and potential spy. Our lives were entwined by the knowledge that a stupid step by either could result in the death of both. It was a powerful bond to have with someone you had only recently met.

Ahmed had been brought up in a middle-class Sunni family. He lived with his wife and four-year-old daughter in the south-western Baghdad suburb of Dora. It was a district that in 2006 would become one of the most brutal fronts in the sectarian civil war as both sides committed the most horrific atrocities in an attempt to oust the other.

He was proud of being a good Muslim but despised the fanatics, and, like most of Iraq's university graduates, he had originally been excited by what the Americans might bring. He liked to write and would occasionally send out messages to his foreign friends that detailed incidents from his life and his thoughts on events in his country. He would sit in front of the computer in our office tapping away with two fingers, hitting the letters with such force that the keyboard would jump across the desk, to provide an insight into the occupation as seen through the eyes of the occupied. In the summer of 2005 he wrote:

The definition of disaster usually means something bad happened or is still happening such as a flood or an earthquake. But my disaster is entirely different. My disaster began when I was working on the computer at my wife's sister's house. At that time I heard my daughter and her cousin from her mother's side as they were playing together saying, 'Let me pretend to be an American soldier and you an Iraqi policeman driving our military vehicle chasing thieves and mujahideen.'

I was shocked when I heard that. I immediately stopped working and turned to them. Asking my daughter what she had said, she answered me by carrying a stick as if she was a soldier carrying his gun. 'I am chasing thieves, dad.'

I asked my four-year-old, 'Where did you see that?'

'On TV,' she replied.

I was about to cry and be angry at the same time. Children play with their toys, and she should be playing with her dolls, but the children of Iraq are playing military games. She is a girl – but what about the boys of the same age especially when they grow up and become the men in charge?

The culture of Iraq could be described as a war culture and I am still wondering how I can change this in my daughter's mind and in the minds of children who were brought up in this bloody period when their life becomes a military life and their playground became a battlefield.

A few days after that incident I was driving my car at 9.30 pm with my family. It was the first time I had been out that late since the fall of the former regime. I was heading back to my house after the wedding party of my wife's nephew was over. It happened that a car was coming on the opposite side of the road, a woman was sitting next to her husband in the front and two children were sitting in the rear seat. It was a few metres away from me when two cars stopped them and started shooting at them, killing the husband and his wife. Fortunately the two children survived.

I was trying to calm my wife and my daughter down by telling them, 'Do not be frightened'. But I had another disaster when my daughter asked me directly, 'Why have the mujahideen killed them dad?'

That means she knows what is going on in Iraq and it means the life in Iraq and the culture are different from everywhere across the world. It means that we have lots of work to do in order to change our children's minds and to change the future of Iraq from a bloody into a peaceful one. I wonder if I will be able to do that and if God will help me to get this done.

Sometimes they were simply nuggets of reality.

There was a referendum on the new constitution on October the 15th. On that day, in the early morning, I went to the polling station to cast my vote against it while friends of mine were casting their votes for it.

We were heading back to our houses together, walking through barbed wire and police vehicles, talking about the vote. Some of us were saying we have to say 'yes' to it because we are in a very critical moment and others were saying that we should reject it because it divides Iraq into three federal states. It was a very strong argument we had that day and people around could hear what we were talking about because some of us were so angry when we talked.

As we got to our houses, and in the middle of that argument, one of us said, 'That's all bullshit, let us play football.' The weird thing was that as usual we listened to him and forgot about our differences and started playing football just as if nothing serious was happening at that time.

Most were short.

Living in Baghdad nowadays is full of strange dangerous stories. Before the collapse of Saddam's regime I was proudly saying to people that I was a translator, but nowadays I usually hide my translation identity cards when I drive my car to anywhere in my home city. I never show my ID to police checkpoints because nobody can trust anyone in Iraq. Unfortunately, this is the reality in Baghdad.

A few days ago I wanted to take my daughter to the funfair but I hesitated because we could be kidnapped at any moment there. Finally my wife and I decided to do it after a long discussion and planning. I noticed everyone there was as scared as I was, but at the same time I was so happy seeing my daughter enjoying herself after almost two years staying in the house.

For a long time I have been trying to convince my brother-in-law to bring his family to one of Baghdad's nicest restaurants for lunch with us. But he has been rejecting this idea for security reasons because if we go to that lunch the kidnapping gangs would infer that we are a rich family and therefore fair game to be taken as a hostage.

This is the reality of the new Iraq. And this is the way Iraqis live nowadays, a life full of fear and nightmares, and no one can understand why this has happened to us – is it because we kept silent against the tyrant's oppression or because of something else we do not know?

In the autumn of 2005 he wrote about his extended family.

She always runs to the gate when I knock on it declaring my arriving in Samarra, a city 125 kilometres north of Baghdad. It is my oldest sister who married a man from that city 25 years ago.

I remember this always, even though I have not seen her since over a year ago due to the security situation and the US military operations in the city. I remember that she was crying on the fall of Baghdad when we were seeing Saddam's statue being taken down on April 9, 2003. I did ask her why she was crying. She replied, 'Because I am seeing my country is being destroyed, and you are asking me why.' I told her the future of our country would be better when the crazy leaders would be overthrown and efficient persons would take over from them. I promised her that the Americans would do their best to make Iraq better.

I am wondering when I will give her a visit again and when she will be able to come down to Baghdad and get here safely. I am wondering what I will say to her when she asks me about the future of Iraq this time.

By 2006 the content of his messages had become darker.

Three years ago I felt hope. Hope that soon I would be free to act and talk as I pleased, without being stopped by the security services. Hope that one day I would be able to travel without asking permission from the government. Hope that my country would be stable and my people happy.

But today, I can see the freedom and democracy I dreamed of are a mirage.

Before the war, I was at least able to leave my family alone in the house for two weeks when I had to guide a tourist across Iraq without having fear for my family being kidnapped or killed by militias or gangs. But now I have to be at my house by sunset time otherwise they will be panicked.

Nowadays I cannot talk in English in front of my daughter when the correspondent rings me on my mobile because she might by accident tell the neighbours and that could cause us to be killed.

I dreamed of a stable, free and democratic Iraq and

I dreamed of very open-minded and trustworthy Iraqis. But unfortunately I see now the elite Iraqis like doctors, engineers and professors fleeing the country since they became the target for the unknown armed groups.

My hopes were up when the Americans stormed the country and overthrew the dictator. I thought all my dreams would come true, but now there is little room for a moderate, middle ground in Iraq anymore. In this time when mistrust, conspiracy and summary justice are the rule, no one is seen as a man in the middle between Iraq and the west.

The Americans say that they bring Democracy and Freedom to Iraqis, but they actually brought instability, poverty and ethnic differences. So the question, my dear reader, is which is better: to have a useless people who run the country or to keep a tyrant who knows how to run the country but harshly?

When we were working there was often time to waste as we waited for some parliamentary session to start or an American officer to be available for interview. Ahmed was fascinated by what life was like in the West, especially how much everything cost, and would bombard me with questions about what jobs people did, what cars they drove, what the weather was like, everything and anything.

He told me stories about his youth and how at university he had his rebellious moments with alcohol and the ladies. In the months before the US invasion he had worked at the Al-Rashid, the eighteen-storey hotel in the centre of Baghdad that had been the most luxurious in Iraq and was now within the Green Zone. He had seen the antics of Saddam's sons and henchmen first hand as they flew in girls from Lebanon and Egypt to dance at the hotel disco and take to the rooms they had hired for the night.

He was in his mid-twenties when he married. Despite his own indiscretions he had made sure his wife was a good Muslim girl, a virgin who had worked as a civil servant when they met but was now a full-time mother. He might have been a modern man but he was still an Iraqi and as such the old traditions continued to matter.

Often he would talk about the future. His dream had been a simple one. He had wanted to run his own tourist company to show foreigners around Iraq. There were going to be no tourists in Iraq for a long time and, perhaps, few architectural monuments left for them to see as buildings that had stood for thousands of years were being stripped by looters and their relics smuggled abroad.

Now he had no idea which direction his life would go. He wanted to visit London and New York but could not see how it could ever happen. He wanted his daughter to receive a full education but felt it was too dangerous to send her to school. It was impossible for anyone in Iraq to plan ahead. No one knew what the future might hold. No one even knew what the next month might hold. The only decision available for someone like Ahmed was whether to stay in Iraq or to flee as a refugee to Syria or Jordan.

In late 2005 he announced that his wife was pregnant and the following spring she gave birth to their second child. The labour started in the middle of the night. This caused considerable problems as the streets were very dangerous by then and the night-time curfew was consequently rigorously enforced.

He helped his wife to their car and turned on the inside light and hazard signals so that no one might think they were attempting something clandestine. They drove very slowly through the streets. At a police checkpoint he was stopped and told to go back. The officers were scared. They knew those out at that time of night were usually involved in far more illicit activities than taking a pregnant woman to hospital. Ahmed opened the door to explain and a warning shot was fired. He had to plead with them for a long time before they finally allowed him to pass.

He came to our office with photographs of his new son. Ahmed was very proud. Normally he appeared older than he was. His hair was greying and his face risked holding a permanent frown, the two vertical lines between his eyes already deeply ingrained. That day he looked young again, the worry temporarily gone.

I had been amazed when he had originally told me the news that his wife was pregnant. It seemed out of character. He was a cautious man who was already worried about the effect the war was having on his daughter and what would happen to her if he was killed as a result of his line of work. It was a strange time to bring a new life into that world.

'My friend, things are very bad as you know,' he said. 'I can honestly tell you that at first I was not certain. It seemed unsuitable in these terrible times but my wife was very keen.

'Then I thought about it. I thought about it for a long time. I realised you cannot stop living. If you do then you are beaten. So I thought, "What do I believe in during these crazy times?" I came to the conclusion I believe in my family. I decided there is hope in that. That will give me my future, God willing, even if my country does not.'

The British, when they gained control of Iraq after the First World War, had sought to hold the country together by introducing Britain's most enduring system of political stability: monarchy. The Americans, now they were in charge, sought to resolve Iraq's problems by introducing the political system that had worked so well for the United States, one built around a written constitution.

Throughout 2005 a series of political milestones were reached. There was a national election to select an assembly that would draw up a new Iraqi constitution, a referendum on whether that constitution should be adopted, and, finally, another national vote, this time one organised under the new constitutional rules to elect Iraq's first democratic parliament, one which would govern the country for the following four years. Washington intended that this political process would result in an Iraqi state where the country's minorities felt protected by the constitution, and where inter-sectarian and ethnic differences would be resolved by political discourse rather than guns and bullets. Its achievement was the total opposite.

The election to determine the composition of the constitutional assembly was held in January 2005. There were problems from the start as the country's Sunni population made clear it intended to boycott the vote. They knew they were a minority, probably as little as 20 per cent of Iraq's 27 million people, although no one knew for certain as there had not been a comprehensive census for more than a decade. The Shia were estimated to be as much as 60 per cent – the rest of Iraq's population being primarily Kurds – thereby ensuring them a majority under any democratic system and the end to the Sunni Arab hegemony over Iraq that had existed since the era of British imperial rule. For many Sunnis the whole exercise was therefore merely an American plot to make them second-class citizens in a state that they were used to controlling.

In the run-up to the vote the Sunni extremists did their best to stop any doubters in their community from wavering. Ballot boxes had to be delivered under armed guard to Sunni districts and, in many places, were greeted by a torrent of gunfire. Graffiti appeared of headless corpses with ink marks on their fingers. The ink mark had been adopted by the electoral board as the method to indicate who had cast their ballot, thereby preventing multiple voting. As a result it had become the most recognised symbol of people's willingness to be involved in the democratic experiment.

In Shia areas, however, the atmosphere was very different. Their moment had finally arrived after decades of repression and the misery that followed the suppression of their 1991 uprising. I was in the south of Iraq to cover the election, the region where most of the country's Shia lived and where Britain's forces in Iraq were based, and ahead of polling day there was every indication that democracy was being embraced with fervour. Walls were covered in election posters proclaiming the promises of myriad candidates. A billboard dominated the centre of Basra, the largest city in Iraq's south. On its left half was a photograph of smiling children; on its right, the picture tinted red, was a sobbing man holding a dead child.

'Vote,' the slogan read. 'It is the way of peace not war.'

For polling day I travelled to Amarah, a Shia city north of Basra in Maysan province. It was a violent place, the most lawless in the British sector of control, and a region where the economy relied on the smuggling of guns, diesel and opium from neighbouring Iran. Most of the local criminal gangs had a lineage that went back generations and they did not like outside interference that might disrupt their activities. Saddam had installed two army divisions in Maysan that tried, and failed, to establish control. The British were now seeking to impose order with a battalion of a thousand men.

During the summer of 2004 the British HQ in Amarah had been mortared and rocketed almost every day for three weeks. The unit deployed there, the Princess of Wales Royal Regiment, was attacked 658 times in seven months. In one engagement the fighting had been so fierce that British soldiers ran out of ammunition and had to fix bayonets.

Maysan was now the responsibility of the Welsh Guards. Things had improved slightly in the months preceding election day as their commander, Lieutenant Colonel Ben Bathurst, had managed to broker deals with some of the local sheikhs and increased the number of patrols to make clear the British would respond swiftly to any attacks upon them. This had resulted in a temporary suspension of hostilities.

'I don't like the term softly-softly,' Lieutenant Colonel Bathurst told me. 'Our men are prepared any day to go into full war-fighting mode. Anyone taking us on can expect us to bear down on them with overwhelming force. Here strength is respected.'

Amarah was nevertheless still an unpleasant place to be posted. The city was one of Iraq's poorest, its streets filled with garbage and the pavements lined with piles of debris. It also held the relic of one of Saddam's most madcap schemes. In the 1980s he had sought to turn this impoverished smuggling haven into the centre of Iraq's Olympic bid. Construction of a stadium and Olympic village had begun. They were now crumbling into disrepair, home to dozens of the region's poorest families who lived in the half-finished shells with no running water or sanitation. It was a fitting monument to Ba'athist vanity.

In built-up areas, stones and bricks would still rain down on passing British vehicles. Children with catapults lurked at street corners to ambush patrols. Soldiers wore Perspex visors on their helmets for protection. Most had their own story of the one that got through and a number had scars on their cheeks to prove it.

From the British base on the edge of town you could hear gunfire most nights: a combination of political fighting, robbery and blood feuds. When one political party, a collection of local technocrats, became particularly popular attempts were made to murder five of its candidates during a twelve-hour period. Two of the assassinations proved successful.

The ballot boxes were delivered 24 hours before polling day. Two lorries filled with hundreds of metal cases raced up the highway from Basra, protected by a British helicopter flying overhead. A British squadron moved north to establish a checkpoint on the main highway to stop Sunni militants moving south to cause disruption. Five hundred new AK-47s were given to the local police to bolster their firepower. A curfew was announced. No cars would be allowed in the city until voting was completed to limit the threat from suicide bombers.

The next morning British troops took up their positions shortly before dawn. None knew what to expect. They had spent months working towards that day, doing all that they could to make sure the conditions were right for the vote to be staged. The question was if anyone would now turn up to assert their new democratic right.

I visited a polling station as its doors opened at nine o'clock. It was located in a primary school. A local barber had been appointed to run it and he had transformed the classrooms into a temple of democracy. Pupils had made coloured paper chains to decorate the walls. Posters extolled the benefits of the election. Women sat behind the desks on which voting cards were piled. Their clothes looked as if they had been freshly laundered. They proudly explained to me how people would be required to first find their names on the electoral list, sign to receive a ballot and then disappear behind a curtain to fill their ballot in and drop it into the ballot box. Everything required was there except for the voters.

It was mid-morning when they came. Until then the streets were deserted, not a person to be seen, and the first pangs of real concern had passed through the minds of the watching British officers. It started as a trickle, a few families leaving their houses and walking to the nearest polling station. Then it became a flood.

I was looking out of the top of a military Land Rover, crossing onto Amarah's main street, when I suddenly saw thousands of people making their way towards me. Some men wore ornate headdresses, others were in their best suits. Women perched toddlers on their shoulders.

Children were running by their parents. Many families had brought picnics. It was a mass of delighted humanity that stretched all the way to the horizon.

At a polling station, the mood verged on the euphoric as long, loud but orderly lines formed outside the voting booths. As they left, people proudly waved their ink-stained fingers.

'I walked here for an hour and then I waited an hour to vote,' one 52-year-old man said. 'But I have waited my whole life for this.'

The millions who voted that day did so because they believed it was their right to have a say in the composition of their country's government. They voted because they had been allowed to as a consequence of the removal of Saddam. That day in Amarah there was a genuine feeling that everything might just end up working out for the best. It was moments like that which made the chaos and blood-shed that followed all the more distressing to witness.

It was religion that determined the election's result. In retrospect it was, perhaps, inevitable. In such troubled and confused times the question of what God wanted must have seemed particularly urgent. To most Iraqis the will of God is an absolute, a force not only to submit to but one that actively guides events. It is the will of God, more than any other factor, that Iraqis believe determines the course of their lives. 'Insha'Allah,' they say after almost any statement. If it is God's will. This is not solely a turn of phrase. It is an affirmation that if God wills it then it will happen. If not, it will not.

The country's imams had been fundamental in providing information to the electorate on whom to support. With the country's institutions neutered or destroyed, and with Iraq's political parties embryonic or led by distrusted former exiles, the Shia had turned to them because, along with Iraq's tribal leaders, the imams had always held the people together during times of crisis. These were usually conservative and traditionalist voices, ones that were deeply suspicious of the new values the US sought to foster in Iraq. Islam and the traditional Arab values of respect, communalism and honour were the foundations they believed would enable their country's recovery.

A week before polling day a Shia friend of Ahmed's was at his mosque when the imam launched into a tirade against the more secular candidates, describing them as American agents who wanted to subjugate Iraq, deprive the faithful of the Prophet's teachings and give the country's treasures, by which he meant its oil, to foreigners.

'It was a very big show,' Ahmed said. 'He told me the imam was shouting and citing examples from the Koran as to why these candidates' promises would lead to terrible times. Everyone afterwards was talking about it as it was such a heartfelt message.'

Did he think, therefore, that they would follow the imam's recommendations en masse?

'They would never do such a thing,' Ahmed said with a tut. 'Imams are respected but the Iraqis are not goats. They can make up their own minds about what is best for them. The Shia will vote as they think best based on all the information they have got, not solely on what an imam advises them.'

He was right, but that did not mean the message coming from the mosques was not a powerful piece of advertising. The Grand Ayatollah Ali al-Sistani, the country's most senior and influential Shia cleric, even let it be known through his representatives exactly which party the faithful should support.

When the election results were released they showed that, as promised, the Sunnis had boycotted the poll. In some Sunni areas only 2 per cent of the electorate cast their ballot. The Shia did vote, but the vast majority ignored the moderate nationalists and secular parties who, if elected, might have been better able to diminish sectarian tensions and find a working relationship with the Americans. Instead they supported the most overtly religious parties. It was the fundamentalist groups – the Iran-linked Supreme Council for the Islamic Revolution in Iraq (SCIRI) and the supporters of Moqtada al-Sadr – that received almost 70 per cent of the ballot.

SCIRI, the election's biggest winner, was rumoured to have received huge donations from Tehran to finance its election campaign. US intelligence reports claimed that its five thousand-strong paramilitary wing, the Badr Brigade, had within it Iranian agents instructed to infiltrate Iraq's security forces. Iraq's Sunnis certainly had reason to distrust the party. Its leaders had spent two decades in exile in Iran and the Badr Brigade fought against Iraq in the Iran–Iraq war. Moreover its agenda was only nominally democratic. It believed Islamic scholars, rather than the Iraqi people, should have the final say on policy matters.

Sadr's supporters were potentially even more destabilising. Sadr preached an ultra-radical view of Islam and had also repeatedly stated that the American occupation must be resisted, by force if necessary. His paramilitary wing, the Mahdi Army, had launched two unsuccessful uprisings the previous year that resulted in fierce fighting

In 2003, I was embedded in a US army tank unit during the invasion of Iraq. There were regular mortar attacks and days advancing under gunfire. This tank debris was pictured on the outskirts of Baghdad.

During the invasion I witnessed an Iraqi army pick-up truck that had been destroyed by a US tank shell. In it was this body alongside six others. It was images like this that I found hard to forget.

The 130-foot high Hands of Victory triumphal arches were dedicated to Saddam Hussein in 1990 to mark his 'victory' over Iran. When I visited the monument in April 2004, it was located within the Green Zone.

Visiting a former Ba'athist headquarters in Baghdad targeted in the US 'shock and awe' bombing campaign at the start of the war. By this point I had begun dressing in Iraqi clothes, and ditched my workbag for a plastic one, in an attempt to blend in with the locals.

In January 2005, Iraq held its first elections of the post-Saddam era. Here I am pictured at sunrise with one of the British officers assigned to protect voters in Amarah, southern Iraq. Note the sewage running down the centre of the street, an indication of Amarah's poverty.

British troops patrolled in armoured Land Rovers. They offered little protection for the soldier stationed to stand guard out of the top.

A reporter from Britain's Daily Mail *newspaper and I writing our articles in an Iraqi army barracks in Majar al-Kabir, a town in Maysan province in southern Iraq. We found the desk in a nearby office and carried it into the courtyard to locate a satellite signal.*

Abu Omar, my driver, celebrates the Iraqi football team's win over Saudi Arabia by firing his AK-47 into the air. Abu Omar's face has been obscured for his safety – reprisals are commonly taken against Iraqis known to have worked with foreigners.

DO NOT FEED THE LIONS ANYTHING!

NO MRE'S!
NO CIGARETTES!
NO METAL BITS!
NO DOGS!
NO PLASTIC!

BY ORDER: COL. HODGES
(CJTF7 HEAD VETERINARIAN)

Saddam's son, Uday, kept three pet lions in his garden. They became a favoured attraction for American servicemen.

Uday's lions nearly starved to death during the first chaotic weeks of the war. During my visit, a South African vet, on secondment to Baghdad Zoo, fed them a dead donkey for their dinner.

Ahmed, my translator, pictured here in Abu Omar's car as we drove through a residential area of Baghdad. As with the picture of Abu Omar, his face is obscured to prevent retribution against him or any members of his family.

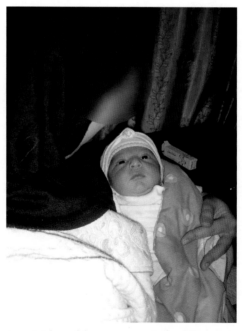

When I first met Ahmed he was married with a young daughter. In spring 2006 his wife gave birth to their son. This is the picture he gave me of his wife, Raha, holding Mohammad, the new addition to the family.

By the Hamra Hotel pool in Baghdad. When the hotel was attacked by suicide bombers at the end of 2005, part of the head of one of the attackers ended up at the bottom of the pool.

This is the view at sunset from the balcony of my room at the Hamra. When the hotel was attacked, the blast walls stopped the reporters living behind them from being killed. Two of the surrounding buildings collapsed, however, and at least eight people died in the explosions.

From left: the card I was required to carry when visiting the US division, known as Task Force Liberty, near Tikrit; my business card, printed in Baghdad – the same details were printed in Arabic on the reverse side; my official press accreditation – carriers of this card were considered bona fide reporters by the US authorities.

with US troops. It had been his men who controlled Kufa when I visited it in the spring of 2004 to see the crater left by the American bomb.

Following his military defeats, Sadr had said he was retiring to read the Koran. In fact he was re-establishing his power base by adapting the social welfare tactics pioneered by the Lebanese group Hezbollah. Sadr's popularity had originally been dependent primarily on his status as the son of a revered cleric killed by Saddam in 1999. Now, seeing the failure of the Iraqi government to provide for its people, he won support among the Shia by helping the poor and building new schools. Food and clothes were provided for refugees and donations handed out on feast days. His militia, the Mahdi Army, also began to assume responsibility for law and order. A system of justice was set up that was independent of the state. The judges appointed by Sadr passed sentences based on Sharia law while his followers acted as police and judiciary. Those who did not accept their sentence were threatened, and, those deemed to deserve it, killed. His militiamen began attacking alcohol sellers and brothels. They slaughtered gypsies for supposedly harbouring belly dancers. In Basra they targeted DVD sellers, threatening any caught selling 'inappropriate' Hollywood films. Musical instrument sellers found their businesses trashed because their wares were considered to encourage inappropriate dancing. Barbers were murdered, their crime being to have insulted Islam by shaving off beards and giving their customers Western-style haircuts.

Before Iraq was invaded, Iraqi political exiles had wooed Washington with tales of an extensive pro-Western, secular middle class that would welcome the

American arrival and embrace its gifts of scientific and cultural modernity. These would be the people, it was promised, whom the populace respected and who would determine the future identity of the Iraqi state. The January 2005 election demonstrated not only how small in number Iraq's secular middle class really was but also the extent to which it could shape how the common man voted. Its influence had proved to be as much an illusion as the weapons of mass destruction whose presence the political exiles had also guaranteed.

It was the Shia from places like Amarah who determined Iraq's future. The Shia I talked to did not necessarily endorse the excesses of the election winners' militias but most of them supported their policies. This was not simply because their imams had encouraged them to do so but because what the religious parties promised was rooted deep within the traditions of Iraqi society. These traditions are rural and religious in origin and they had remained strong even after millions of Iraqis migrated from their villages to the country's cities during the great wave of social and economic change caused by the oil-funded boom of the 1970s. At the heart of these beliefs was a distrust of many aspects of the modern world that are unquestioned in the West, where people more readily prioritise the individual over the community. Recent events had only made the Shia more distrustful of innovation and change. Most feared the Sunni extremists after months of insurgent bombings, wanted Iraqis not Americans to control their country and above all hoped for an Iraq governed in line with the teachings of the Prophet Mohammad.

I might have feared that any government formed by

the parties they backed would be unable to bring the country together, indeed that the very policies they wished to implement could only rip it further apart, but the Shia voted as they did for reasons which were not only logical to them but were fed by their own spirit of optimism. The Shia had gained their freedom from Saddam and they had now made their decision about what to do with it. Iraq would have to live with the consequences of their choice.

The months that followed January's national election brought into sharper relief the changes wrought by it. The largest Shia religious parties put aside their rivalries to form a coalition with the Kurds that gave them control of parliament. A former Kurdish guerrilla fighter, Jalal Talabani, was appointed to the largely ceremonial post of president and a Shia politician, Ibrahim al-Jaafari, was named prime minister, the political post which now held the greatest executive power in Iraq. A dainty man with a receding hairline and greying beard, Jaafari had fled Iraq in 1980 and, although he had now returned and assumed his homeland's highest office, he still had the demeanour of the family GP he had been while living as an exile in north London. A week after his appointment I interviewed him amid the splendour of the Saddam-era luxury villa that he had adopted as his residence. He talked of the need for inclusion, reconciliation and the importance above all of fostering national unity. The policies his government introduced, however, appeared designed to achieve something very different.

The ministry for education was handed to Sadrists who hung pictures of Shia martyrs in its entrance.

Children began saying that teachers were asking them in class if they were Shia or Sunni, something inconceivable only a year earlier. SCIRI was placed in charge of the interior ministry, and consequently became the party responsible for establishing the new police service. The result was claims of widespread infiltration of the security forces by Shia militiamen and of Sunnis being murdered by armed men dressed in police uniforms.

I visited an Iraqi jail, one that was reputed to be among the best in the country. The entire facility smelt overwhelmingly of bleach, which was probably a good thing considering the alternative as prisoners were packed five to a cell. They jammed up against the bars as I was shown around and, through Ahmed, I questioned them about how they were being treated. Even though we were accompanied by a prison guard, the Sunnis held there told me that they wished they were being detained in a US facility, despite Abu Ghraib, because of their fear of what might happen to them in a prison run by the interior ministry.

In November their rationale became clear when American troops discovered a secret prison in the middle of Baghdad. They found it by chance after being led to it by an Iraqi woman who was worried about what could be happening to her imprisoned 15-year-old son. The prison was located in a former bomb shelter that had been turned into an interior ministry operations centre. Inside were 173 prisoners – many of them teenage boys – all of whom were starving and terrified. The US authorities kept the press away from the facility, but they made public that interrogators had peeled the skin off the bodies of some of the prisoners and beaten two so violently they were left paralysed. One prisoner had been blindfolded for three months and electrocuted almost every day.

A Sunni welfare group contacted Ahmed saying it had photographs of Sunnis who were tortured after being arrested by the police. The pictures' provenance was impossible to verify but the mutilation was sickening. One figure had burn marks on the chest, welts on the ribs, scars across one arm and two bullet holes in the head. Another had had both legs broken and his nose smashed. It was reminiscent of the worst Ba'athist excesses. However, this was now happening in a country supervised by American and British forces.

Unsubstantiated rumours circulated among Iraqis of secret Swiss bank accounts into which government funds were being diverted. Corruption was certainly endemic. After one flight into Iraq I was asked at the airport for a bribe by one of the customs men if I wanted to avoid the laborious process of him going through my bags. When Ahmed had to secure the immigration documents that allowed me to work as a journalist in Baghdad, a process he had to go through every time I arrived in the country, he took with him a pile of dollars to smooth over complications. 'Give praise to the new Iraq,' he would say as he disappeared out of our office.

Throughout 2005, ministers routinely made trips to Najaf to seek advice on legislation from Grand Ayatollah Sistani. Politicians would use parliamentary sessions as a stage on which to expound the depth of their religious convictions. Imams were invited to comment on proposed legislation. Religious programming began to dominate parts of the state television network. Asmaa, Abu Omar's sister who I had met while watching the Iraqi football team's match against Saudi Arabia, and for whom not wearing a hijab was a point of principle, said she was now sometimes called a 'whore' if she walked outside unveiled. On Shia festivals crowds of worshippers took to the streets, at times with catastrophic consequences. A thousand people died during one pilgrimage when there was a stampede on a bridge over the Tigris. After that incident bodies were being pulled from the water for days.

Unable to sack anyone or move ministers around due to the delicate state of his ruling coalition, Jaafari was rarely able to assert his authority in the cabinet. Government departments became political fiefdoms that rarely communicated with each other and had their own security forces that operated at their minister's discretion. Despite his office's theoretical powers, Jaafari was often reduced to merely adjudicating on who would live in which former Ba'athist mansion.

The debate during the summer of 2005 on what should be included in the text of Iraq's new constitution confirmed the impression of a political system in crisis. The Americans had gambled that the constitutional process would unite the country. Instead it appeared only to harden divides.

Shia politicians, with the help of their Kurdish political allies, used the overwhelming parliamentary majority they had secured as a result of the Sunni election boycott to force through what they wanted against all objections. The American ambassador pleaded with them for moderation, saying his country had already expended too much 'blood' and 'treasure' for an equitable solution to be abandoned. When the draft constitution was published at the end of August it was clear he had been largely ignored. There was little in it to imply the future would not be just as painful as the present. The US even had to accept its failure to establish Iraq as a secular state. The document's second article sanctioned Islam as a 'basic source of legislation'.

The draft constitution contained a system of federalism that would make Iraq one of the most decentralised states in the world. If approved, any of the country's eighteen provinces could hold a referendum on whether to become a semi-independent region. They would then have the right to ensure their 'internal security'. This clause had been demanded by the Kurds to preserve the autonomy of their peshmerga fighters, the Kurdish warriors who throughout the 1980s had fought a war of independence against Saddam's soldiers. It raised the spectre of regions having their own paramilitaries operating under the label of specialist local police units. With most of the Shia popula-tion in the south, Sunnis in the west and Kurds in the north, each region could potentially have its own private armies and be sanctioned by the state to do so.

Shia politicians maintained that federalism was neces-sary to prevent another Saddam emerging as it neutered the centralised powers he had exploited to subjugate the entire country. To its Sunni opponents, however, it simply looked like a plot conceived in Iran to break up Iraq and gain de facto control over the Shia south and its vast oil reserves.

Three days before polling day I watched a group of election workers, tasked with encouraging Iraqis to vote in the constitution, visit the Baghdad district of Karrada to hand out baseball caps and badges featuring pro-democ-racy slogans. The authorities had promised it would be a neutral 'go and vote' exercise but the atmosphere changed as 200 people swarmed around the electioneers, becoming one that reflected the real issue of the campaign: sectarian rivalry. This was a largely Shia area and the traditional folk songs being played turned into Shia religious songs. Women in black robes appeared on balconies as the crowd whipped itself into a frenzy. 'Shia, Shia, Shia, vote yes, vote yes, vote yes,' they chanted.

The government had created a lavishly produced pro-constitution advertisement to be broadcast on Iraq's TV stations. It was as glossy as any that might be seen in Britain or the United States during an election campaign. To the sound of nationalist music, a young boy first gathered stones in the desert and placed them to form an outline of Iraq. Dozens of men and women in different ethnic and religious dress then emerged with their own stones, each coloured a lighter or darker shade of brown, which they placed to form a wall. As the music reached a climax, the camera pulled back to reveal a crowd of smiling, embracing people and the coloured bricks spelling the word 'constitution'.

The problem, as the local press reported, was that none of those joyful figures were Iraqi. The advert was as much an illusion as its message of unity. Due to fear of revenge attacks, no local actors had been willing to appear in it and therefore the advertisement had been filmed abroad.

The Sunnis did vote when the referendum was held in October on whether the constitution should be adopted. Their exclusion from the parliamentary debate on the constitution's content had made clear that their previous boycott had been a major mistake. It had left them with no legitimate say in the country's political future. The result of the poll, however, only exposed how deep sectarian divides had become. The Shia and Kurds voted overwhelmingly for the constitution, the Sunnis overwhelmingly against it. The constitution passed. The lesson many Sunnis drew from this was that they were unlikely to gain anything through the ballot box.

In December 2005 another national election was staged so that a parliament could be elected under the new rules approved by the referendum. Once again I saw thousands of people lining up to cast their ballots. This time I was watching Sunnis vote as, despite their disillusionment with the referendum result, most were giving the ballot box one last chance. They did not have much of an alternative. The Sunnis' electoral boycott at the start of the year had led to a parliament dominated by their enemies. At the very least they wanted to ensure that this time they had some say in its composition.

I was in Tal Afar, a town in northern Iraq which only six months earlier had been one of the most dangerous places in the country. Located 30 miles west of Mosul, it had been controlled by Sunni extremists who used it as a staging point for suicide bombers coming in from Syria. According to the Americans, horrific atrocities had been committed. There were beheadings and executions. People were grabbed from their homes and tortured if suspected of being Western sympathisers. A mass grave was later found containing twenty-one bodies, nineteen of which had been shot through the back of the head.

In May, the American 3rd Armoured Cavalry Regiment was dispatched to restore order. When US soldiers first approached the town scores of gunmen stood in their path firing rocket-propelled grenades. Taxis had brought up reinforcements. The American commander, Colonel H. R. McMaster, responded by building an embankment around the city. He stationed guards to stop anyone hostile going in and out. His troops then moved into the town itself, using barbed wire to close off each district and clearing them house by house.

The impressive thing about the job McMaster had done was that he had expended as much thought on how to get the town up and running again as he had on the killing of the enemy. In Fallujah, which the US had stormed more than a year earlier, many people were still living in the ruins of their former homes. In Tal Afar the streets were filled with building sites. Shop windows that had been destroyed during the US assault were replaced and new sewers laid. Two thousand goats were distributed to farmers. These were little things but such steps were not normal and that tells its own story of the American failure in Iraq.

The evening before election day, I arrived in the US base on the outskirts of Tal Afar in a military helicopter. As in Amarah the previous January, the soldiers stationed there were nervous that night, uncertain if anyone would come out the next morning to vote and what violence might accompany the ballot. They need not have worried. The following day was mostly peaceful in Tal Afar, bringing only a few mortar rounds and a sole rocket-propelled grenade attack, and the Sunnis came out in their tens of thousands as soon as the polling booths were open.

The polling station I was taken to visit was in a secondary school in the district of Zahawi. It was one of the largest structures in the city, a four-storey concrete block with horizontal windows framing the main entrance and brightly coloured murals of palm trees and oxen lining the corridors. As in most of Tal Afar, work had already started to repair the marks of combat. Bullet holes had been cemented over and walls decorated. A new lick of paint, however, could not hide the gaping holes left by two American Hellfire missiles. They had struck four months earlier, an American soldier told me, when Sunni gunmen turned the school into their command centre. In the aftermath of the fighting to capture the building, mangled bodies had lain in the school's corridors, bloodstains marked the tiled floors and the playground was left pockmarked with craters. Now the school was filled with hundreds of people waiting to vote. It was the smell of drying sweat, not burned flesh, that pervaded its crowded rooms. Similar scenes, I was told, were occurring across the city and in Sunni areas throughout the country. In Fallujah demand for ballot papers was so high it risked outnumbering supply.

Due to concern about suicide bombers, those seeking to vote at the school in Tal Afar had to be frisked three times before they could reach the ballot box, which slowed down the process and left many voters waiting for hours before they had their chance to join the democratic process. The queue stretched from the classrooms where the polling booths were located, through the school's entrance, around the building and down the street. I walked the length of it, trying to gauge the number of people. There were six hundred, maybe a thousand, though it was difficult to judge as families clustered together and individual Iraqis moved from one part of the line to another as they sought out friends with whom to chat. The atmosphere was one of patience and contentment, despite the gaps in the queue that the US had instructed be left every thirty yards to try to limit the carnage that would follow if anyone did fire a mortar shell at it. Seeing me, many of those waiting smiled and waved.

A week before election day, I had interviewed Iyad Allawi, an Iraqi politician who headed one of the country's largest secular parties, the Iraqi National Accord. He was a committed opponent of the religious political parties and was a confidant of both the American and British ambassadors. His analysis of what would happen if the coalition of Shia religious parties that had won January's vote was again victorious was little less than apocalyptic. Iraq would descend into civil war, he said, unleashing a wave of 'evil forces' around the world.

'The stakes are very high,' he warned. 'Imagine that the same group comes to power for a further four years and maintains the current situation. Everyone will get hit. You can't have the streets of Iraq split between terrorists and insurgents on the one hand and militias on the other.

'If Iraq continues down this route it may dismember and fragment. If it fragments, God forbid, it'll be quite bloody. Not only for Iraq. It will trigger a chain in the whole region, and perhaps beyond, which could not be controlled and this will unleash evil forces throughout the world.'

What would he do, I asked, if the same parties won? 'I'll relocate abroad,' he said, throwing up his hands to indicate he would have little choice.

On election day, similar warnings were repeated by the voters I talked to in Tal Afar. Even in a place that had experienced first hand the worst insurgent excesses, they were still more terrified of the Shia religious extremists than their own fanatics. They were voting, but they were doing so in desperation.

'We want to change the government because this government is attacking Sunnis,' said one man, a 29-year-old Sunni Turkoman who worked as a construction worker in a nearby street. I asked him what would happen if the current government remained in charge. He stroked his moustache. 'I do not know,' he said. 'Only God knows but I fear it will be very bad.'

When the election result was announced the following month it revealed that the same Shia political parties had won. Iraqis had again chosen to vote along ethnic and sectarian lines in overwhelming numbers. The secularists were nearly annihilated. Allawi saw his party's parliamentary seats reduced to half the number won in the election at the start of the year. The coalition created by Ahmed Chalabi, a former Pentagon favourite who had put together a list of secular and nationalist candidates, failed to win a single seat.

This time it was not only Shia but also Sunnis who ignored the moderate political parties. The Shia gave the religious parties backed by their clerics another overwhelming victory. Four-fifths of Sunnis voted for the Islamic Party, the Sunni political party with the most fundamentalist agenda, ensuring it became the largest opposition body in parliament.

The Americans had launched the political process with the objective of giving all factions in Iraqi society a stake in Iraq's future so that they would unite in working together to ensure its stability. The result was a parliament filled with zealots who hated each other. Perhaps it was inevitable. The chaos that had engulfed Iraq was now feeding popular fundamentalism because it made people angry and desperate. This was no environment for promoting moderation.

Throughout 2005, when senior officers in the US military talked to each other about the possibility of civil war they referred to it as the 'subject of which we do not speak'. With the announcement of the December election results came the expectation that they would not be able to avoid speaking about it for much longer.

6. Insurgency

Ahmed did not need an alarm clock. First light would come through the windows of his flat and wake up his daughter, Labibah, who slept in the same bed as her mother and father. Although she was four-years-old, and had her own room, after the war started she became frightened of sleeping by herself, often having nightmares built around the snippets of news about killings and bomb blasts that she had overheard. So it had become the family routine for her to sleep with her parents. Ahmed said he had come to prefer it because if anything bad happened at night – a raid by soldiers or an explosion nearby – he knew immediately where all his family were located so would not lose precious time establishing if they were safe.

When his daughter woke she made sure everyone else was awake too. It was not an unpleasant rising. Labibah, Ahmed told me, would start hugging her mother and father until they gave up their slumbers. They would then take turns to cuddle her. He would hold Labibah to him, place her between his arms and kiss her on the forehead. Their day started with a moment of comfort and love.

By September 2005, the first hour was usually spent trying to preserve the family's propane gas to ensure there was enough to make breakfast, and transferring water from the tanks on the apartment's balcony into the bathroom so the family could wash. The price of gas was rising fast. It had doubled during the previous two months to 20,000 Iraqi dinar a cylinder, which was about $17, a lot in Iraq where the average wage was $300 per month, especially as each canister rarely lasted more than three or four days. In order to limit wastage, as much food as possible would be cooked in the same pan at the same time. This inevitably challenged the skills of the cook, who in Iraq is always one of the women of the household, and therefore in Ahmed's family his wife, Raha. Water was a different problem. As supply could be intermittent, many Iraqi families, Ahmed's included, directed it into tanks so it could be stored in preparation for when nothing came out of the taps. Shortages usually occurred at the time of most demand: the early mornings and late evenings. Ahmed had to carry water in plastic buckets from the storage containers to the bathroom, where those who wanted to wash could scoop it over their bodies.

My day started later. I did not want Ahmed or the rest of my Iraqi staff to arrive at the office too early. The early part of the day often brought some of the worst explosions as roadside bombs buried overnight were detonated by passing US patrols. I asked them to arrive at work at ten. My alarm went off at nine. In my suite at the Hamra I always had electricity, provided by the hotel's generators, and the vast tanks on the roofs of the hotel's twin towers ensured there was a steady supply of water. My morning consequently began with a long shower. I would then usually make myself a cup of coffee and eat a bowl of cereal while watching the news bulletin on BBC World. I was not able to buy either of these food items for myself. Visiting shops was dangerous as I might be identified as a foreigner. Buying a packet of Shredded Wheat did not seem a good enough reason to risk being kidnapped or killed. Instead I drew up a shopping list for my driver, Abu Omar, and every few days he would go and buy me food and also the office supplies I needed.

Even though Ahmed did not have to be at work until ten o'clock, he still left his house at nine. In safer times Dora, the district of Baghdad where Ahmed lived, was only a fifteen-minute drive from the Hamra but, with roads closed off by the war and checkpoints routinely set up by the military to try to catch suicide bombers and those carrying illegal weapons, it now normally took four times as long to complete the journey. Ahmed was always insistent that he did not like to make a big deal of the goodbyes as he headed out of the front door. If he did it would make him and Raha more emotional, which did neither of them much good because he had to work and she knew it. Raha and their daughter would nevertheless come out onto the balcony to watch and wave as he climbed into his car and started his drive across Baghdad.

It normally took him an hour to get to work but it could take longer. On one day in September 2005, Thursday the 8th, it took him almost two hours. The roads on the route he normally took were chaos because four checkpoints had been set up. When he finally arrived at the Hamra he was stressed out and cursing. I was at the computer in my office, trawling the internet to see what had been written about Iraq that day and what developments were being reported on the news wires, when he came in to apologise for being late.

'This wounded country of mine is becoming unbearable,' he said. 'Four checkpoints today. Four! I would not mind if they were not so useless. At the bridge [crossing the Tigris river] the Iraqi police had closed all the lines on the highway except one. It was a terrible crush as everyone tried to get through. And when we arrived at the checkpoint what do you think was happening? They were not even checking any cars. The policeman liked to sit under the shade of their awning and wave everyone through. I became so mad. They are so useless!'

The rest of the team, Abu Omar, my security guard Marwan, and the second driver Sajad, had come from different parts of Baghdad and had already been at the Hamra for almost an hour. They were sitting watching al-Jazeera on the television, drinking strong coffee from espresso cups. Ahmed began organising them. Abu Omar was asked to go to the offices of Iraqna, the local mobile phone operator, to pay our bill. Marwan and Sajad were instructed to read through a pile of documentation we had received from a Sunni religious welfare group detailing a rise in child malnutrition. Ahmed wanted them to highlight the most pertinent and shocking bits so he could later translate them for me.

I rang the *Telegraph* office in London on the satellite phone. The foreign desk had just arrived at work, the time difference between Britain and Iraq being three hours, and they wanted to discuss what stories I was going to put forward that day. Things were quiet, merely a few routine reports of a US patrol attacked near Ramadi, rumours of a gunfight in Kirkuk, nothing particularly major or out of the ordinary, so the conversation was short. It was arranged I would ring back in two hours to give an update on how the day was developing.

I rang back far quicker than that. Almost as soon as I put down the phone there was the sound of an imploding blast and we knew that somewhere in the city a bomb had gone off. The news reported that the explosion had been in Kadhimiya, a district in north Baghdad that was one of the few Shia enclaves to the west of the Tigris. A car filled with 500lb of explosives had apparently driven into a crowd of unemployed labourers, killing 114 of them and wounding a further 156.

Baghdad's unemployed often gathered in the city's main squares in the hope of picking up some work for the day from a building contractor or factory boss. They knew that if these companies found themselves temporarily short of staff they would drive to where labourers congregated and single out those who looked the most fit and strong. The economic collapse caused by the continuing violence had resulted in thousands of labourers gathering across Baghdad each morning. It appeared that they had now become too tempting a target for the bombers.

This was a big explosion even by Baghdad standards. We prepared ourselves to go to the bomb site. The procedure was that Marwan and Sajad left the office first. They drove around the block outside the Hamra's entrance in our second car to see if anyone appeared to be waiting for us and if anything looked suspicious or out of the ordinary. If it was safe they contacted us on their walkie-talkie and Ahmed, Abu Omar and I would leave the office and climb into Abu Omar's car. Once we had driven around 50 yards from the hotel, Marwan and Sajad would emerge from a side street and slot onto the road behind us. The intention was that the two cars would not be seen leaving the Hamra together, and then stay far enough apart so that anyone watching would not realise they were associated.

The traffic was still terrible and it took us forty-five minutes to get close to Kadhimiya. We were on one of the main highways headed north through the city, an overpass that enabled us to look down on the streets around us and which had only a handful of entry and exit junctions, thereby limiting the likelihood of someone taking us by surprise. Ahmed was in the front passenger seat, I was in the back. He held the walkie-talkie between his legs. To avoid looking suspicious, he would not look down at it as he spoke to Marwan about the vehicles around us and their likely intent.

We could see the smoke from the fires started by the explosion, the black plume drifting up into the still air, dissipating and curling into mutating clusters. Lines of US and Iraqi army vehicles were visible ahead as they approached the bomb site. Marwan reported that some of them seemed to be slowing down and he was concerned that they might be about to close off the road to secure the area. That would leave us stuck in a traffic jam for hours as the damage caused by the explosion was examined and cleared. Ahmed pointed out that even if we did reach the attack site there would already be so many soldiers at the scene that we would never be able to get close to it. We decided to turn off the highway and head to a nearby hospital to see if there were any wounded there who could talk about what had happened.

The Yarmouk hospital is one of the city's main casualty centres. From the outside it looks like almost every other building in Baghdad, the bricks of its walls covered by an expanse of concrete into which are inlaid rows of domed windows. There was no mistaking the building's function that day as the road in front of it was filled with ambulances and cars dropping off the injured. We had pulled over and parked when a police patrol truck appeared. Half a dozen officers were standing in its back and they started firing their Kalashnikovs into the air to tell the vehicles in front to clear out of their way. When the truck stopped at the hospital entrance, three of the policemen picked up a figure who had been lying in the back, the blood seeping through his blue police uniform visible from where we sat, and carried him into the building. Another officer followed them, turning just before he disappeared inside to fire another burst of gunfire into the sky.

Ahmed turned around from the front seat to look at me. 'Wait in the car,' he said. 'Do not get out. This is not a good situation. I will go inside and find out what it is possible to discover.'

I did as I was told. Abu Omar and I watched him disappear, notebook in hand, into the building. It was twenty minutes before he returned, twenty minutes during which a parade of vehicles dropped off their dying cargos. Ahmed reappeared, notebook still in hand, climbed into the front seat and said, 'It is time to go. I have a good interview. I will tell you about it when we reach the Hamra.'

Back at the office we learnt that there had been other bombs going off, none of which we had heard about or been aware of. It appeared as if they were co-ordinated attacks, intended to feed Baghdad's fear and chaos. A suicide bomber had killed eleven people waiting to fill their gas canisters in the north of the city. An Iraqi police convoy had been hit near the Baghdad offices of Moqtada al-Sadr, killing five and wounding twenty-four. Soldiers training to join the new Iraqi army had been targeted near the northern district of Shu'lah, killing at least two people. In Adhamiya, a Sunni district to the east of the Tigris, gunmen opened fire on a car, killing four. As passers-by rushed to help, a suicide bomber detonated, killing seven more. This was proving to be a particularly bloody day.

Ahmed described the situation in the hospital, reading back his notes. 'It was very bad,' he said. 'Many police were around and they were very angry. I found one of the injured unemployed labourers. His name is Hassam Jabar. He is 32 years old and has five children. He said he considers himself lucky if he gets two days' work a week. He was wearing black baggy trousers that had been cut just below the groin. His left leg was broken and his right leg almost severed at the knee. He was the only one I could find conscious on the ward to talk to. The man beside him had terrible facial injuries.' He grimaced and then gave a little laugh. 'It really was terrible in there!'

He looked back through his notebook. 'Jabar said to me that he had seen the car come in from the east side of the square. It looked normal. "Cars might mean work," Jabar told me. "Everyone moved towards it. There must have been a thousand people. The crowd pushed closer as news spread that the driver was saying he had jobs. People started shouting 'I am a carpenter' or 'I am a painter'. Some were so close to the car they were touching it." At that moment its driver detonated his explosives.'

Ahmed continued, 'Jabar said to me, "I found myself on the ground. There was blood on me. Then I saw there were bodies – many, many bodies – and severed limbs lying around me. Then I heard shooting and I was frightened but my legs could not move. People were running away screaming and shouting. I realised the police were shooting into the air to get people away but I still could not get up. Then people started to grab me and pull me away. I found myself in a minibus. The first hospital was chaos. They could not take any more people so they took me here."

'That was all I got,' Ahmed said. 'A doctor came and told Jabar they had to take him to surgery to have his right leg amputated. The police were starting to look at me in a strange manner so I left.'

For the next few hours, Ahmed and I tried to gain additional information and kept the office in London updated on developments. Abu Omar provided us with cups of tea, while Marwan and Sajad monitored the TV. There was another attack: a US patrol rammed by a suicide bomber. No one at the US military press centre would tell me about the extent of casualties but the Iraqi news channels were showing the burnt-out shell of a Humvee.

At five o'clock, I told everyone to go home. It would get dark soon and the most important thing was that none of them were still out on the streets after dusk. When night came the situation in Baghdad was always particularly dangerous as those seeking to cause harm used its anonymity to conduct their business.

Ahmed arrived home at six, he later told me, just as the sun was beginning to set. His wife had spent the day cleaning their flat. Her work had used up all the water so he could not wash. He did not mind, however, as he knew his wife liked to clean on days when she heard that the situation was particularly bad in Baghdad: it distracted her from worrying about her husband's safety. Ahmed's daughter, Labibah, had not been allowed outside because of the day's events and was consequently restless. She demanded her father play with her and for the next hour he sat on the floor pretending to have tea with her and her dolls.

I spent the evening at my computer. Due to the time difference between London and Baghdad, my final deadline was 9 p.m. On days like that I would work right up to it because casualty counts had to be updated and new facts incorporated into my article. In total 152 people died and 542 were wounded in Baghdad on 8 September 2005. It was one of the worst days in the city since the defeat of Saddam. Al-Qa'eda in Iraq claimed responsibility. At around 8 p.m. its leader, Abu Musab al-Zarqawi, released an audio tape in which he promised 'all-out war'.

Once my work was finished I was too tired and stressed to want to meet up with anyone else staying at the Hamra for a drink or a meal. Instead I ordered a kebab through room service and put on a DVD while eating my dinner. I usually watched boxed sets of American TV series, something that would absorb me and transport me as far away as possible from where I was. When I first arrived in Baghdad I had started with slightly more cerebral programmes like *The West Wing*. However, I quickly found myself becoming addicted to *Buffy the Vampire Slayer*. On nights like that one in September 2005, it was all that my brain had space left to take on board. I saw a lot of undead get staked during my time in Iraq.

Ahmed and his family turned on their diesel-powered electricity generator that evening to watch an Egyptian comedy film, sitting in the light of the TV screen because all the other lamps were turned off to limit the amount of electricity used. They went to bed at around ten. Every evening he liked to hold his daughter to him before she went to sleep, placing her between his arms and kissing her on the forehead, so that the day ended as it started: with a moment of comfort and love.

In April 2005 there had been a real fear that civil war, Iraq's greatest nightmare, was about to break out. Reports emerged that Sunni extremists had seized control of Madain, a city just south of Baghdad, and were giving the Shia who lived there two days to leave or be killed. Jalal Talabani, Iraq's newly appointed president, warned that the stretch of the Tigris that passed through the city was awash with bodies. At least 58, some of them women and children, had been pulled from the water in recent weeks. The cabinet's national security advisor announced that Sunni insurgents wanted to massacre peaceful Shia families in order to turn the city into a fundamentalist Islamic bastion.

As three battalions of the Iraqi army, supported by US troops, were dispatched to restore order, I began to explore what had gone wrong in Madain. It took a long time, weeks of work, as anything like that always did in Iraq. At one point I ignored Ahmed's protestations and risked the journey south to knock on doors to see if people's stories confirmed the reports of what had happened. Often in Iraq, the deeper I dug, the more confused I became but this time my efforts paid off. A picture emerged and it bore little resemblance to the Iraqi government's neat description.

During 2005 the situation in Iraq deteriorated with every passing month. While US High Command outlined their programmes for success, and soldiers on the ground sought to control their areas of operation, a void had emerged where the mechanisms of government once stood. Security, food, electricity, water, medicines: these basic necessities could no longer be relied on. The state was failing to look after its people. What I learned in Madain gave me my first indication as to what was filling the gap it had left. It is worth explaining in detail what I discovered because it was in Madain that I realised events were developing a dynamic of their own and that the situation was moving beyond anyone's ability to control. Madain was not merely a story about ideology or nationalist conviction. It was about power, money and people's overwhelming instinct for survival.

Although aspects of what happened in Madain remain unclear, its problems appeared to have originated in the aftermath of Saddam's defeat. Before then it had been a relatively tranquil place, somewhere to which families from Baghdad would travel on a day out in order to picnic in the lush fields that surrounded it. Then, in the second half of 2003, tens of thousands of Shia moved to the city from Iraq's impoverished south. The Shia had missed out on the best economic opportunities during Saddam's time, the real prizes being kept for Sunnis, particularly those who came from Saddam's hometown of Tikrit, and they had grown up hearing how much richer people were in Baghdad and in its Sunni hinterland. With the Ba'athist regime now deposed, they were moving north to see if they could secure some of that bounty for themselves.

At first, conditions in Madain had been relatively peaceful, despite the large number of Shia moving to the city. In Iraq, Shia and Sunni had lived alongside each other for generations and were used to focusing on their common identity as Iraqis and Muslims rather than the difference of their sects. Madain's local Sunnis even paid to have a new Shia mosque built to accommodate the Shia's growing numbers. The situation started to deteriorate in late 2004. A new, predominately Shia, police unit was sent from Baghdad and there was an influx into the city of Sunni fanatics fleeing the US military's November assault on Fallujah. These newly arrived Sunni extremists believed the Shia to be apostates who had turned away from the Prophet Mohammad's true message and therefore deserved to be killed. Frustrated by their defeat in Fallujah, they attacked Madain's Shia and its local symbols of government, such as its municipal offices. The police, a unit of Shia that had come from the Shia district of Sadr City in Baghdad, apparently took out their anger at these attacks on the city's entire Sunni population.

On a Shia feast day, local Sunnis told me, the police drove through Madain firing guns into the air and playing Shia religious songs. An officer grabbed a 14-year-old girl from the street, sat her on the back seat of his car and threatened to rape her. A Sunni wedding was being held that day. The police gathered outside and one of the officers started shouting at the wedding party, saying no one could leave because he wanted to molest the women. Many of his colleagues joined in, flinging insults of their own. There was a riot, gunfire and numerous police cars were burned. The police responded by taking refuge in the police station and, in the following weeks, limited patrols to a minimum.

The Sunnis from Fallujah continued their fundamentalist vendetta. With the police essentially having handed over control of the city, the Shia had little choice but to look to their own for security. Shia armed groups began to emerge across Madain and its surrounding region. The most powerful came from a nearby village, Hurriah, and was led by a 16-year-old Shia, Fadil. The techniques he adopted will be familiar to anyone who has ever seen a Hollywood gangster film. Local people claimed that anyone who wanted his gang's protection had to provide them with money or sustenance in order to secure it. Those who refused risked a knock on the door and a warning of what would happen if they did not co-operate in future.

It was perhaps inevitable that the Fallujahists began to exploit this money-making enterprise just as enthusiastically as the Shia gangsters. The local Sunnis, now terrified of both the Shia armed groups and the police, had concluded that they alone could provide any form of defence. The Sunni extremists had experience of fighting and the weapons with which to do so. As a result they were able to start their own protection rackets.

By March 2005, the situation had deteriorated to a level where assassinations were routine, tit-for-tat kidnappings commonplace and businesses regularly burned out as the Shia and Sunni gangs struggled for supremacy. In the midst of all this, an arms race had begun as each side tried to outdo the other. They amassed rocket-propelled grenades, AK-47s, and mortars. One Shia group was even reported to have got its hands on an old Iraqi army artillery piece.

The crisis reached its conclusion when a Shia group ransacked a Sunni mosque, an affront that brought all sides onto the streets, prompting the Iraqi government's claims that Sunni extremists had taken over the city, the Shia were being butchered and the Tigris filled with bodies. It had been the final showdown, the moment when it was concluded that one sect had to leave for good or there could never be peace. This was what had been interrupted by the sudden influx of Iraqi and US soldiers, who were now desperately trying to work out how they could possibly pacify such hatreds.

This was not the Iraq I heard about from officials in Baghdad, or in the reports being issued by governments back in the West. In these reports armed Iraqis were known as 'former regime elements' or 'Islamo-fascists', hostile forces labelled 'insurgents' or 'terrorists', and their motivation primarily said to be nationalism or a desire to defend a radical view of Islam. The situation in Madain did not fit any of these labels. It fact using them could only hide the reality of what was happening and give an unwarranted credibility to what was essentially mere banditry or a struggle for survival that bordered on anarchy.

In the coming months, the more I learned about what was going on in Iraq, the less the situation in Madain seemed exceptional. It soon did not surprise me that I would often arrive at a US base to find the senior officers working their way through boxed sets of *The Sopranos*. It was, they would tell me, one of the best guides to understanding the mentality of those in their area of operations.

At times I would read analysis by commentators based in America or Europe that described the strategy of the 'insurgency' in detail. 'Baghdad is now under siege', they would say, or 'the insurgency is preparing for its own Tet offensive'. As far as I could see the insurgency did not exist as they understood it. There was no phantom Ho Chi Minh figure pulling the strings. There were extremists out there motivated by loyalty to Saddam or religious conviction who were stoking the chaos. However, much of the violence was the work of the unscrupulous exploiting the weak for their own benefit, or countless individuals taking up weapons for their own protection, protection that was sometimes against the Americans barging around their villages kicking in doors. The American-led invasion, and the subsequent misjudgements of the CPA and heavy-handed approach of the US military, had created the circumstances that enabled such a situation to flourish. But what was now happening appeared increasingly separate from any action being taken by the Americans or those who had originally taken up arms against them. This was a breakdown of society being fuelled by fear and the necessity for self-preservation.

Moreover, the Sunni armed groups who did claim to be pursuing political objectives, and who propagated them through web sites and leaflets, defied easy categorisation. According to the US authorities there were three main players and a dozen smaller ones in the Sunni insurgency. The largest ones were Al-Jaysh al-Islami fil-Iraq (the Islamic Army in Iraq), Al-Jabha al-Islamiya lil-Muqawama al-Iraqiya (the Islamic Front of the Iraqi Resistance), and Jaysh Ansar al-Sunna (Army of the Partisans of the Sunna). The smaller ones included Jaysh al-Rashidin (the First Four Caliphs' Army), Jaysh al-Ta'ifa al-Mansoura (the Victorious Group's Army), Harakat al-Muqawama al-Islamiya fil-Iraq (the Islamic Resistance Movement in Iraq), Saraya al-Ghadhab al-Islami (the Islamic Anger Brigades), Saraya Suyuf al-Haqq (the Swords of Justice Brigades) and Jaysh Mohammad (Mohammad's Army).

The fighters in one group would have separate objectives to those in another and often strikingly different interpretations of their responsibilities as Muslims. Most also had their own protection schemes and smuggling rings that they ran alongside their more obvious insurgent activities. It was often hard to determine which they considered more important, or even if either aspect could be separated from the other. In some cities there could be half a dozen of these insurgent groups. At one point the US announced it had identified 24 different militias in Baghdad alone.

In addition to all these warring and shifting paramilitary organisations, there was al-Qa'eda in Iraq, the official al-Qa'eda franchise in the country, under its terrifying leader Abu Musab al-Zarqawi, the man who all Westerners in Baghdad knew wanted to put them in an orange jumpsuit and behead them, just as he had Ken Bigley. This was the organisation that was widely accused of being responsible for the worst atrocities and the most horrific suicide bombings, and was the ideal that most of the young men flooding into Iraq from across the Arab world had come to join.

As with so much in that conflict there was far more confusion than fact surrounding al-Qa'eda in Iraq. This was partly due to the very nature of al-Qa'eda itself, which is as much a state of mind as a terrorist organisation. All anyone has to do is accept its beliefs, adopt its particularly violent solution to destroying materialism, and they become a member. This made it difficult to judge how closely involved al-Qa'eda was in guiding those who fought under its name in Iraq, particularly as Zarqawi's loyalty to Osama bin Laden was tenuous. It was known that the two of them had argued in the past, Zarqawi refuting bin Laden's right to be the symbolic head of militant Islam. Occasionally the Americans would release messages that they had intercepted in which bin Laden or his closest lieutenants would plead with Zarqawi to alter or moderate his tactics. These instructions were clearly being ignored as his organisation's attacks on soft targets, such as markets and mosques, continued unabated. It was possible the organisation's adoption of the name al-Qa'eda was merely a marketing technique rather than a symbol of close affiliation.

So scarce was information about al-Qa'eda in Iraq that the Americans were not even sure if Zarqawi had one leg or two. It was debated whether he had lost one while fighting in Afghanistan. Al-Qa'eda in Iraq was clearly operational. It was clearly nasty. It was probably responsible for many of the worst attacks. Yet it was unclear how many people were operating under its name. It could have been five hundred or five thousand. Nobody seemed to know for certain.

When al-Qa'eda in Iraq claimed culpability for a bombing or an attack it did not necessarily mean it was responsible. Other insurgent groups would also often claim responsibility, sometimes with far more credibility. Determining who was to blame was only made harder by the Americans' apparent penchant for publicly blaming al-Qa'eda in Iraq if it was at all possible. This played well back in the States and avoided them having to admit that the people primarily shooting at them were Iraqis rather than foreign jihadists.

Some Iraqis were so cynical about the whole situation that they would argue al-Qa'eda in Iraq did not even exist and that Zarqawi was merely a CIA creation to justify America's continued presence in their country. It was, in its own way, as justifiable a conclusion as any other.

Amid this chaos and confusion the Americans announced plans to create a new Iraqi army and police force to remove responsibility for security from the US and its allies. In 2005, the US hoped it would be the establishment of this force, combined with the rallying effect of the political and constitutional process, that would pacify Iraq. An ambitious timetable was announced in which these new security forces would be up and running within two years, by which time it was intended that Iraqis would be leading the fight against the insurgency and securing the nation's borders. There is a military truism, however, that I repeatedly heard from officers in Iraq, both American and British, which states that it normally takes ten years to win an insurgency, and fourteen years to lose one. This new plan intended to stabilise Iraq far quicker and this brought its own dangers.

The pressure for prompt action was particularly acute in the case of the new army. The US desperately needed Iraqi soldiers if it was to have any hope of stabilising the country or of reducing its own casualties. Iraq's Saddam-era army had been abolished on 23 May 2003 by a stroke of Paul Bremer's pen. During 2004, the Americans first attempt at creating a new Iraqi army failed when a battalion turned tail when ordered to go into Fallujah and 40 per cent of its recruits deserted. The remainder of the force had largely been disbanded and a new training programme drawn up to ensure the soldiers it produced would be willing to fight. In 2005 this was now being implemented. Thousands of Iraqis were recruited and millions of dollars spent on salaries and equipment. American and British soldiers were taken off combat operations to whip the new military into shape. A staff college opened south of Baghdad.

The need for fast results meant many Iraqi recruits were placed with active units after only six weeks of training, so keen was the coalition to get Iraqi boots on the ground as quickly as possible. Doubts were raised in some quarters as to whether they could possibly have the discipline and skills needed. The American response was that there was a war going on and therefore no alternative to a significant degree of on-the-job training.

It was not easy to gain permission to spend time with the troops in the Iraqi army, even though by mid-2005 there were meant to be 57,000 of them. The Americans knew they were a work in progress, and that what was being reported back by those who had managed to see them in action was not always favourable. Nevertheless, in late May I managed to secure approval to visit a brigade based near Muqdadiya and accompany it on an operation. It was to be the first time Iraqi soldiers had been allowed to operate independently of American troops and US High Command wanted to show off this achievement to the media. I was told I would be joining an Iraqi army unit commander called Captain Haider in one of the white pick-up trucks that at that point were the Iraqi army's only mode of transport. A US army Iraqi translator would be assigned to accompany me.

On the day of the operation, five of us squeezed onto the front seats of the pick-up truck – myself, my translator and three Iraqi soldiers – while six more Iraqi servicemen sat on the metal benches fitted to the back. Despite the supposedly multi-sectarian composition of the army, all the soldiers were Shia. They were dressed in second-hand uniforms donated by the US military. These were of the same design as the ones the marines had worn while fighting the Iraqi army during the 1991 Gulf War. The Marine Corps had been told to pass them on now that their own uniforms had been upgraded to a new computer-generated camouflage design. Few fitted their new owners properly, the average Iraqi soldier being far smaller than his American counterpart. Leather belts held up trousers and sleeves hung to the tips of fingers. None of the Iraqis had any body armour and weaponry was largely limited to second-hand Kalashnikovs.

The operation was to be a sweep of local villages that for months had been considered home to the prime suspects for the roadside bombs which kept hitting American patrols in the area. As we waited for it to start I asked my companions what had drawn them to the military life. The answer seemed to depend on their rank.

For the officers it was apparently patriotism. 'I am aware I could be killed but there can be no room for fear in my heart,' a Lieutenant Mohammad told me. He had the stare of a true believer. 'I must protect my family and country. When I went on my first raid I let my soldiers enter the house first and I could see they were scared. The second time I led the way so they knew my strength and now they fight like lions.'

Captain Haider, his commander, nodded in approval.

A private sat on my left, a man hairy even by Iraqi standards with black curls covering the backs of his hands and pushing out of the top of his camouflage jacket. He had a far more pragmatic reason for enlisting. 'There are no jobs so I become a soldier,' he said without a hint of embarrassment. 'I dream of owning a little shop but it is impossible with the present conditions in Iraq. In two or three years, when I have saved money, I will leave. This job is very dangerous and my family begs me to finish it, but for now I need to work.'

Captain Haider nodded again, though this time not with approval but rather with an air of resignation to the fact that it was true and a common story.

Haider was a rotund man, his stomach falling over the front of his trousers, who was hardly ever without a cigarette. He was a committed patriot and keen to assure me that the new Iraqi military was the right organisation to bring stability to his country. Its soldiers, he insisted, were among the bravest in the world and had some of the best training methods.

'I am special forces,' he said. 'To finish our training we must catch a wild rabbit or cat with our hands, kill it with our hands and then eat it raw. I have eaten five cats. That is how strong the Iraqi soldier is.'

Haider's role in the operation was to gather information for his commanding office and, once it started, the first few hours involved him listening to the radio so that he could report what was going on. The situation was mostly quiet. There were a few mortar rounds, a rocket-propelled attack and some gunfire, but the impression was that most of the local armed groups had been fore-warned that the operation was coming and had disappeared before it began.

This, I was told, was not an unusual occurrence in operations that involved the Iraqi army. The links that existed between the soldiers and the local communities in which they lived resulted in confused loyalties that made secrecy difficult. Due to the speed with which the new army was being put together there had been little time for adequate screening of people's true motivations for joining the force. Sometimes this problem went to the highest levels. The previous month a battalion commander had been arrested for feeding information to local extremists.

It was mid-morning when we were finally ordered to visit the villages being searched. A number of Haider's troops donned balaclavas even though the temperature was around 35°C. This, I learned, was so that no one could recognise them and later take reprisals against the soldiers or their families. My translator, a local university student who could not have been more than 19 years old, had kept his balaclava on from the moment we had joined the Iraqi soldiers, such was his view of their integrity.

The countryside was lush and well irrigated by a series of slow-moving streams and ditches. Reeds lined the road-side and the fields were dotted with groves of date palms and poplar trees. Haider drove fast, the speedometer rarely dropping below 70 mph. The roads were not good, mostly dusty tracks beside irrigation canals, but there was no regard for tyres or shock absorbers as he pushed the accelerator to the floor.

'We go fast so they do not hit us,' he reassured me. 'There is no need to be worried. Iraqi soldiers are very brave.'

We began to meet other units. At road junctions groups of Iraqis sat or squatted on the ground, most of them smoking. At one turning the private on my left waved and shouted a hello. 'He is my cousin,' he said, indicating a figure waving back. Everyone seemed remarkably relaxed.

In the first village we reached, more than a hundred soldiers were milling around the streets, many sitting on benches or walking into and out of houses. It was a typical Iraqi village. These, like almost all Iraq's built-up areas, were rarely attractive places: featureless in their repetitive-ness – lines of houses, one or two shops selling bottles of water and vegetables, a few trees, a couple of sad-looking shrubs – and drab in their colouring of brown and grey. The buildings were mostly concrete blocks, most less than thirty years old, with the roofs flat in case someday the money miraculously appeared to enable another storey to be built on top. However, those who lived in them had rarely travelled far and as a result they had the atmosphere of entrenched communities, places where the villagers knew with unthinking familiarity every corner and pot-hole. Families had usually lived there for generations and so understood, for better or worse, all that was good and bad about each other.

A half-dozen local Iraqis stood to one side, silently watching. There was the sound of a shot and for a moment every soldier was alert. It became apparent that it had come from one of their own and the target had been a dog. A soldier was gesticulating and pointing at it. The animal had blood coming from its haunch and was lying on the ground, trying to pull itself up on its front legs. The soldiers started laughing and a few ran forward. They trained their Kalash-nikovs and started shooting. Not one hit. Then a soldier produced a pistol and shot the dog in the head.

'It tried to bite them,' my translator explained.

In the next village two prisoners were waiting outside a house, their hands bound behind their back. They looked like farmers. We stopped beside them and an Iraqi soldier came over and said something to Captain Haider. He got out of the truck and slapped both the prisoners hard across the face. He thrust them against the side of the truck and started shouting at them.

'These insurgents pushed some of the soldiers when they entered the house,' my translator said.

An old woman, presumably the men's mother, ran over. She was pulling at her clothes and wailing. The soldiers started laughing again.

I looked around. Soldiers were coming out of a building carrying a locked chest which they then smashed to see if it held any weapons. Another group were taking a loaf of bread from a shop. Some villagers were having their hands secured behind their backs by plastic binders. Trucks were roaring up and down the road. Captain Haider was still shouting at his prisoners and pushing them in the chest. Two hoods were placed over their heads but he did not stop pushing them.

A US patrol drew up. A colonel, a man at least six foot three inches tall, tanned and oozing confidence, stepped out of the middle Humvee and started congratulating the Iraqis on a job well done. The American soldiers guarding him had black bands for sunglasses and webbing weighed down with weaponry. The colonel went on a walkabout accompanied by two female GIs, both of them blonde and so beautiful they could have stepped out of a TV show. The women had bags of sweets which they offered to the villagers. The children took them but the men stared back with such hatred it was numbing to behold.

'These are brave men,' the colonel told me as Iraqi soldiers gathered to have their photograph taken with him. 'Iraq has a golden future.' They liked that, when it was translated for them. Soldiers started hitting each other on the back and flexing their muscles before raising a cheer for the colonel's benefit. It felt like quite a carnival for a moment there.

7. Home

Abu Omar, the *Telegraph*'s driver, was a Sunni from the Dulaimi tribe, one of the largest tribes in Iraq and the one from which many senior military and intelligence officers in Saddam's regime had been drawn. He held no affection for the Americans and saw their occupation as a national humiliation, but he cared even less for those Iraqis who were killing Iraqis.

'Kill an American and you're a hero, kill an Iraqi and you're a criminal,' he would say.

He was the oldest son and, with his father dead, took his filial responsibilities seriously. His family was originally from the city of Baqubah, an agricultural centre on the Diyala river 30 miles north east of Baghdad. It was the scene of some of the heaviest guerrilla fighting but he still insisted on seeing his relatives regularly, despite the journey's hazards, as it was of fundamental importance to him that the family remained emotionally close to each other. He would bring back figs from a tree in his uncle's garden that were the most delicious I have eaten anywhere in the world.

He prayed regularly and kept a prayer mat in the office to ensure that he fulfilled his duties as a good Muslim. He once gave me a collection of writings explaining the teachings of the Prophet Mohammad that emphasised the peaceful nature of Islam and the spirit of shared humanity that underlined much of their message. On the front, written in English, were the Prophet's words, 'A Muslim is the brother of a Muslim. He neither oppresses him nor disgraces him, he neither lies to him nor does he hold him in contempt.'

When I first met Abu Omar in the summer of 2004, he ridiculed the idea that there could be a civil war in Iraq. Indeed he laughed at the possibility. Sunni and Shia had lived beside each other for generations, he said. They worked together, inter-married and lived as neighbours in many districts of Baghdad. Their most important sense of identity was that they were Iraqi above all else. That was what foreigners needed to understand. Sunni and Shia were both Iraqi and Iraqi Arabs might fight foreign invaders but not each other.

By the middle of 2005, when Iraq's newly elected Shia politicians were beginning to misuse their power to settle old scores and exert their authority, Abu Omar began to talk darkly about the influence of Iran. One of his cousins had been a pilot in the Iraqi air force and scores of pilots from the Iraq–Iran war era were now being assassinated. These people were particularly hated by the Iranians as they were the ones who had dropped the chemical weapons that Saddam had used against Iran. His cousin fled to Syria after the most famous Iraqi pilot of his generation, Ismael Saeed Fares, whose repeated raids in the Iran-Iraq war had earned him the nickname 'The Hawk of Baghdad', was shot dead. He was hit by 24 bullets as he sat in the garden of his north Baghdad home.

Abu Omar was convinced, as many Sunnis were, that the pilots' personal details were being taken from old records in Iraq's defence ministry. He blamed the Badr Brigade, the paramilitary wing of the Shia political party SCIRI, for the killings and viewed it as an instrument of the Iranian military. To him, the influence of Tehran was everywhere. He was not alone in that. As a result of the close links that existed between Iraq and Iran's political leaders even some US State Department officials liked to say, only partly in jest, that 'the war's over – and Iran has won.' However, for Abu Omar this belief began to cloud every facet of his thinking. The Iranians and their acolytes, he said, had assumed senior positions in Iraq's police force in order to arrest, torture and kill innocent Sunnis. It was they who were murdering Sunni clerics and were responsible for the worst excesses occurring in his country.

By late 2006, a time when the sectarian civil war was being fought in earnest, Abu Omar did not view many Shia as fellow Iraqis any more. They had betrayed their right to such an honour by siding with the Iranians to help them destroy the Iraqi state. He lived in an area of the capital called New Baghdad. It was a mixed sectarian neighbourhood and by then Shia militias were breaking into Sunni houses at night to threaten and kill their owners.

Abu Omar's wife suggested they leave the city, maybe even get out of Iraq itself. If he wished to continue working, she said, then he could stay behind while his family sought sanctuary and visit them whenever he could. He would not tolerate this idea. For a start he would not allow the social impropriety of his wife and daughters living apart from him. More importantly, he would not accept that the enemies of Iraq could force him from his own home. The family, he said, would live together and if necessary die together. What they would not do was betray their principles by escaping the land that was their birthright.

Marwan, Ahmed's brother who was my security guard, and Sajad, the second driver, became good friends after they started working for me. It was an unlikely pairing. Marwan was a Sunni who was proud of his military background and was extremely patriotic. He had served in the Iraqi army and still sported a closely clipped military moustache. He had been in two of the nastiest fights of the Iran-Iraq war: the one in which the Iranians first gained Iraqi territory when they seized the al-Faw peninsula south-east of Basra, and the one two years later when the Iraqis drenched that same peninsula in chemical weapons while taking it back. After that he had lost faith in Saddam, refused to join the Ba'ath Party and had his army career curtailed.

Sajad was a Shia, and like most Shia had never had much time for Saddam or the Iraqi military. What linked the two of them, other than a basic good humour, was the knowledge that they did not take their religion too seriously. They considered themselves Muslims, fasted at Ramadan and noted their sects' holy days, but neither seemed to spend much time praying.

Marwan had a Shia wife, a not uncommon situation in Iraq where – as Abu Omar had so rightly told me – before things got out of hand Shia and Sunnis had lived alongside each other for generations. His wife was the daughter of the family that lived next door to his. While in his early twenties and still in the army he had returned on leave and spotted her walking along the street. He had gone to his parents that very day and told them he had seen the woman he wished to marry. They organised for her family to visit. It was the first time the future husband and wife had met properly. They were not permitted to talk to each other in private while their families discussed the suitability of the pairing.

Marwan's future wife was asked by her father if she was willing to go ahead with the match. She said she was. Marwan and his bride-to-be had barely spoken a hundred words to each other by the day of the marriage ceremony but both had been the ones who had permitted the wedding to go ahead once their families had agreed it was acceptable. It was the traditional way of doing things for the educated Iraqi middle class. They now have five children.

Neither of their families had considered religious differences a stumbling block. What primarily mattered to both was that their child was marrying into a respectable family, and as they lived beside each other they already knew that to be the case.

When, during 2006, conditions got really bad in Baghdad and Shia and Sunni armed bands were killing each other with real enthusiasm, I asked Ahmed if the situation had made any difference to Marwan and Sajad's friendship.

He looked at me as if I was an idiot.

It was during that period that I came into the main room in our office and found Marwan repeating phrases as Sajad looked on, nodding encouragingly.

Sajad was checking Marwan's knowledge of Shia religious history and customs. Marwan's wife had been teaching them to her husband so that if need be he could bluff his way through the illegal checkpoints that the Shia death squads were setting up across Baghdad. When an Iraqi was stopped at one, and if those manning it identified him as Sunni, the likely result was torture and death. So Marwan was practising his newly gained knowledge of the twelve imams revered by Shia Muslims, the sect's key historical dates and the significance of its festivals. Sajad corrected any mistakes.

I asked Sajad how Marwan was doing. He was doing okay, I was told, 'for a soldier'. Marwan stared at him. Then he stood up and started to pretend to whip himself. It was a parody of the Shia faithful who would commemorate the anniversary of the death of Husain in the Battle of Karbala by publicly beating themselves with ropes and metal strips until the ground was covered in blood.

He hopped around saying, 'I have become a good Shia now.'

Everyone, Sajad included, loved it.

It was a strange life, the one I led at that time. To give me opportunities to relax the *Telegraph* let me take regular three-week holidays from Iraq. I would finish a stint, board a flight out of Baghdad airport, arrive in Amman, and the next morning be en route to Heathrow for the start of a break back in Britain. After landing I would find myself on the tube, sitting alongside the commuters as we passed under central London, they on their way to work, me on my way home. It seemed incredible that life in these two cities could be going on at the same time in their own very different ways separated only by two short bursts of reading a book on a plane.

London has been the one constant location in my life. I was born there, and though I have lived away from it I have always come back. My friends and family live there. I know many of its streets so well that I do not even need to look to see where I am going. It is predictable and consequently reassuring.

In the Middle East a country was dying. In London people were preoccupied with the usual talk of house prices, dating and jobs. I would spend weeks living in Iraq, then fly back and find the conversations were still exactly the same. People knew that the war was going on, most knew it was not going well, and a number had demonstrated to try to stop it from even taking place, but it was not – thankfully – the most important thing in their lives. It was, in fact, rarely mentioned. There would be moments when what was happening in Iraq would come to the fore when another squaddie died or something catastrophic happened. Even then people's reaction seemed to focus back on themselves, dealing with how they hated the hypocrisy of Tony Blair or wondering how a Labour government had gone so wrong.

During my first week in London I would largely stay at home, watching TV late into the night, so that I could shake off the residual stress before I started meeting up with people. During the second week I would go out and enjoy myself, delighting in the simple pleasure of being able to go to shops and bars. Often during the day I would walk for miles, revelling in the sense of movement and the sight of people going about their everyday lives. Nothing I saw seemed predictable. It was as if I had hyper-vision, every person fascinating me as they went about their normal routine. In the third and last week I would feel the tension coming back into me and I would start waking up earlier, becoming more frantic about trying to fit what I could into every day. Then I would find myself on the tube with my bags. A day later, there I would be, back in Baghdad.

There were moments in Britain when I could not escape

the effect of Iraq, however hard I tried. Normally it would come when I was sitting around people who started complaining a little bit too much about stresses such as a pushy mother-in-law, a delay at an airport while going on holiday or a washing machine that kept on leaking. I did not have much sympathy at the time for such problems. It seemed to me that people in London had life pretty good and that they should enjoy it as much as possible, though to give them credit, most of the people I knew did. I kept my mouth shut when those moments came. It was normal for people to be dwelling on such details; lucky even.

Then I met a girl. Previously London had been a place in which to relax and forget. Now I had a reason to be there. On my breaks back in Britain we would swim in the pools on Hampstead Heath, sit in pubs during cold nights, go and see films together, do all the good stuff normal people do. We had a lot of fun. In fact, it was fantastic. The more I got to know her the more I realised that she somehow already knew the most important lesson that living in Baghdad had taught me. She understood that all the inconsequential strains of life were not things to get caught up in and distracted by, that only the really big stuff mattered and the rest was too often merely an impediment to actually living.

Until then I had enjoyed a pretty self-centred life. Being a foreign correspondent often does that to you because when things get tough you can simply weigh anchor and move on. I had made homes on three continents and travelled around the world at least twice. There had been a period in my youth when I had happily partied too hard, and another in my twenties when I probably drank too much. I had never given much thought to where it would all lead. The priority had been what might be the next exciting place to visit or story to cover.

Being in Iraq changed people. Some it made angry and too quick to snap. Others it left feeling invincible because they believed they had seen the worst and survived. I saw a lot of that, especially among the troops. They would get through their tour of duty, arrive home, and then be killed in a road crash. They could not conceive how they could be hurt in such familiar surroundings and as a result drove far too fast. A private in the unit I had been placed with during the invasion had died that way. He arrived back to Georgia in July 2003 after having spent a year training in the Kuwait desert, fighting his way to Baghdad and then coping with the first stirrings of the insurgency. A month later he was dead after he refused to ease off on the accelerator and his motorcycle hit a tree.

A significant minority were left feeling that they needed to find ways of escape; that they wanted to forget everything and let alcohol and drugs make them live only in the moment. To me, however, it did the opposite. For the first time in my life I did not want to find fresh distractions. Doing so seemed a way to waste time and no one has much of that. That was another lesson I learnt in Iraq.

It was an amazing feeling to get on a plane, circle up above Baghdad airport and then head west, knowing it was taking me to someone who wanted to see me, and whom I wanted to see just as badly. In Iraq I witnessed people's emotion as they lost everything and everyone that they had cared about. That was a powerful thing to behold. While on breaks in Britain I started looking carefully at the lives of my friends with families, people who had settled in one spot and made the best of it. I realised they had made a choice and, for the most part, they were content. More than that, it had made them who they were and what they would be. My time in Iraq had a surprising effect on me. It was terrifying and terrible but it did finally make me grow up.

I was on one of those breaks in London when, shortly before the December national elections at the end of 2005, the Hamra hotel was attacked and my office destroyed. I was watching Fern Britton on *This Morning* discuss a comb that was supposed to cure baldness when my boss rang to tell me the news. When I first heard it, I could not believe it. That building had been my safe space, a refuge where I could pretend I was somewhere sane. Two cars, piled high with explosives, had driven into the perimeter blast walls. There was nowhere sane in Baghdad any more.

While I digested the news, I wondered for a moment if it was worth going back. That dilemma did not last long. In fact it was gone almost as soon as the question had been raised. I had got too involved in what was happening in Iraq to be able to step away now. I needed to know what happened next, whether the catastrophe that I feared was approaching would unfold or if the Iraqis and Americans could somehow pull the country back from the brink of total collapse. What was happening in Iraq was important and even what had happened to the Hamra was not enough to make me want to stop reporting on it. I rang Ahmed and he said the team were already organising themselves to drive to the hotel to see what remained and that they needed me back soon as they did not know what to do next. I booked a ticket and, a couple of days later, was waiting at Heathrow for my flight.

The Hamra escaped being totally destroyed because the bombers got their calculations wrong. The first explosion not only took down our defences but blew such a colossal hole in the tarmac that the second vehicle could not drive over it. The bombs still caused considerable damage, however. My office was on the side of the building that bore the brunt and afterwards it resembled the collapsed shacks one sees in photographs taken after a major earthquake. The ceiling had come down, windows were blown in, cupboards reduced to tinder and the metal front door was buckled and left hanging by one hinge.

The Iraqi houses around us suffered the worst. They did not have any blast walls to protect them. I used to watch the people living in them from my window: the women stepping onto their balconies to hang up their washing, or the children gathering to kick a football around on an adjacent stretch of wasteland. They had found themselves targets solely because the international press corps had decided to move into the hotel next door. No one asked them if they minded. Afterwards those of us at the Hamra, myself included, did not like to talk about that too much. Everyone sought to put this knowledge to one side, the knowledge that they were hit due to our presence.

Two apartment blocks disappeared in the bombing to be replaced by a pile of rubble and a couple of stubbornly standing supportive struts. At least eight people died, among them the little boy who had ferried hot pastries to the hotel bakery. He had been making a delivery just as the bombs went off. They never found his body. Indeed the strange thing was that the only bodies people could locate in the immediate aftermath were those of the bombers themselves. Bits of them had gone everywhere. One of the Westerners hired to supervise security at the hotel claimed to have found a penis in a shrub. Half a head was left lying at the bottom of the swimming pool, its one eye staring up at passers-by. Someone fished it out but I noticed that even on the hottest days people seemed to use the pool less after that.

8. Tea and Sympathy

The cockpit of the helicopter ferrying me from Amarah to the British base in Basra was baking hot. The cooling system had shut down and the pilot turned around to show me that the back of his green flight suit was black with sweat. He pulled an expression of mock surprise. The few helicopters the British had available were being worked all hours. Many dated back to the 1970s, had been flogged around the world for decades and were now at constant risk of breakdown or worse. It would probably have been more noteworthy if there had not been something on that helicopter which was broken.

He gave me a headset so we could talk. With his cut-glass accent and chin that bobbled when he spoke, he would have been more suited to a Kensington drinks party than a Mesopotamian desert. In fact he had flown across Iraq almost every day for three months and he talked of some of the recent trips he'd undertaken. It was the height of summer and he had spent most of the previous weeks ferrying soldiers with heatstroke to hospital. This was not the kind of heatstroke that might be picked up on holiday, he was keen to emphasise, but the kind that risked causing people's internal organs to boil.

'The amazing thing is that these boys never seem to

complain,' the pilot said of the soldiers he had been called on to evacuate. 'They're in a terrible condition, barely able to say a word, and often going into and out of consciousness. But despite that I've seen them raise themselves enough to give me a thumbs up as they get carried off on a stretcher. I've seen that so many times and it is always a touching sight. They're such young chaps but they're brave.'

It was scenes like that which had made him angry. 'No one has ever told me exactly what we're doing in Iraq and what we're meant to be achieving,' he said. 'I pick up these boys and they're in a terrible condition and nobody has made clear to me what it's for. The government doesn't care even though they sent us here. All it wants to do is suck up to the Americans and we're the collateral damage for that.

'Nor does anyone back home really give a toss,' he continued, for the first time an edge of real bitterness coming into his voice. 'They haven't got a clue. I was back on leave and went to get my hair cut. The girl doing it was asking what I did and so I told her. She said she wouldn't like that. It sounded dangerous. She said, "Do they attack you?" Can you believe it! I told her they threw mortars at us the whole bloody time. She kept quiet after that.'

It may not have been comfortable but it was nevertheless comforting being with the British Army in southern Iraq, surrounded by soldiers whose behaviour and preoccupations were familiar and easier to comprehend than those of the Americans and Iraqis. I was instinctively sympathetic to their situation but the respect I developed for them was based on more than that. It was the very scale of the terrible failure that unfolded under their watch and the lack of tools they had been given to prevent it that, perversely, made it impossible not to be impressed by their fortitude. As the war went on, and the situation deteriorated, British troops knew only too well that they were losing control over their area of operations but they never gave up. Missions were planned and executed right to the end, even though their impact was often little more than that of a pebble in a raging sea. Among the servicemen I met there was none of the evangelical belief in the need to fight terrorism abroad that marked the average American serviceman but there was a keen pride in their ability to soldier.

In Iraq, British soldiers often worked eighteen-hour days, regularly put their safety on the line, and had to cope with the most oppressive heat and humidity. They did not have anything but the most basic living conditions. There were no Ben and Jerry ice-cream stands or Xbox game rooms here. Variants on sausage, beans and chips were normally as far as the daily menu stretched. At the main British base at Basra airport, which was probably the best-equipped camp Britain had in Iraq, accommodation was limited to tents into which the soldiers were packed by the half-dozen. I would find myself in accommodation areas in which scores of people shared the same washing facilities. The air-conditioning systems were so feeble they made the clunking 1970s set-up at the Hamra seem positively luxurious. When the sun came up the temperature inside would rise with it. While staying in these buildings during the summer months, the sweat would be pouring off me by mid-morning.

Conditions at the smaller bases were even more spartan. Soldiers slept on military cots or metal-framed bunk beds. There was rarely internet access and few forms of entertainment were on offer. One camp adopted a stray goat to provide a distraction from the daily routine. When the troops pulled out in 2006 the goat was given to a local sheikh to look after. Despite his assurances of the loving home awaiting it, there was a general acceptance that it was most likely destined for the pot.

While the US military patrolled in its low-slung Humvees with their armoured sides, the British looked as if they were off to a Scottish shooting party as they careered about in their outdated Land Rovers. These risked toppling over if taken around a corner at too great a speed and provided little protection for the soldier stationed to stand guard out of the top. Those assigned to the position were only too aware of its dangers. Whenever you have read about a roadside bomb going off and it having left one British servicemen dead or maimed, it would nearly always have been the soldier poking out of the top who was the one hit.

The troops did not have adequate body armour until well into 2005, protection previously limited to a paperback-sized slab of Kevlar that barely covered the heart. The rubber soles on older boots disintegrated in the heat. Soldiers consequently often preferred to buy their own boots, as they did many items of personal kit, particularly desert goggles. There were not even enough pyjamas to give the wounded basic personal privacy when airlifted back to the UK.

Despite this the soldiers I met in southern Iraq were always good company, even when they were doing their best to stop me finding out quite how much was going wrong, and committed to honouring the Army's traditions by demonstrating the competence of their force. That was why it was so hard to take that Basra was no better off than it had been under the Ba'athists by the time the British started to pull out of their bases in Iraq during the summer of 2006. One kind of dictatorship had been uprooted but another, one more fragmented and one which manipulated an interpretation of Islam to justify its excesses, was establishing itself in its place. Conditions in the city may even have been worse than before the war. Certainly many Iraqis in Basra told me as much and they were people who had really hated living under Saddam.

I make that clear now as it explains why what follows was so depressing to behold. I had trusted that at least we, the British, would not betray the promises made when our troops crossed the border into Iraq from Kuwait. But we did. I would hear officials back in London say that at least the locals were now under the control of their own sect. That was not really the point. What mattered was that nobody living there knew what was going to happen next because the situation was so chaotic, although many suspected that it was going to be bad.

Basra had become a city where rival militias, with their own power structures and differing fundamentalist Islamic beliefs, fought for dominance over the systems of political patronage and the spoils of Basra's economy, particularly the supply of oil. For the people of Basra this meant a life of constant insecurity. The bullet was the ultimate determinant of policy and rival gangs used it to protect and expand their turfs. The police were as likely to be members of militias as they were to be attempting to stop them. Politicians were often merely the public face of those who relied above all else on armouries and foot soldiers for their hold on power. The local people had little choice but to acquiesce. The long list of those assassinated in the previous few years was lesson enough to anyone thinking differently.

The British troops understood this, even if government politicians back in London did all they could to obscure from the British public the full extent of what had been spawned in Iraq's south. The troops knew they were not pulling out because they had done what they had been sent to do but because they had failed to create the better society promised by Britain's political leaders when they arrived.

Southern Iraq was more stable than much of the rest of the country, but this was primarily because the local armed groups controlled their areas of jurisdiction so absolutely. It was these organisations, rather than the Iraqi state, that restricted the general lawlessness, limiting it to the times when it served their own purpose.

British troops had become a magnet for the violence, even a generator of it, but that was because they were almost the only ones in a position to stand up to the thugs and extremists who, as a result, did everything they could to force them to pull out. By 2007 the British were withdrawing as quickly as the Americans would let them, while the people of Basra remained to face what had been left behind.

It was for this reason that there was such an impassioned response from many in the armed forces when the British government originally refused to offer their Iraqi translators asylum in the UK. These were the Iraqis the soldiers had worked alongside, the ones with whom they had developed close personal bonds. The military knew exactly what their fate would be if they could not take them out of Iraq. The Army had accepted it could not save Basra but it at least wanted to save its own.

The reopening of Iraqi Airways in May 2005 provided the first real insight into what was happening down south. Before that it had been hard to reach Basra other than by spending time with British troops. The road from Baghdad was a treacherous one, a route that took travellers through the insurgent-dominated areas south of the capital and on into the marshland north of Basra where bandits robbed and kidnapped motorists. It was a journey that Iraqis baulked at attempting, and was potential suicide for any foreigner.

The British military had a poor reputation among the press pack for its media management, though its behaviour was perhaps not surprising to anyone familiar with the perfidy of Britain's newspapers. The Army's attitude was far removed from the laissez-faire approach of the Americans who, if your embed was approved, would send you on your way with only the name of the unit who would look after you. The British insisted that any visiting journalist had a press officer accompanying them at all times and their movements were limited.

These restrictions caused considerable resentment, particularly among American reporters who considered it an infringement of their right to freedom of speech, and many bristled at the military's ham-fisted attempts at spin. One colleague of mine, interviewing a captain about the influence of militias on the local police force, was told the problem was that many police officers felt greater loyalty to the anti-Western cleric Moqtada al-Sadr than to their commanders. The press officer assigned to accompany him butted in and said that what the captain was trying to say was that, while there were problems, the situation was not that serious as efforts to expel the militia-loyal officers had been stepped up. The captain told him bluntly that he knew exactly what he was saying and it was not that.

It was the spring of 2005 when Iraq's national airline took to the air once more, its inaugural flight celebrated with the killing of a goat on the runway. In the coming months a procession of reporters paid their £84 for a return ticket to Basra, all of whom came back with stories that made clear that it was not only fear of the tabloid press that had caused the British to try to assert control over the flow of information. It was also because things had begun to take a turn for the worse.

On any flight on any airline there is a sense of relief when the aircraft completes take-off and levels out at its cruising altitude. On Iraqi Airways, however, the ping as the fasten-seatbelt sign was switched off brought with it something approaching euphoria. Not only did it signal the successful completion of the corkscrew ascent from Baghdad airport, it also proved that the plane could fly.

The airline was a far cry from what it had been in its heyday in the 1980s when its fleet swelled to 23 aircraft and destinations included London, Paris, New Delhi and Bangkok. The first Gulf War had caused most of its planes to be flown out of the country for their safety, and two could still be seen rusting by the runway at Amman airport. The start of the present war had marked the airline's nadir. An American missile hit one of the terminals at Baghdad airport, the airline's offices had been set on fire and its remaining aircraft were stripped during the looting that followed Saddam's fall. Its revival came after Iraq's transport ministry loaned the airline the money to buy two second-hand planes with which to provide a distinctly basic service. Entry to the terminal involved dogs sniffing your luggage for explosives. All passengers were patted down for concealed weapons after receiving their boarding cards. The plane's interiors were pure 1970s with seats upholstered in purple check. Stewardesses in crisp green uniforms handed out pieces of stale cake.

On my hour-long flight to Basra that May the cabin ceiling appeared to be held up by adhesive tape and there were no laminated cards detailing what to do in an emergency. The flight attendants indicated which way nervous passengers could pray towards Mecca, which I found less than reassuring.

At Basra airport's main entrance, a maze of blast walls and razor wire, I was met by Haider, the *Telegraph*'s translator in the city, and his friend, Abbas, who was to act as our driver. Haider was a delicate man, his arms almost as thin as cricket stumps, and with soft skin that caused his face to belie his 28 years. Abbas was his opposite: fat and jolly and with stubble so thick it was almost a beard. Haider, who was dressed in a bright white short-sleeved shirt, greeted me with a deferential smile. Abbas' shirt was of tattered check, unbuttoned almost to his navel and he put an arm around my neck and pulled me towards his car, loudly promising that I had nothing to worry about while in Basra as he would look after me. Once I was sitting in the back he indicated, in a gesture intended to reassure me, the AK-47 he kept by the gear stick in case of trouble.

Basra was once known as the Venice of the East and with imagination it was still just about possible to see why. The city had its own beauty with boats skimming along the Shatt al-Arab waterway, the point where the Euphrates and Tigris rivers met and which marked southern Iraq's border with Iran. Its golden domes shimmered in the sunshine and coffee shops bustled in the old quarter. Indeed, on that first day, I was quite bewitched by Basra. The contrast to Baghdad was striking: there were fewer of the blast walls that surround the capital's governing buildings and Basra's markets and streets thronged with people. At sunset we went for a walk along the Corniche, the road in the centre of the city that bordered the Shatt. The light was fading and I was dressed, like many of the locals, in faded jeans and a red-and-blue-checked Iraqi shirt so Haider thought it safe, although he was vehement that I should not speak a word in case anyone realised I was a foreigner. For me, walking about in public was a liberty precious in Iraq by that time and I revelled in the opportunity. There were kebab sellers and ice-cream stands. People sat on chairs grouped on the sidewalk to smoke hubbly-bubblies. Children picked at candyfloss. Beneath one street light a crowd had gathered to watch two men squatting on the ground playing chess. As the sun disappeared it cast a pink glow across the water while the waves lapped against the shore.

My hotel was considered the safest in the city. It was not the Sheraton, once the city's only five-star hotel, now empty after having been gutted in the fighting that accompanied the British arrival and the looting that followed. Nor was it the four-star Shatt al-Arab hotel, which had been turned into Britain's main base in Basra. My hotel was a small guest house prized by foreign visitors for the visibility of its guards with their assault rifles. It was called the Mirbad, but everyone knew it as the Morbid as, though safe, the rooms were far from palatial with their rickety fans above the beds and TVs with only one viewable channel.

It was there that I got my first indication that Basra was not all candyfloss and sunsets. Steven Vincent, an American journalist, had been living in the hotel since early spring, the only Western reporter to be permanently based in Basra. He, like a surprising number of people I met working in the American press, was in Iraq because of 9/11. He had been a 46-year-old living in New York when the Twin Towers were hit and he had watched them fall from the roof of his East Village co-op. Formerly an art critic, he decided he needed to understand how such a thing could have occurred and had consequently left his wife behind in the States to undertake stints as a freelance foreign correspondent. It was a calling that took him to Baghdad in late 2003 and early 2004 to witness what the US forces were doing, and now it had taken him to Basra, where he was damning about what the British had created.

He was not an easy person to talk to. His unwillingness to tolerate any opposing argument made it a very one-sided conversation. He talked and I listened, his angular frame folded into a chair in the hotel lobby. When recalling stories of the worst abuses occurring in Basra, he would rub his goatee beard with real aggression, sometimes tapping the table to make sure I was concentrating.

It was, nevertheless, a fascinating evening. I had only been to Basra once before, during the January 2005 elections when I stayed there a few days while using it as a stopping point en route to Amarah, so I knew little of the city. I took notes as he described Basra as a place where religiously conservative Shia were turning an open, liberal society into something closer to that found in Iran with alcohol banned and women harassed if they refused to wear the veil. Moderate Shiites were being assassinated and Western music effectively outlawed. Dozens of students from Basra University had been injured when their picnic was attacked by militiamen for the sole reason that the two sexes were mixing in public. I could not yet judge if what he was saying was true but this was a very different Basra to the one the Army and politicians back in London were describing. It provided a rival template to the official story, one I could explore for myself as I sought to determine what was happening.

According to Vincent, Basra's police had been infiltrated by militias who were using their position and its resources to carry out their own vendettas. As evidence he cited the city's chief of police, Hassan al-Sade, who had recently gone on the record to warn that he believed half his 13,750-strong, British-trained force secretly worked for political parties, that he could only trust a quarter of his officers, and that politicians used police vehicles, weaponry and personnel for party business, much of it nefarious.

'The militias are the real power in Basra, and they are made up of criminals and bad people,' Sade had said. 'Some of the police are involved in assassinations. I am trying to sort this out, for example by putting numbers on police cars so they can be identified. I wish I could sack bad people but I do not have the authority.'

The immediate cause of these problems was January's elections, Vincent explained, which in Basra had been won by religious parties with close links to Iran and even closer links to the city's criminal gangs. Adopting *The Sopranos* allegory favoured by so many in Iraq, he said it was as if Tony Soprano had been elected mayor and then tasked with creating the New Jersey police force from scratch.

The elections had left the city's 41-seat political authority dominated by members of SCIRI and officials loyal to the Ayatollah Muhammad Yacoubi, a radical cleric renowned for his friendship with Moqtada al-Sadr. Under the supervisory control of this body, militiamen were increasingly able to impose their leaders' fundamentalist agenda with impunity. The local SCIRI leader, Furat al-Shara, had even said there was no need to enshrine Islamic law in the country's legal code because it was already being done 'culturally'.

The people Vincent blamed the most, the people he really raged against, were the British. He could not stomach how British officials were keeping up their human rights rhetoric while tacitly supporting figures whose actions contravened it in almost every way. It was the hypocrisy that got him. He viewed the British as having made a modern-day deal with the devil. They would ignore what was happening – even if it was the oppression of women, brutality in the police and the killing of the few remaining Iraqi moderates – as long as those in charge did not directly challenge the British presence.

The alternative, he believed, was to attempt what Vincent viewed the Americans as doing and actually confront the extremists now running things; challenge the militias rather than recruiting and training them as a new police force. That would have stirred things up, however; caused the number of British casualties to rise and delayed any hope of withdrawal. So he saw it as a trade-off. Britain would get itself an exit strategy to appease the disgruntled electorate back home, but in return it would abandon Basra to gangsterism and intolerance.

Everything I saw during the following week made clear that Vincent was not exaggerating the extent of Basra's problems although I was far from convinced that it was a conscious conspiracy. It seemed to me that British forces could not have acted very differently even if they had wanted to. At least 20,000 soldiers were probably needed to have had any chance of filling the power vacuum created by the end of Ba'athist rule. With only 8,000 men in southern Iraq, the Army simply did not have the resources to take on the fanatics and maintain law and order. This was why Tony Blair and his cabinet were a constant source of ridicule among the soldiers. I lost count of the times that a British officer mentioned to me, with an arched eyebrow, how appreciative he was that Blair had sent them to Iraq but had never once found the time to publicly visit the wounded being treated in hospitals back in the UK.

In Baghdad I had a friend who had been one of Saddam's colonels and was now paying the bills by free-lancing as a driver for one of the newspapers at the Hamra. He liked to reminisce about the trips he took to Basra in the 1970s when on leave. The city had been rich then, its people made prosperous by the oil wells that surrounded them and the trade that flowed across the border from Kuwait, Saudi Arabia and Iran. In Basra the bars were so plentiful, my friend said, that he never had to go onto the pavement to get from one to the other. He would instead climb to the roof, walk onto the adjacent building, make his way down through the prostitutes working the upper level, and expect a bottle of Johnny

Walker Black Label to be waiting for him on the bar, his order having already been phoned across from next door.

I visited one of Basra's markets and saw the building which had once sold alcohol but was now burned out. Haider introduced me to a group of music and video sellers that he trusted. We met in the back of a shop down a side street from the main market. None of the half-a-dozen people present were willing to give their names nor have their photographs taken but, in the light cast by a bulb hanging from the ceiling, a DVD seller told how a gang of masked men had raided his shop and rummaged through his stock for signs of inappropriate content. A musical instrument salesman described how, when it was the turn for his shop to be searched, guitars and recorders were smashed and torn apart. The militiamen told him that his wares turned those who played them into the 'servants of Satan'. During lunch at a local family's house a woman described how she had received an envelope with bullets in it and a note telling her not to allow her 10-year-old daughter to practice athletics outside. The fanatics considered such activities unsuitable behaviour for women, even young girls.

I heard how, in recent weeks, the bodies of women had begun being discovered dumped by the roadside. Three were found at first, then another two, and six more the week before my arrival, each victim riddled with bullets. The Iraqi police insisted they had no strong leads but everyone I talked to said the reason for their deaths was an open secret: they were prostitutes and their killers were one of the city's armed militias enforcing its strict code of Islam.

I visited the area where the latest bodies had been dumped. It was one of the city's poorest. Sewage ran beside the pavement and through holes in the walls of the surrounding buildings I could see thin mattresses and battered pots and pans.

Abbas, who I had discovered was not one to hide his immoralities, described how he had been in the same area a few weeks before, visiting a house of 'belly dancers' because it was the only place he knew that still served alcohol. While he was there a dozen men had broken down the front door. 'They started hitting the girls, shooting the walls and breaking the furniture,' he said. 'They brought boxes of vodka and beer outside to smash them. One of the girls ran outside and she had stones thrown at her. Everyone in the place was too frightened to help.'

I visited a senior policeman to discover more about militia infiltration of the force. We met at his house, a freshly painted bungalow surrounded by a carefully tended garden in one of the city's suburbs, and he was happy to talk about anything – anything except that. 'They would kill me if they found out,' he explained.

I gained a crash course in the labyrinthine range of militia operating in the city. As well as the usual suspects – SCIRI's Badr Brigade and Sadr's Mahdi Army – Basra had its own homegrown forces. There was a group that owed allegiance to the memory of Sadr's uncle (who had also been assassinated by Saddam) rather than to Moqtada or his father. There were the fundamentalist Vengeance of Allah, who were blamed on the streets for the prostitute murders, and the particularly violent Master of the Martyrs. There were others so small they only oper-ated in individual neighbourhoods. All were believed to have members entrenched in the police force, while also having civilian shock troops who would attack their enemies with only their eyes visible above the scarves that hid their faces.

The most popular show in town was a running tap in a house in one of the outlying districts. Someone had claimed to see the image of a particularly revered dead Shia cleric in its flow and crowds were now lining up around the block for a glimpse of it. It was in an area Haider deemed too dangerous to visit but I saw a DVD recording of the phenomenon. It looked to me like a stream of water refracting the paint on the wall behind in a way that, from one angle, did slightly resemble a face with a long white beard. However, I was not looking for a sign that God had not forgotten me. For the masses queuing to view this miracle it was a symbol of hope that there was some divine plan behind what had happened to them and to their city.

On the last night of that trip the three of us – Haider, Abbas and I – ate at the restaurant in my hotel. It had been a particularly dispiriting day. In an attempt to try to get the British interpretation of events, we had gone to their main camp by the airport to see if anyone might be free for an interview. We had waited six hours at the entrance and not been able to talk at length to anyone. All we were given was the standard official line that the British were responsible for the security of the sector but did not intervene in domestic matters that were political or involved law and order. That did not justify my expectations as to how my taxes should be spent.

Haider sought to cheer me up, and to do so he told me his life story. He had the most gentle of demeanours and a character that seemed unable to accommodate the hatred required for conflict. He was, however, clearly tougher than he looked because throughout the late 1990s Haider had been in trouble with the authorities after refusing to conform to the dictates of Basra's Ba'athist rulers. He was fascinated by the West and managed to get an illegal satellite dish fitted to his home so he could watch foreign TV stations. He read banned books and listened to modern British and American music. At one point he flirted with radical politics and met some Shia dissidents who, unknown to him, were being watched by the authorities. His involvement drew the security forces' attention and for five years he had been in and out of prison.

During that entire time he had been in love with a girl. She was his teenage sweetheart and when young they had courted each other. Unfortunately, when her parents heard of Haider's brushes with the law, they labelled him a hooligan and a bad influence. They banned their daughter from seeing him. For almost half a decade the couple had not been able to meet. She had kept the romance going by sending text messages from her friends' mobile phones whenever she could.

Haider said that when in prison he would think of her and the life he had dreamed they could have. He could see no way that her parents would ever accept him and he would be overcome by despair.

When the British arrived in April 2003 everything changed. The Ba'athists were gone. Haider was no longer some sort of minor dissident but a modern man perfectly positioned for the modern world many now expected to dawn. By chance he met the *Telegraph* reporter assigned to cover the British forces at the start of the war and his excellent English resulted in him being hired as a translator. When the fighting moved north Haider kept providing the newspaper with stories from Basra. My *Telegraph* colleague had also introduced him to representatives from one of the British security companies setting up in the south. They too hired him as a translator and he was now earning good money. Seeing this, his girlfriend's parents suddenly forgot their opposition to the match. Haider and his childhood sweetheart were to be married the week after my visit.

'So you see,' he said, 'for me the arrival of the British was the greatest thing that has ever happened in my life. Before that no one could see any hope for the future as Saddam was all-powerful. Now, every dream I have ever had has come true. For that I have them to thank.'

Steven Vincent, the American journalist I had met on my first night, was killed that summer. It happened on 2 August, two days after the publication of an opinion piece he had written for the *New York Times* in which he accused Shia militia in Basra of infiltrating the police force and assassinating their opponents.

Vincent and his translator, a notably vivacious Iraqi woman called Nour Itais, were leaving the Mirbad hotel when they were kidnapped by men in police uniforms driving a white police truck. Bystanders said the kidnappers shouted at them not to get involved as it was official business.

Itais survived, despite having been shot twice in the leg and once in the shoulder. She told how they had been taken to an undisclosed location and were beaten and interrogated for five hours. They were then ferried to the outskirts of Basra. Their bodies were found the next morning. Vincent was already dead, shot once in the back at close range. Itais was taken in by the British and treated for her wounds at a military hospital. Vincent's body was returned to the States and he was buried at a cemetery in Brooklyn.

On my next visit to Basra in early 2006 the British were no longer claiming that things were going well. The illusion had been shattered the previous autumn when troops broke into an Iraqi jail in order to secure the release of two SAS men who had been arrested and beaten by local police. The television footage of the rioting that followed their rescue, particularly the images of the crew of a Warrior armoured vehicle leaping from it in flames after being surrounded by a mob, had gone around the world. People across Britain had watched their soldiers under a barrage of petrol bombs and stones. They had wondered, unsurprisingly, why British forces were being attacked by the people they had been sent to liberate and why they now had to act against a police force they had created and trained.

The answer, the British government said, was that the extremists were whipping up anti-British sentiment among the populace. Parts of the police force, it was admitted, were now effectively being run by the same militias that the British forces were fighting. The station where the SAS men had been held, al-Jamiyat, was considered a centre for their work, even though it was officially home to one of Basra police force's most elite sections, the major crimes unit. British officers had nicknamed it Gestapo HQ, officials said, because of the number of detainees believed to have been killed there.

By the start of 2006 there was a real feeling that the situation was going from bad to worse. Official figures showed crime in Basra had risen by 15 per cent. Sixty people were being murdered a month. The number of roadside bombs had tripled since the end of the previous year. There were reports that Sunnis and other minority groups were being driven out of the city. For foreigners such as myself there was now little likelihood of staying in hotels in Basra or driving around with only a local as a guide. The militias had put out word that any lone Brit should be kidnapped and used as a hostage to try to secure the release of the men arrested by the Army in the aftermath of the SAS fiasco. As with almost all the rest of Iraq, the only way to get even the most limited impression of what was going on was by spending time with the military. There would be no more trips to the south for me on Iraqi Airways.

The deterioration in Basra had come as a shock to Ahmed and my team of Iraqis. They had always held a touching belief that the British would be efficient and effective. Ahmed in particular had argued that, owing to Britain's imperial history in Iraq, they better understood the Arab mindset and could therefore make the reconstruction of southern Iraq work. This conviction had come from his elderly relatives who had told him stories about honest and respectful British administrators in Baghdad after the First World War. It was this view that had probably drawn him to work for a British newspaper. I suspected that he found the reality of the modern-day Brit something of a letdown. He would always seem disappointed when I turned up late for appointments, my tardiness conflicting with notions of Britons' impeccable timekeeping that dated back to the era of empire.

Abu Omar, my driver, would always support Ahmed in the discussions we had about Basra, brushing aside my protestations that the British had it in them to be just as incompetent as anyone else. He was a committed monarchist who believed that only the restoration of Iraq's Hashemite royal family, presently in exile in London, could save his country. It was a viewpoint largely based on the fact that the 1958 military coup d'état that overthrew the monarchy had ushered in decades of instability as military strongmen and Ba'ath Party leaders conducted revolutions and counter-revolutions. As a result Abu Omar had romanticised Iraq under the Hashemites as a tranquil and secure place, somewhere he would like to have lived. He was also, due to the enduring nature of Britain's monarchy, instinctively pro-British. Britain's prosperity was for him indicative of the stability and good government that royalty ensured. Both he and Ahmed were consequently bemused by what had happened in southern Iraq. It was no longer only the Americans who could get it wrong.

After the December 2005 suicide bombing of the Hamra I was considerably less keen to be anywhere near the hotel if at all possible. The blasts had forced out most of the few remaining freelancers and caused the newspapers that remained to cut their staff in Baghdad to a minimum. There were rarely parties or dinners on the terrace any more, indeed it was possible to go days without running into another journalist, there being so few of them. Inevitably conversations focused on whether the bombers might try again, and their likelihood of greater success. The building where our office had been located stood at the far end of the pool, the cracks in its walls caused by the explosions a visible reminder of the fragility of our situation. To get away from the complex I organised a number of visits to troops outside of Baghdad in the following months.

In March I joined the British in Basra. I found that the troops were pretty glum. On my first day at the British military HQ at the Shatt al-Arab hotel in the centre of the city a procession of officers detailed the extent to which the situation had deteriorated. The most immediate problem was that their relationship with the city's governor, Mohammad al-Wa'eli, had completely broken down. Five weeks earlier he had severed all ties with British personnel in the city and imposed a boycott stopping any local government officials or council members from dealing with them. The governor's reasons were twofold: pictures had appeared in a UK Sunday newspaper supposedly showing British soldiers beating Iraqi suspects and cartoons had been published in a Danish newspaper that ridiculed the Prophet Mohammad. These caricatures heightened anti-Western feeling across the Muslim world but particularly in southern Iraq where a small contingent of Danish troops operated alongside British forces.

The British Army maintained that the boycott had been introduced because the governing council's political supporters were linked to the criminal gangs whose activities were being curtailed by the crackdown on the police that followed the events at al-Jamiyat prison. The governor himself was either in hock to these same criminals or he did not want to threaten his power base by confronting them. Using comparisons drawn from their experience in Northern Ireland, the Army detailed how the armed groups were smuggling oil, running protection rackets and routinely kidnapping for ransom while pretending they were primarily motivated by nationalism and religious ideology.

Whatever the cause of the boycott, the result had been administrative paralysis. The British were banned from contact with any of the institutions of regional government, meaning efforts to root out militia infiltration of the police had stopped. Troops were not even allowed to deliver air-conditioning units bought for the city's secondary schools. Educational institutions were under the remit of the local politicians so access to them was denied.

The British Army, the force which for centuries had been one of the greatest military bodies in the world with battle honours won across four continents, was reduced to driving around Basra with little idea of what was going on, and with orders to avoid doing anything that might cause further harm to their relationship with Basra's political masters. The soldiers' anger at this was what was fuelling their frustration.

The force's intelligence expert, Major Toby Christie, was the glummest of the British officers I met. He had the clearest understanding of the overall situation and knew what this softly-softly approach meant for British influence. He had concluded there could be no happy ending for Basra.

His office was at the end of one of the Shatt al-Arab hotel's main wings. It was a building that was supposed to have once been a luxury venue, but either Ba'athist standards for hotel comfort were lower than those in the West, or years of war had taken their toll, for it was a very basic establishment. Paint was peeling off the walls and few of the toilets worked. The lights in Major Christie's office flickered with the beat of the generators and the window was covered to prevent flying glass in the event of a mortar attack. There was a good supply of tea, however, which was provided while Christie discussed the situation on the ground.

'The number of police who actively seek violence is no

more than 10 per cent but the number intimidated to support them is immeasurably more than that,' he said, cradling his cup. 'After thirty years of Saddam Hussein people will not put their head above the parapet to oppose them. Nor can you blame them, they know at some point we're going to leave.

'That's why everyone else is fighting so hard to position themselves. What you have to understand is that we're merely one tribe here amongst many. For a while we were the most important tribe, and still we're the best armed. But our position is weakening as time goes on because the other groups know that we will leave soon and, when we do, it will be one of them that will become top dog.

'It's all about power. The police are corrupt, the government is corrupt. There's a lot of money at stake due to the oil. The foot soldiers may be influenced by anti-Western feeling or religion, but those at the top are simply manoeuvring for a slice of the cake.'

It did not get any better. 'I do not believe the system we leave behind will be the same one that is here ten years later,' Christie said. 'When we go there'll be a lot of flag-waving and those people who actively fought us will be able to play the nationalist card and set themselves up as the heroes of Iraq. These will be the people who are going to be running this place. There's going to be a certain amount of killing and someone's going to come out on top. In that there will be a strong religious dimension and there'll be little sign of real democracy.'

He put down his tea. 'Put it this way, I don't think we will be seeing Iraq clamouring for entrance to the Commonwealth anytime soon.'

The next day I moved to the only British forward operating base, or FOB, still active in the heart of the city. It was in the old Ba'ath Party state building and was known by the soldiers as Rorke's Drift. It was not difficult to appreciate why. The camp was surrounded by the enemy. Barely the size of three football pitches, it was partly overlooked by buildings on two sides. The perimeter consisted of blast walls made from Hesco barriers and the watchtowers dotted along it were manned throughout the day and night.

A tour of the site involved my guide pointing out the holes in the walls and the craters in the ground that stood as reminders of previous attacks. There had been a lot of them. The Old State Building, as the base was officially called, would soon have the infamous distinction of being the most attacked military location in the entirety of Iraq. Even then it had been targeted 37 times in the previous ten weeks. Throughout the day a group of children usually stood at the corner near its main entrance so they could throw stones at any vehicles that came in or out. At night I watched the green flares rise up into the sky as the guards sought to spot potential attackers.

I went out on patrol with a team who were trying to maintain contact with the local police units that they had previously worked alongside. The hope was that those they had known the best would still be happy to talk to them. Some, I was told, would still meet with British soldiers despite risking the governor's ire by doing so. The unit we visited that day, however, proved not to be one of them.

We had travelled in a line of Warrior armoured vehicles along Basra's main street and then down into the al-Asmaoi district where we stopped. Climbing out of the metal, windowless box that is the back of a Warrior, I found myself by a rubbish-filled river on a dirt track marked with the deep ruts of tyre tracks. Three policemen stood by the gate leading into a two-storey concrete block, which I was told was the district police station. Their blue jackets were open at the front and the bottom of their white shirts were hanging over their trousers. Another officer was siphoning petrol from a nearby car.

A British lieutenant, only 23 years old and more used to navigating the shops and pubs of his home town of Sutton Coldfield than these back alleys of Basra, first tried to talk to them in pidgin Arabic, and then through his translator. He had with him a photograph taken in easier times of his troops with the police officers stationed there. It had been hoped that offering it as a gift might prompt a thawing.

A police captain was called to receive it. He was very polite. There was a shrug to mark his embarrassment at not being able to repay the kindness of the gesture with an offer of hospitality and a brief smile as the lieutenant said he wished that things were different. Then the request for us to leave. Now. Which we meekly did. Back to driving around the roads of Basra seemingly doing nothing more than showing that the British were actually still there.

During my three days at Rorke's Drift I spent most of my spare time with the two officials sent out from Britain to train the local police. They were the only other non-military people on the base, which created a certain camaraderie. In their mid-to-late fifties, both balding and with the start of pot bellies, they were from Northern Ireland, former RUC men, as were almost all Britain's police trainers in Iraq. For them this was a final swansong before retirement. Due to the governing council's boycott there were no police available for them to train. While it lasted they spent most days sunbathing, sitting on chairs placed against the strongest wall in the base for protection. It was March and the temperature was what one might hope for on a good English summer day. I would finish my work and wander down to see them, the two men enjoying the weather, dressed in shorts and reading detective novels.

They were not only excellent company but also a mine of fascinating, if possibly unreliable, information. They told me that the Americans had paid to provide the police with computers but had not trained them how to use them. Nor had there been any spare parts made available for when they broke. The equipment the local police most urgently needed, the trainers said, had been notepads and pens. They described how life was now so cheap in Basra it only cost around $150 to have someone murdered. They were convinced that the governor was an Iranian agent put in place to make life hell for the British.

In their opinion, one of the greatest threats that would ultimately come out of Basra's collapse had not yet been widely appreciated. Like many policemen, they were particularly concerned by drugs and had been petitioning the Foreign Office for more funds to stop them being smuggled through Iraq. Already, they said, medical-grade heroin and amphetamine could be bought freely in the city. Basra was both on the route that led west from the poppy fields of Afghanistan and at the mid-point between South East Asia's Golden Triangle and Europe. In the city there was rampant corruption, little law and order and the criminal gangs were consolidating their control both economically and politically. In their view this was the perfect combination for Basra and its port to turn into one of the key staging posts for the drug smuggling trade in coming decades.

On my last day at that base, the two police trainers had to go to the British consulate on the other side of the city for a meeting. They returned with a story they recounted with particular glee. Apparently a British legal expert had been sent out by the Foreign Office to advise on the rebuilding of the local judiciary. He had never been out of the compound but enjoyed lecturing those who did, walking around in tan chinos and a linen jacket as if he were at an exclusive tropical hotel. Then, the previous week, he had finally gone out with a patrol. There had been gunfire and a rocket-propelled grenade attack. The next day, the linen jacket had disappeared and he had come down to breakfast in body armour. He refused to take it off, even when inside.

'He's telling everyone that no one should be allowed out as it is so bloody dangerous,' one of the trainers said. 'As if we didn't already know.'

The British are not used to losing wars. It is ingrained in our sense of national identity that we win them, indeed not only that we win them but the greater the odds the more likely we are to overcome and vanquish our enemies.

Losing in Iraq was therefore a shock for the senior officers sent to fight there. Many dwelled on how Basra had gone so wrong. Some sought historical or sociological explanations that would make clear it had been an impossible task. Others blamed the Americans for provoking instability in the north. Most railed at the government that had sent them without enough troops or equipment to do the job properly.

One of the most erudite explanations I heard came from Brigadier Patrick Marriott, commander of the 7th

Armoured Brigade, who was in charge of all British forces in southern Iraq during the latter part of 2005 and early 2006. He had concluded that believing the worst of authority was deeply ingrained in the people of Basra, making it impossible for the British to have ever won their trust. Basra was on the front line of Saddam's war with Iran, during which it suffered regular bombings, and at the heart of the repression, torture and murders that followed his suppression of the 1991 post-Gulf War uprising by Iraq's Shia. When the Army arrived in 2003, it did not understand how used to barbarity the citizens of Basra had become.

'The people were immersed in cruelty. There's a sad culture of mistrust, especially of authority,' Brigadier Marriott told me when I interviewed him in March 2006. This explained, he said, why the British attempts to win hearts and minds had failed so dismally, despite the tens of millions of pounds poured into reconstruction.

The people of Basra survived Ba'athist rule by turning to what they could trust, which was not only religious and tribal ties but also the militias: small, tightly knit groups created to oppose Saddam that members could rely on for protection. They became the bedrock of political association within the city.

The British thought the way to secure the city's future was to reform the police. However, a people who had previously been terrorised by its police for decades were wary about letting others take control. So each militia made sure its members were selected to the new force, and then recruited their comrades to join them, creating paramilitary cells whose loyalty was above all to each other.

The same process was repeated when the local council was elected. After so many decades of repression the groups that had resisted Saddam's Ba'ath Party were not willing to let rivals dominate them, so had joined the political process, putting forward candidates and cajoling the electorate to support them. This did not mean that the groups behind these new politicians gave up their weapons, Marriott explained. They knew they needed them in case their enemies re-grouped and were also waiting for the British to leave, which would produce a power vacuum that they intended to exploit. It would be then that the struggle for control would start again. The cycle of cruelty that had created modern Basra would continue, defining its future generations as the past had created the present.

I met Corporal Kevin Douglas at Rorke's Drift, the forward operating base in the heart of Basra. He had the steady humour and self-possession of the battle-hardened, one of those who has seen fighting at first hand and understood what it was about. However, he was more contemplative than most, a result partly of his job as liaison officer to the local sheikhs. He had been in the Iraqis' houses and therefore knew them as more than mere figures seen through a visor or the slit window of an armoured vehicle.

One afternoon we stood on the roof of the camp's main building. In front of us stretched Basra: a collage of yellow-stained apartment blocks topped by palm trees, their fronds oscillating in the slight breeze. On the main road we could see the cars making their way forward as best they could amid the traffic and by the camp's entrance stood a group of children, presumably waiting with their stones. Then there were the British blast walls, the tanks lined up in rows behind them, and the soldiers standing guard duty at their watchtowers, rifles to hand, staring out, as we did, at the city we were in but not part of.

'Often we go out on patrol, have to talk to people and do what we've been instructed,' Corporal Douglas said. 'Then we come back to base, and you sit down and have a think: "What did I actually achieve today?" But then you've got to concentrate in order to dispel that thought. There's no point thinking about whether we did good or bad, what the people back in Britain are thinking or what we're actually achieving. That doesn't get you anywhere because whatever you think it doesn't stop you being here. You're here to do a job and you just have to do the best you can. But God, it's frustrating. There's no escaping that. Frustration – that's the credo of everyone here.'

9. Armageddon

Ahmed recounted a story a friend told him about what happened when she was on a coach passing Abu Ghraib. The passengers had suddenly realised they were surrounded by Opel Vectras, the car favoured by suicide bombers for being cheap but fast.

The driver turned around and said, 'My dear friends, now we are finished.'

The result was a coach filled with laughter.

Such a reaction was not unusual. Laughter was a surprisingly common sound in Baghdad. Iraqis loved their black humour. Newspaper cartoons routinely mocked their nation's plight with barbs at everything from Iraqi politicians' incompetence to the anonymous tip-offs that resulted in military raids on the homes of innocent people.

The most famous cartoonist in the country was Muayad Naama, who was proud of his ability to make his readers 'smile but also cry'. I cut out one of his drawings from an edition of the local paper and stuck it on the wall of my office. It featured two men drinking tea in a cafe when a car bomb explodes behind them. As body parts fly through the air, one of the men looks shocked. His friend tells him not to be alarmed. 'That's not our car,' he says.

Once, at the main gate into Baghdad's Green Zone, I

saw that the Iraqi soldiers guarding it had gathered around a mobile phone. They were all smiling and laughing. One had received a text featuring a fake wedding invitation from Abu Musab al-Zarqawi, the head of al-Qa'eda in Iraq. 'His sheikh humbly invites you to the marriage of his son, TNT, to his bride, Miss Roadside Bombs,' it read. 'He promises the celebration will be a blast.' This was at a spot where suicide bombers were striking on a near-monthly basis, normally killing many of those on guard.

Iraqis knew only too well that the joke was ultimately on them. Ahmed shared with me one of the most popular jokes among Sunnis, a voice message that had been sent to his mobile phone. As in most humour the references were cultural. In it a man mimicked Saddam to play on Arabs' ridicule of the Kurds, the fact that the country's president, Jalal Talabani, was from Kurdistan, and the way that Iraq's poorest people traditionally survived by weaving reeds into mats to sell.

'You abused me but now you have neither cane nor reeds. And, despite this, you still let your new president be a Kurd,' the voice said, before breaking into peals of mocking laughter.

I suspected that the joke was also on me. I had come back to Iraq in the hope that all the violence I had witnessed might have been for something worthwhile. I was now in a country suffering far worse than it had ever done during those first few weeks of the war. By 2006 the situation in Iraq appeared painfully simple. The country had been reduced to a level where a basic truth was being played out on a grand scale. All the talk of development schemes and rebuilding operations was just talk, there to feed the politicians' conceit that they were in control. It was the power of the gun that was absolute and people were doing all they could to make sure they were not on the receiving end of it.

I would see the celebrity correspondents come in from America and Europe and be flown by their military hosts into the Green Zone. They would receive their high-level briefings, all those statistics and graphs, and leave fully confident in the knowledge that there really was a plan that would make it OK after all. Those correspondents out beyond the blast walls were brave folk, I imagined them thinking, but they had got a bit too close to it and could no longer see the wood for the rather more scary trees.

I did not blame them. I often wished I was them: it must have been reassuring to feel that certainty once again. They could only go on what they were told and what many officials in Iraq liked to claim was shocking if you knew what was really happening. I would be informed that the rising violence was a good thing because it showed that the insurgency was being beaten. The extremists were, apparently, merely redoubling their efforts in a desperate last attempt to try to destabilise Iraq as they knew they would soon be smashed forever. Diplomats would publicly pledge that the Iraqi government was finally on track to resume responsibility for the country, while privately admitting that even their own security details were so nervous of the interior ministry's paramilitary death squads that they did not like to go onto the streets outside.

In Iraq, however, reality could never be avoided for long and what occurred at 6.55 a.m. on 22 February 2006 left no room for contrivance. It was a time when the official talk was of incremental progress and final objectives, with the US claiming that the political process had been a success and the soldiers were going to be able to start coming home soon. The events of that day, however, pitched Iraq into an orgy of bloodletting that would defy anyone's attempts to downplay.

Beyond the general lawlessness, the violence until then had been primarily caused by the efforts of the Sunnis to resist the American occupation that had marginalised them in a country they had once ruled. The Shia government was settling scores against their former Ba'athist political enemies and intimidating Sunnis to try to stop them aiding insurgents, the Kurds were doing what they could to force Arabs out of Kirkuk so they could one day incorporate it into their new Kurdistan, and the religious extremists were busy trying to bomb and brutalise the Shia, whom they had labelled apostates and therefore worthy of being killed. Before that day in February the Shia had not properly fought back, however, certainly not en masse. The majority had ignored the provocations and heeded the instructions of Grand Ayatollah Sistani, their most senior cleric, for restraint rather than retaliation. It had been a heroic act of fortitude for which they never really received enough credit.

On 22 February, shortly after midnight, half a dozen men overwhelmed the guards at the Shia's Golden Mosque in Samarra, forced their way inside and set explosives on the building's five supporting pillars. It was a lengthy job and one that took considerable skill. To ensure the structure's collapse holes had to be drilled into the stone supports and the explosives packed inside. Then the firing mechanisms were set to detonate simultaneously.

The work took five hours and it was dawn by the time it was finished. The mosque had stood for more than a thousand years, though the golden dome from which it now took its name was a relatively recent addition, having been constructed shortly before the First World War. It was one of Shia Islam's holiest sites, a centre of pilgrimage and prayer, exceeded only in veneration by the shrines at Najaf and Karbala. The explosions sent up a cloud of dust that hung in the air for almost ten minutes. When it cleared, the crowd that had gathered could see that the dome and most of the mosque's side walls had been destroyed. Wails of lamentation went up. In the following months such cries of anguish were repeated across Iraq as the consequences of that act became apparent.

Outraged, the Shia came out in force. It was unthinking and unplanned. No one controlled it at that point as throughout Iraq vengeance was enacted. Convoys of Shia roamed the streets of Baghdad. Sunni mosques were targeted and a number set on fire. In the coming weeks, Sunnis with no sympathy for the more extreme elements of their sect concluded they had no choice but to fight back in order to defend themselves. Neighbours who had lived side by side for generations turned on each other as fear of proximity to a member of the rival sect overtook their previous bonds of fellowship. Thousands piled their most treasured possessions into cars and fled their homes. The city's morgue brought in freezer trucks to cope with the number of corpses.

No one knows the full death toll from those first few days after the bombing of the Golden Mosque. Mixed Sunni-Shia areas surrounding Baghdad were off limits to any Western reporter. Even Iraqi journalists found themselves under attack if they ventured too far from the capital. Atwar Bahjat, a correspondent for the al-Arabiya

TV station, was lynched in Samarra, her body and that of her cameraman later found mutilated. What was certain, however, was that the whole dynamic had altered. The civil war in Iraq had begun.

It was the bodies that denoted how much had changed. Suddenly they were everywhere, each day bringing reports of the latest discoveries. Iraqis were being killed before, of course, but now the danger was constant and in every quarter. The militias were not only guarding their own districts but rampaging through surrounding streets. Homes were broken into and the men in them rounded up and marched away. In the months after the Golden Mosque was destroyed vehicles were stopped in broad daylight, identity cards checked and those from the wrong sect rewarded with a bullet. A bus carrying Shia and Kurd students was raided, everyone on board told to leave their seats and line up outside where they were summarily shot. Gunmen slowed down as they passed a Sunni market, stuck out their guns and killed 23 people. Rockets fell into a Shia neighbourhood, killing 62 people and wounding more than 100. In the Sunni area of al-Jihad the gunmen did not even bother to make an event of it. One afternoon Shia militiamen simply took to the streets, firing into shops and killing whoever they wanted. By the time Iraqi security forces arrived the streets were littered with the dead, the bodies of men, women and children left lying in the dirt.

Night-time was worse; the time of mystery when the real work was done. The police were supposed to be the only ones out, the whole of Baghdad under curfew, but it was still between dusk and dawn that most killing occurred. The corpses would be found dotted across the city the following morning. You had to draw your own conclusions as to what the police had actually been doing and who their friends really were.

Pathetically, there was not even a functioning Iraqi government that could act to try to stop what was happening. The politicians chosen in the previous December's election still could not put aside their bitterness and rivalries. They continued to wrangle that spring over who should get which post in the cabinet.

I went to the city's morgue. No one knew exactly how many bodies it was dealing with. Previously I had relied on the director of the facility, Faik Bakir, to provide me with the number of victims of violent death that it processed. That was no longer possible because, following the bombing of the Golden Mosque, he had been forced to flee the country, reportedly for revealing to the media the unprecedented number of dead being delivered to the morgue.

The stench of corpses rotting in the heat reached me before the sight of the pale-yellow brick medical centre where they were stacked. The refrigerators were full and bodies were now being piled in rows on the floor. A group of armed men were checking the identity papers of all those going inside. They were Sadrists, representatives of the Moqtada al-Sadr supporter now in charge of the country's medical services. They scared me.

Ahmed went to find out what he could. The narrow, crumbling lane that led to the morgue was filled with people. They had all come, as we had, for answers. In their case though they sought answers to what had happened to those they had lost: the husbands, the sons, the cousins or the friends who had disappeared amid the slaughter. An old woman was standing by the metal gate that marked the entrance, her sorrow so total that she had to be held upright by two male relatives. A young man was shouting at the sky in anger. Those passing him barely acknowledged his pain, so preoccupied were they by their own fears.

Pictures of the dead could be seen on computers placed in the morgue's lobby. Families were clustered around them, scrolling through the photographs in the hope, and the dread, that they might recognise someone. It was acutely unpleasant viewing. People in Baghdad were not simply being killed; they were being beheaded, garrotted, and tortured. Victims were having electric drills used on them and cigarettes stubbed out on their flesh. Eyeballs were being gouged out. Bones were broken and body parts hacked off.

It was said to be the Shia who preferred the drilling and gouging. The drill bits pressed into the temples of Sunni heads would apparently 'destroy their stupid minds'. The Sunnis preferred beheading because it was believed to be the Prophet Mohammad's method of dealing with apostates. As a result of the level of mutilation being inflicted, tattoo parlours began offering customers 'death tags' featuring names and next of kin as a possible safeguard should they end up among the facially unidentifiable.

Those who had recognised someone in the photographs told their stories. Four brothers living in Mansour had been taken from the home they shared with their wives. Their bullet-ridden bodies were found in a drainage ditch, their toes and fingers cut off.

Jabar al-Azawi's face was covered in purple welts, he had drill holes in his legs and both shoulders broken. He had been working in his shop in southern Baghdad when he was grabbed by a carload of armed men.

Ahmed did not say much as we drove back to the office. In fact he did not say much at all during that time, focusing instead on his work, busy pushing his contacts and travelling the city to interview those he trusted to gather the information we needed. It was as if by putting in the hours covering what was happening he could avoid worrying about what it meant for him and his family.

When, weeks later, the Iraqi government finally released a figure for the number of people killed in Baghdad in March 2006, the month after the bombing at the Golden Mosque, it was 1,294. By mid-summer the official monthly death toll in the city had reached 1,500. More Iraqis were being killed in Baghdad every couple of months than the number of American soldiers who had died in the entire conflict. Plans were announced to build two new morgues so that Baghdad could cope with the influx of bodies.

What was really haunting, however, was the knowledge that even these numbers did not tell the whole story. There was no way of knowing how many more bodies were simply being thrown into the Tigris or the city's sewer system. The 4th Infantry Division, the American unit unfortunate enough to have the Iraq rotation at that time, announced that its men were going to plug the holes where the sewers could be accessed from ground level. This would not do anything to limit the slaughter but it would at least mean that families were more likely to have a body to bury.

Families of the wrong sect in the wrong place woke in the morning to find letters pushed under their front doors telling them to get out by nightfall. The message would sometimes be delivered by someone simply shooting at the building. No one with any sense needed to be told twice. It was not a time for stubbornness. Around thirty thousand people became refugees in those first few months. By July there were 180,000 of them. Eighteen months later it was approaching three million. Whole streets in the bloodiest districts had been abandoned.

The Western security contractors in the Hamra, the ex-Special Forces men hired to provide guidance to the press corps, began providing regular updates on where the latest militia checkpoints had been spotted. Roads that I had previously driven along dozens of times were now firmly out of bounds. A reporter from the *Washington Post*, and he must have been half mad to try it, attempted to get into the Shia bastion of Sadr City. He came back with stories of children as young as twelve standing at road junctions, dwarfed by their AK-47s, checking everyone who went past.

Abu Omar, my driver, lost his eldest sister. She was five months pregnant, a teacher who had been at the front of her class when a bomb went off outside the building. The brother of Sajad, the driver of our second car, disappeared while driving on a highway near Ramadi that he had to use for his job as a truck driver ferrying goods to the Syrian border. As he was Shia it was presumed he had been taken by Sunnis and was being tortured or had already been killed. The elders of Sajad's tribe sent a delegation to the Sunni tribes around Ramadi seeking information about what had happened to him. They pleaded ignorance. I worked my contacts in the American military to see if there was any chance that he had been accidentally arrested. They knew nothing.

His eight children and wife moved in with Sajad's family. Sajad already had six children of his own. He now had sixteen mouths to feed and sixteen lives to protect from the madness.

Ahmed was at home when the gunmen came to his street. They stopped outside his house and he heard them break into the building next door. He sat with his family in their living room praying that they would be spared. There was gunfire. He heard the gunmen leave and then a tap on his door. He opened it and there was his neighbour, his hands clutched over his chest to try to stop the bleeding. He could not even speak to ask for help but instead collapsed on the floor. Ahmed tried to put into effect the medical training our team had received, while his five-year-old daughter watched a man die in front of her. Ahmed moved his family to his parents' house that night. They did not even bother to pack, so desperate were they to get away.

I went to one of Baghdad's psychiatric hospitals with the hope of finding what effect this might be having on the mental state of the city's population. It was a small building beside a roundabout in the centre of the city accessed through a metal gate covered in flaking green paint. Inside the walls were covered in white tiles. There were only four doctors working in the facility with half a dozen nurses to help them, the rest having fled abroad.

They had almost no medication with which to treat their patients. Instead they relied on more antiquated solutions. In a small room on the second floor was an electroshock machine. It had leather straps to hold the patient down and a metal headset was attached by two wires to a wooden box. Patients were given two to three sessions of electroconvulsive therapy a week, a plastic mouth guard placed between their teeth before each treatment.

When we arrived, the patients, watched by their supervisors, were wandering around a whitewashed courtyard. The doctors, in their white jackets, chain-smoked. They were notably introspective about their task.

'In Iraq 90 per cent of people have some form of mental problem due to the lives they face,' the duty consultant, Dr Nour Bassim, said. 'We, the doctors here, have diagnosed each other and know that we ourselves are suffering. But is that necessarily madness or is it a rational reaction at a time like this?'

He pointed at a man standing by a small statue of the hospital's founder. 'He is delusional. He is convinced that if he leaves this hospital he is destined to die. It is acute paranoia, so much so that he cannot even step outside.'

'That man,' he said, indicating a middle-aged Iraqi with a bald head and bushy moustache. 'He has concluded he must be divine as he was in a bombing but survived.

'How can I say with certainty that neither is right? Is it correct to say they are clinically unwell? That they are wrong to believe they will be killed outside these walls or did not only live due to a miracle of divine favour? How do I know the answer when nothing seems certain? I could be the person who is delusional, they the ones who are sane.'

Despite the suicide bombing of the Hamra most of the press corps stayed in the hotel, moving into the main tower that had escaped the worst of the damage. I checked out, partly because the staff had been seen looting the worst-damaged rooms but primarily because, in the aftermath of the bombing, the locals living beside the Hamra had made clear that they had had enough of our presence. When reporters drove in and out of the main entrance they started having stones thrown at them. There was a whip-round of all the media bureaus to raise money for those affected by the blasts, which for a while did pacify the more aggressive instincts of our Iraqi neighbours. Nevertheless I could still only feel embarrassment and apprehension when I saw them.

I moved the office to another hotel in the compound. It used an alternative entrance to the Hamra and was in a spot where the surrounding buildings had been unaffected by the bombing. The hotel had been the Australian embassy until the general security situation deteriorated to such a level that it had been thought sensible to join the other diplomats in the Green Zone. During their time at the hotel, however, the Australians had renovated it to ensure the building had proper escape routes and this made it feel secure.

The only other alternatives within the complex surrounding the Hamra had been a hostel, which had exotic, if frayed, decor that betrayed its former use as a brothel, and the faux-Classical Greek glamour of a hotel opposite the Hamra itself, which seemed to me the most exposed of them all because it was closest to the main road. Not staying there proved to be the right choice. A few months later its staff became convinced that it was only a matter of time before the whole compound was overrun. One night they stole everything they could get their hands on and disappeared.

I liked our new residence. It was clean and the owners friendly. The family who ran it lived in rooms on the ground floor and I often spent time with their children and relations who would tell me the latest gossip from their day. The Australians had built a pool table that sat in the basement. The Iraqis were extremely good at pool but played in a style of their own. There were no tactical soft shots or snookers in their game. Every ball had to be hit as hard as possible into the pocket otherwise it did not really count.

The building in front of it had been taken over by a security firm run by an Iraqi-American who had come to Baghdad from New York. There was an uncertainty about what his company did, although whenever you asked people working for it they answered that they were in the 'packaged food transportation' business. This was clearly more of a money-spinner than might have been expected. While staying overnight in Jordan waiting to go into or out of Baghdad, members of the Hamra press corps routinely said they had spotted the Iraqi-American outside the Four Seasons hotel in Amman in a white Rolls-Royce.

I was concerned that this firm was a likely target for attack. There had already been a failed bombing attempt on it the previous year and, a month after we moved into our new office, a half-dozen or so of his people were shot while they were out in the city. In response the Iraqi-American brought dogs in to patrol the perimeter walls at night. In the autumn of 2006 the Iraqi police raided the company and seized an arsenal of weapons said to include heavy machine guns and a storage room filled with AK-47s. The Iraqi-American fled the country while leaving instructions for his remaining men to mount extra guards to overlook every exit.

I heard recently that the company left Baghdad in 2007, finally forced out of Iraq, only to be replaced at their old base by a new set of security contractors. They are Russian and they can apparently be heard singing at night as they work their way through cases of vodka.

Iraq's old institutions of state had been stripped away when the American administrator Paul Bremer disbanded the Ba'athist instruments of rule. The new organs of government that the US established in their place had largely failed, a result of the security situation, the unrealistic expectations introduced at their inception by the American ideologists who governed Iraq in the year following the US invasion, and the incessant political wrangling caused by the country's year of elections.

As Iraqis now flailed in the knowledge that their lives were under acute and imminent threat, the traditional Arab bonds of charity, tolerance and communal responsibility finally started to fray. These had done much to maintain social cohesion despite the strains caused by the war, but the enemy was now their own countrymen not a foreign invader. After the bombing of the Golden Mosque individual people in individual districts concluded that the only logical response to what was unfolding was to seek their own defence. If that meant taking out the family in the neighbouring street before they got to you, so be it.

The militarisation of Baghdad was taken to the next inexorable step. While the number of tit-for-tat killings continued to spiral and the death squads prowled the streets with ever more menace, Iraqis sought to protect themselves. The price of an AK-47 trebled to $350. People talked of burying rocket-propelled grenades in the garden. Women began carrying pistols in their handbags.

In the worst-affected areas individual streets started organising their own paramilitary groups for security. This was neighbourhood watch, Iraqi-style. When the sun set, zigzags of obstacles – palm trees, old air-conditioning units, unused cars – were pulled across roads to slow approaching vehicles. The men of the street would take turns to stand guard, some at ground level and others on the roofs of surrounding buildings to give them a better angle of fire.

I talked to members of a group in a Sunni neighbourhood in the south-west of the city who were adamant that, with so many people having suddenly developed a taste for killing, they could not trust anyone but those who lived in the same row of houses as themselves. Their mistrust was particularly directed at the police whom they considered nothing more than a legalised extension of the Shia militias. They were deeply concerned about the extent of their present weaponry. They only had Kalashnikovs and they wanted much more firepower, particularly heavy machine guns and rocket-propelled grenades. Feelers had been put out to a street a dozen blocks away whose defenders were rumoured to have got their hands on a collection of mines. Laying them across the entrance at night was considered an attractive precaution.

In the Adhamiya district, Sunni guards fought a two-day pitched battle when police tried to enter the neighbourhood. A rumour had spread that the officers were members of the Badr Brigade, the paramilitary wing of the Shia political party SCIRI, a name synonymous for Sunnis with murder and kidnapping. Omar bin Abdulaziz Street, Adhamiya's main thoroughfare, was racked by assault rifles, machine guns and the occasional grenade as the police were caught in crossfire from the surrounding buildings. Loudspeakers in the Sunni mosques shouted slogans praising 'the heroes of Adhamiya' and calling on them to 'defeat the aggressors'.

The US army, accepting the inevitable, began to issue weapons licences to those guarding their homes. Some groups did not survive long enough to be accredited. One north-western Sunni district had to disband its neighbour-hood watch after eight of its members were killed in the first two days.

Across the capital, battle lines were drawn up as the two sects faced each other. Zones of control were guarded and raids launched into bordering districts. Members of a minority sect living on the wrong side of these new demar-cation lines were expunged for the perceived safety of the majority. Tens of thousands of people were threatened, killed or forced from their homes. By August the scale of this sectarian cleansing meant that 95 per cent of Shia were believed to have fled the southern Sunni stronghold of Dora. Sunnis had left the Shia parts of Zafraniya. A similar cleansing of Sunni occurred in Mashtel, while in nearby New Baghdad, where the sects were more matched in size, they fought nightly battles in a desperate attempt to gain control.

One man, a Sunni, told of what had happened when rival gunmen succeeded in infiltrating his area. 'They started firing at our houses,' he said. 'They didn't expect a very quick response, but we gave them one. We surrounded them. They were in a trap and gunfire on them was from everywhere.

'We killed a lot of them. After defeating them, it was our turn to attack. We followed the ones fleeing and we saw them entering a mosque, which we shot with two rocket-propelled grenades. And then we returned home.'

Very occasionally there were people who tried to preserve the old ties that had once appeared so enduring. A Shia community leader in the central commercial district of Karrada publicly issued a warning against anyone intending to hurt the Sunnis who lived there. 'If anyone touches them, they touch us,' he said.

In a city where fear now ruled that was the exception, and anyway I heard later that he had been tracked down and killed.

Working in Baghdad was relentless and exhausting. To have a break from its terrors, Ahmed and I flew on Iraqi Airlines to Irbil, the capital of the Kurdish region in the north of Iraq. It was the first time Ahmed had been on an aeroplane and the corkscrew ascent did little for his confidence. Every few minutes he asked if it was normal for the plane to be wobbling so much. I did not have the heart to say no.

Kurdistan was different to the rest of Iraq. The presence of the peshmerga, the guerrilla force who for decades had fought Saddam from strongholds in the mountains, was felt across its four provinces as they guarded checkpoints and scrutinised strangers. It was why, along with the relatively homogeneous nature of the local population, the area was relatively peaceful.

The result had been a building boom. Where Baghdad was a place of blast walls and debris, Irbil was one of new shops and emerging high-rises. There was even a five-star hotel in its centre where you could sit by a pool and drink cocktails. It was a hotel where a concierge opened the front door in welcome, bell boys carried your luggage and waitresses in fitted suits drifted around taking orders. It truly was a different world.

I caught sight of myself in the line of mirrors that covered the wall opposite the hotel's check-in desk. There was a short, dirty figure in Iraqi-style lime green stonewash jeans, the hems too long so that they came down over his shoes. The shirt was from a shop in Baghdad, short-sleeved and long-collared, brown with thin orange stripes in a zigzag motif. I did not like to shave, the Iraqis being so naturally hirsute that I thought it helped me blend in, but I had never been able to grow a good beard so there was merely an embryonic moustache in the making. I had cut my own hair, barbers being in short supply in Baghdad by then and ones who would risk touching a foreigner even more so. I had trimmed the top and back but had clearly not done a good job as parts were sticking out in chunks. Sweat stuck dirt to my face. My skin was burnt by the sun, my nose red, and my eyes tired so that they squinted slit-like against the electric lighting.

Previously starved of investment, Kurdistan was being pulled out of poverty and into the modern world. Seventy-eight international companies had invested hundreds of millions of dollars in the previous two years. The area's previous poverty made it a blank slate while its oil reserves promised rich rewards. Roads were being blasted through mountains, bridges built, underpasses created and the edge of the city ringed by new housing projects. It was an indication of how events might have unfolded across the rest of Iraq if things had worked out differently.

My aim was to spend time at Lake Dukan, a reservoir

in Suleimaniya province where the altitude provided relief from the summer heat. A cousin of Ahmed's, who was half Kurd and half Arab, had agreed to be our driver. On the evening before we set off, we drove to a pizza restaurant for a meal. Some children dropped firecrackers on the road beside us. Ahmed and I hunched automatically. Our driver was in hysterics. 'This is not Baghdad,' he said. 'This is Kurdistan.'

When we arrived at the lake we found families picnicking along the water's edge, while on the surrounding roads cars deposited their cargo of delighted children. It was a beautiful spot with the aquamarine water ringed by mountains whose cliffs had been eroded into sharp peaks and whose lower reaches had been softened by centuries of alluvial deposits. Heather tipped with rose-coloured flowers grew by the lake's edge. Men and young boys had stripped to their underwear and were splashing in the water.

Most of the visitors were Arabs who had also come north for a break from the violence. One group was preparing food on a small camping stove, a blue rug laid out beside them. 'Have some, please,' said the women in charge of the cooker, a simple gesture to two strangers. It was chicken and okra piled on fresh rice. Tea was poured for us into thin glasses and three teaspoons of sugar stirred in.

The family had not had a pleasant drive up. 'It was terrible,' the cook, Bekal, told us. 'All the way I was berating my husband for taking us on this trip. When we went through Baqubah there was a bomb in a car on the road in front. I was sure the whole way we were going to be killed. But it was worth it. I cannot put into words what I feel to be here. It is wonderful – quiet and full of water. At home I feel myself to be in a prison. Here I feel a different person. I feel happy.'

There was only one clear winner from the chaos that gripped Iraq that year and it was Moqtada al-Sadr. His position was one that had always relied to an extent on violence. It dated back to the moment he emerged as a key player in Iraq, when his supporters killed the traditional hereditary holder of the keys to the Imam Ali mosque in Najaf, Haidar al-Raifee, and America's favourite Iraqi cleric, Imam Abdul Majid al-Khoei, days after the US troops entered Baghdad in April 2003. Sadr's followers viewed Raifee as a Ba'athist collaborator and Khoei as an American stooge. When the two men approached the mosque to try to broker a peace agreement with the Sadrists who now controlled the site, they were attacked by a mob. Raifee was killed, stabbed with bayonets and knives, and Khoei was bound and taken to Sadr's head-quarters. Witnesses later told the investigating judge who examined the case that Sadr had appeared at the entrance and told them: 'Take this person away and kill him.'

Sadr's supporters were fundamental in propagating the sectarian violence now spreading across the country. His personal responsibility for these attacks was ambiguous. In public he would often call for restraint, saying that civil war would only play into American hands by giving the US an excuse to prolong its occupation. No one knew what he was saying in private, however, and the men in his Mahdi Army militia were the ones seen attacking Sunni mosques and forming the illegal checkpoints that now ringed Shia districts. They were the people who the Sunni said were telling them to abandon their homes and were rumoured to be carrying out much of the night-time killing. Whatever Sadr's rhetoric, his followers' actions increasingly had the appearance of an orchestrated assault.

In the absence of a functioning state it was to Sadr that the Shia turned for security. He had already started building up his mechanisms for a state-within-a-state the previous year with his religious schools and programmes of welfare relief. His followers now took on the responsibility of protecting swathes of the country from Sunni attacks. Visitors to Najaf reported that Sadr's followers were manning roadblocks accompanied by the police officers whose task it was officially supposed to be. In Sadr City, the Baghdad Shia neighbourhood named after Moqtada's father, it was his supporters who acted when a bomb went off, killing dozens of people. Members of his Mahdi Army militia seized two suspects, judges he had appointed tried them, and his followers hanged them from a lamp-post. The Iraqi government, let alone US forces, had little influence in these places. It was Sadr's face that stared from posters on street signs, in shop windows and from the walls of people's homes. He was their protector and the one to whom they were willing to publicly pay allegiance in exchange for the security he brought.

There were times when Sadr's organisation appeared to be fragmenting and the authority he held over his supporters seemed less than absolute. In late 2006, the Americans said they had identified at least twenty former Sadr militia leaders who were now acting independently of him as they sought to carve out their own little fiefdoms. The most feared of these was Abu Deraa, or Father of the Shield, a man known as 'the Shia Zarqawi' because of his acute viciousness. One of Baghdad's new self-styled emirs, his favoured method of murder was to have his followers hold his victims down so that he could crush their heads between cinder blocks. A video was circulated on mobile phones of him laughing as he heaped bodies onto a rubbish heap. However, groups like Abu Deraa's were small, maybe made up of a few hundred men at most. Sadr had around ten thousand men in his Mahdi Army.

The bombing of the Golden Mosque had moreover given Sadr's status within Iraq a unique boost because it was widely seen as having been partly directed at him. The particular reverence given to the mosque was not only due to the fact that the tenth and eleventh imams were buried there but also that it bordered the shrine of the twelfth imam. This figure, known as the Mahdi, is one of the most sacred in Shia Islam.

After the death of the Prophet Mohammad, and the schism between the Sunnis and Shia over who were the correct leaders to preserve the purity of the Prophet's message, there was a succession of twelve imams to whom the Shia alone paid allegiance. These rivals to the Sunni's Caliphs were known as the Infallible Imams or the Guided Ones.

Muhammad al-Mahdi was the twelfth imam. He was born in AD 868, the child of the eleventh imam and, legend says, either a Byzantine princess or a Nubian slave. At his father's funeral, when only 5-years-old, he commanded his uncle, who was supposed to have led the funeral prayers, to step aside. As he began the prayers, he suddenly disappeared. The Shia regard this as the moment that marked the start of the occultation, the period when God concealed the Mahdi from humankind.

A crux of Shia belief is the certainty that Muhammad al-Mahdi was the prophesied redeemer of Islam. They believe that he will be the one who will rise before the day of judgement and institute a kingdom of justice after triumphing against the Antichrist. This battle will supposedly occur in modern-day Israel at Tel Megiddo, a place 20 miles from Nazareth that is known more commonly in the West as Armageddon. According to Shia tradition the Mahdi's reappearance will come when the world has fallen into chaos and civil war rages. It will be a time when every leader and government has failed. True believers will ride from Yemen to Mecca carrying white flags, while more will emerge from Karbala carrying black ones. Then the Mahdi, no longer a five-year-old child but a force of divine power, will reappear wielding God's sword, the weapon known as the Blade of Evil's Bane, Zulfiqar, or the Double-Bladed Sword.

It was at the shrine beside the Golden Mosque that Muhammad al-Mahdi had disappeared. It was in his honour that Sadr's followers called themselves the Mahdi Army and, in the Iraqi mind, it was Sadr who was most closely linked to the expectation that his return was imminent.

Sadr preached that the day of judgement was drawing near. He insisted that he was not the Mahdi himself, despite some claiming he was, but he left no doubt that the moment of the Mahdi's return was fast approaching. He cited current events as proof. There was no law, there was no order, the true believers were being persecuted, the foreign *kuffar* controlled Iraq. What else could this be but the end of days?

This conviction was the basis of Sadr's power. It was a message that was preached from mosques and informed the actions of millions of Iraqis. For them the countdown to the Mahdi's return provided the context for the war that had consumed their country. To most political commentators what was happening in Iraq was about terrorism, or oil, or imperialism, or power. To many Iraqis, it was the prelude to the apocalypse.

In late August I was being driven back from the Green Zone when we got caught in traffic a few hundred yards from my hotel. No one was going anywhere. It was a Shia festival and hundreds of worshippers had gathered outside the offices of one of the religious parties located on the roundabout adjacent to where I lived. We had seen them being bussed in all day but had wrongly thought we could get back before the procession started. Now it was gridlock. It felt dangerous to sit where we were and Ahmed and I decided to leave Abu Omar in the car and walk west towards the safety of our office. The journey only took about five minutes but it provided me with one of the more memorable sights from my time in Iraq. Halfway to the Hamra compound, I looked down a side road and caught a glimpse of part of the throng that had gathered to give praise. At the road's far end was a mass of figures, dressed in white robes, dancing, twirling and jumping in utter delirium.

Back in our office I asked my team what they considered to be the religious dimension to what was occurring in their country. There were American troops out there who believed that the Second Coming was imminent; there were millions of Iraqis who believed the fighting anticipated the return of the Mahdi. My team were educated and Westernised Iraqis and I was intrigued to know their perspective.

There were five of them present, Ahmed, Abu Omar, Marwan and Sajad and also Abu Omar's younger sister, Asmaa, who since the death of her schoolteacher sister had been working with us as a distraction from her grief. Three were convinced that this time marked the advent of the apocalypse. The 'qiyamat', they called it, and it was what they now believed God willed. Only Marwan, my security guard, and Sajad sneered at the idea. The rest were certain. They could see no other way to explain what had happened to their world.

10. Tell Them of Us

In the centre of Baghdad is a war cemetery that serves as a reminder that this was not the first time British troops had fought in Mesopotamia. When built, it must have been a well-tended site. An ornate iron gate stands at its entrance. Rose bushes and ordered rows of graves can still be made out. By the time I was there, however, it had become a broken and ridiculed place. Grass and thorns grew wild. Gravestones had been toppled. Others were smashed. Locals looking for a convenient spot to dispose of their waste had covered the cemetery in rubbish. Plastic bags, bottles and the other detritus of modern living were now among its most visible markers.

The bodies buried there date from nearly a century ago when Iraq played its part in the First World War. With the Ottoman Empire siding with Germany, British forces under Major General Charles Townshend had landed near Basra in November 1914 to wrest Mesopotamia from Turkish control.

It was not a successful campaign. The British deployment, primarily made up of men from the British Indian Army, advanced north along the Tigris to within sight of Baghdad. There, at Madain, the Turks attacked. Townshend was forced back towards Kut, where he and his men were besieged. The fighting was prolonged and painful. Three times the British tried to raise the siege and three times they failed. Townshend and his men were reduced to eating their mules and horses. In April 1916, he finally surrendered and his remaining 8,000 men were forced to march, with little food or water, to Baghdad in 120-degree heat. Half of them did not survive the journey or the hard labour they were required to carry out for the remainder of the war.

The British finally took Baghdad a year later. A new commander, Lieutenant General Frederick Maude, had been installed and for six months he drilled his troops in southern Iraq before leading them along the Tigris. His offensive was methodical, organised and victorious. The Turks were this time smashed at Kut and when the British troops entered Baghdad they were greeted by ecstatic crowds.

A week later, the General released the 'Proclamation of Baghdad', his pledge of fair government to the Iraqi people that uncannily mirrors the promises that the Americans brought with them when they sought to define Iraq's destiny a century later.

'Your city and your lands have been subject to tyranny, your palaces have fallen into ruins, your gardens have sunk in desolation and your forefathers and yourselves have groaned in bondage,' the General wrote.

'Your sons have been carried off to wars not of your seeking and your wealth has been stripped from you by unjust men and squandered in distant places. You have suffered under strange tyrants, who have endeavoured to set one Arab house against another in order that they might profit.

'I am commanded to invite you to participate in the management of your own civil affairs in collaboration with the political representatives who accompany the British army, so you may be united with your kinsmen in realising the aspirations of your race.'

The British suffered 92,000 casualties, 30,000 of them fatalities, in their Mesopotamian campaign. Half these lives were lost in combat, the rest died from disease, primarily cholera. It was cholera that killed Maude eight months after he had entered Baghdad.

The pledges of his proclamation did not survive much longer. Whatever Maude may have said the British would do in Iraq, they were not primed to rule with anything but a heavy hand. By 1920 the Iraqis were in revolt, a revolt that started in Fallujah, and though the rebels were beaten back they took up arms again in 1922 with fresh demands for a representative government.

By 1932 Iraq was nominally independent although it was still ruled by the Hashemite monarchy Britain had installed and London kept a close watch on its interests there. In 1941 British troops were back fighting in Basra. A military coup had resulted in an Arab nationalist government taking control and Iraq sided with the Nazis. Finally, in 1958, the last vestiges of British influence were removed as the monarchy was overthrown. The king and his family were shot in their garden and their bodies paraded to the public.

It was mid-afternoon, late in 2005, when I visited the British war cemetery in Baghdad. Ahmed and I climbed through a hole in the railings. General Maude's mausoleum, a dome-topped structure edged with four pillars, stood in its centre. It had been used as a public toilet and anti-British graffiti was scrawled on its sides. On the surviving gravestones were faded names, a few lines of poetry, promises that 'At the going down of the sun and in the morning, We will remember them.'

A group of children were playing football with Maude's mausoleum as the goal. They saw us and started to come over, shouting at us and looking for conversation. The children were only around 10 years old but I was worried about the attention they might attract. We tried to get them to be quiet but they wouldn't stop so we did the only thing I could think of and fled.

The graveyard in Baghdad is not Iraq's only British war cemetery. There are others scattered across the country. There is a cemetery in Habbaniya, another in Mosul and one in Amarah. In Basra there are two: one for the British and the other for the Indian soldiers. Nobody knows how many were buried in the Indian cemetery because at the time it had not been thought necessary to record their names or numbers. Whatever the hierarchy that once divided them, both have now suffered the same degree of neglect. The cemeteries came under sustained shellfire during the Iran–Iraq war and looters stripped them of brass and stone in the aftermath of the 1991 Shia uprising. After the British entered Basra in 2003 the War Graves Commission announced an ambitious restoration programme. Security concerns prevented the work from taking place.

The cemetery at Kut suffered the worst. Four hundred and seventeen people had been buried there in a small grass square shaded by palms and pomegranate trees. A steel cross was erected by the British authorities on a red plinth at its centre. The cemetery was kept in relatively good condition until 1991 when Saddam ordered it to be used as a rubbish dump. A pump, which had kept it dry when the Tigris flooded, then broke. The guard who looked after the cemetery went mad and was taken to a mental asylum in Baghdad. The local sewage system deteriorated, pouring waste over the graves.

When the Americans arrived in April 2003 they pledged to repair the site. A team of Seabees, the US military's construction engineers, was assigned to the job. Within weeks it had been overhauled and a new cross built and mounted. A rededication ceremony was held. Senior officers from both the British and the American armies gathered at the spot. A bagpiper played 'God Save The Queen', and the Union flag was hoisted beside the memorial.

That night it was vandalised. Gravestones were pulled out or pushed over. The flagpole was bent to a 45-degree angle and the Union flag was ripped down and burned. The inscription on the memorial, which had been attentively restored by the Americans, was chipped and scratched. The quote on it was a version of the words by John Maxwell Edmonds, the Edwardian poet, favoured for so many war memorials of that era. It had read, 'When you go home, Tell them of us – and say, For your tomorrow, We gave our today.' Now it was once again illegible.

The British retreat from southern Iraq began in earnest in the summer of 2006. First their base near Samawah in Muthanna province, west of Basra, was handed over to the local authorities – then Camp Abu Naji, the base outside the smuggling haven of Amarah in Maysan province, was abandoned.

It was the first time I had visited Abu Naji since being sent there to witness the January 2005 national election in which the Shia had come out to vote in such numbers. Maysan had lived up to its image as the most difficult area within the British zone of control, with pre-election politics as often revolving around the judicious use of Kalashnikovs as it did around pamphleteering.

Little had changed. The British officer now in charge was a Lieutenant Colonel David Labouchere of the Queen's Royal Hussars. He had a reputation as a bit of a maverick, someone who would deviate from traditional military thinking if he believed it could provide a greater chance of success, and he cut a romantic image, a tatty brown scarf usually wrapped around his neck for protection against the sand and dust. Labouchere clearly loved his responsibilities in the desert, enthusiastically describing the province as Iraq's 'problem child', and was full of stories about the local blood feuds and tribal squabbles that he had witnessed. He seemed a character from a previous era, a modern Beau Geste in his own desert outpost, someone who had been given the chance to live the Boy's Own tales I could only imagine he had grown up on.

Labouchere's favourite tale to illustrate the nature of life in Amarah was what he called 'the story of the pigeon that killed five people'. A girl had a pet pigeon which she loved to play with. It would insist on squawking and cooing all day and night, which drove the neighbouring family to distraction. One day the head of the neighbouring household barged into the girl's house and killed the bird. Her father came home to find his daughter in tears and his wife outraged by their neighbour's intrusion into their property. He grabbed his gun and shot his neighbour and wife. The victims' brothers picked up their guns and shot the man, his wife and their daughter. The matter had not ended there. The extended families on both sides had been required to flee Amarah amid promises of further reprisals. 'These people are rather like Texans, but even more stubborn,' Lieutenant Colonel Labouchere said. 'Armed and against anyone who's not one of them.'

The people of Maysan province did not like interference from outside and Britain's military operations in the area during the previous few years had spawned umpteen blood feuds against its soldiers. Attacks on British forces grew until they reached a level that was unbearable for those based at Abu Naji. The British were sitting ducks, stuck in one place to be picked off by the mortar and rocket teams prowling outside. There had been 281 attacks on the camp since the Hussars arrived in April, ensuring their time in Iraq had been marked with blood and lost limbs.

In the first years of the British presence in Amarah, attacks had been limited to one or two rounds a night. They now came in barrages. On a night in May, 54 rounds detonated one after another. On the day before my arrival seventeen had come in, causing such fires that the camp ran out of fire-suppressant foam.

'We've been here too long,' Labouchere said. 'We said we could bring reconstruction and new police forces and democracy, and that was all very well three years ago. But we needed to deliver the goodies. They never really wanted us here. Now we're excess to what is needed.'

Labouchere had decided that enough was enough. He was not having his men remain as stationary targets any longer and had come up with an adventurous solution.

His force was going to leave the camp and drive into the desert where they would become an ever-shifting force, sleeping under the stars and fighting on the move in a fleet of stripped-down Land Rovers. Resupply would come from air drops or transport planes landing on temporary runways. 'Labouchere of Arabia', they were calling him in the British base at Basra airport. I suspect he liked that.

His men's mission would be to patrol the Iranian border, over which there were a growing number of reports – but little hard evidence – that weaponry was being supplied to Shia militias in Iraq. The plan was reminiscent of the long-range desert group who in the Second World War had caused so many problems for the German field marshal Erwin Rommel. However, the main reason for its adoption was to stop the British being mortared so routinely. Recent months had been, as one captain observed, 'very wearing on the nerves'.

When I arrived at the camp on 21 August it was a hive of activity. Everything that could be removed was being packed up and placed in a convoy of lorries to be ferried to Basra. A number of convoys, each 160 vehicles long, had already made the journey in the preceding weeks and only the most essential items now remained. Ammunition was boxed, air-conditioners were taken out and the accommodation tents collapsed and stowed away.

I was surprised to find all this work being done. The line from the British government was that the base was being vacated because the local security forces had been brought up to a level where they could handle things by themselves. The camp, I had been told, would be given to the Iraqi police for them to use as a training centre, the implication being that it would be handed over as a functioning facility.

There was considerable hilarity when I mentioned this. The operations officer who was organising the removal of Abu Naji's equipment asked if I had not heard what happened at Camp Smitty, the base near Samawah that Britain had vacated at the end of July. I had not. The events following that departure had not been made public and when I heard what had happened it was clear why, for this was not the ordered retreat, leaving working camps to a grateful people, being described in the official briefings.

British officials had said that Smitty was only vacated after a rigorous assessment of the competency of the local government and police. Des Browne, Britain's Defence Secretary, had hailed it as a step in 'building a stable and democratic future' for the country. In fact Smitty was looted bare as soon as the British left. As the last Army vehicles drove out of the main entrance those in them could already see pick-up trucks being filled with tens of thousands of pounds worth of equipment. Water filtration systems, chairs, bedding, air-conditioners and kitchen utensils were removed, rendering the site uninhabitable. Even light switches were taken off the walls. Locals said they saw off-duty soldiers and the governor's own staff loading their official vehicles with booty. Some of Smitty's air-conditioning units were now understood to be in the governor's private office.

The mob had then moved on to a nearby Japanese base, which had been vacated the same day. They were accompanied by hordes of people from nearby Samawah, word having spread of the easy pickings on offer.

The Japanese base had always had a near-legendary status among the coalition forces in Iraq. The Japanese government was determined that nothing untoward should happen in what was the country's first, and highly controversial, deployment of troops to a war zone since the end of the Second World War. Consequently every possible measure was taken to ensure the protection and comfort of the 600 Japanese troops stationed there. Soldiers who had been inside the base described it as like something from a James Bond film with lasers and infrared beams crisscrossing the surrounding terrain to detect potential attackers. There were even electronic massage chairs for the Japanese soldiers to relax in should they ever feel stressed after a tough day.

Whatever had been left was gone within hours. In the following weeks markets popped up along the main streets of Samawah selling the goods that had been pilfered and attracting customers from as far away as Najaf and Nasariyah.

'They will be like ants going over this base,' the operations officer at Abu Naji predicted when asked what would happen there when his unit pulled out. He had already overseen the removal of eight thousand tonnes of material to avoid it falling into the hands of looters.

Shortly before the British troops final departure, a ceremony was held at the war memorial that honoured the soldiers at Abu Naji who had been killed since the Army's arrival in Maysan in 2003. It was in the centre of the camp, five whitewashed walls with a gravel bed and a six-foot-high cross in front. It was to be taken to Basra and rededicated in the British base at the airport. The service was being held to mark the significance of the moment and pay respect to the sacrifices that had been made.

Around three hundred troops were still in the camp and almost all of them attended. The sun was going down, silhouetting them against the falling light. Male and female soldiers slouched against walls, many cracking jokes, while they waited for the service to begin. They then stepped forward, formed a semi-circle, and pulled themselves to their full height as their commanding officer signalled the start of proceedings.

They sang 'Guide Me O Thou Great Redeemer' and listened to the reading of Psalm 54, 'For strangers have risen up against me, and the ruthless seek after my life.'

There was a pipe lament and then Labouchere addressed his soldiers.

'These men,' he said, indicating the memorial, 'came here, like you did, to be the best they could be. They came here to do their duty, and they died for their country. Here, on the roads and the desert, you have been attacked, you fought back. Even here in our camp you faced the most extreme dangers. You have fought a determined and fierce enemy who came at you in numbers and with a will. Yet you endured.

'You are soldiers for your country and the greater good. The most important thing you can do is your bit to make this country a better place. By doing so we honour the men honoured here for they died in that endeavour.'

As the soldiers drifted away and the final preparations began for the memorial's removal, I walked over to have one last look at it. The brass plaques on which the names of the dead were written had been freshly polished.

'Far from here,' said an inscription, 'families have borne the heavy price of the loss of their loved ones, in order that the people of Maysan might enjoy a safe environment in which to rebuild their country. May their sacrifice bear fruit.'

On the day Labouchere and his soldiers at Abu Naji climbed into their Land Rovers and drove into the wilderness, the people of Maysan did, as predicted, swarm over the base like ants. Around five thousand ransacked the site. They were jubilant as they did so. Everything that had been left was pillaged, from doors and window frames to corrugated roofing and metal pipes.

Three companies of Iraqi soldiers, who had been hastily stationed within the base, at first tried to hold back the mob, firing shots into the air to disperse them. The crowd came back with AK-47s, some even with rocket-propelled grenades, and the soldiers were quickly overwhelmed. A number of them were later seen joining in the looting, accepting the opportunities presented by a bad job. At nightfall a spokesman for the local Iraqi army division confirmed that 'everything' had gone.

In Amarah a throng gathered around the local offices of Moqtada al-Sadr as a loudspeaker repeatedly broadcast the triumphant message, 'This is the first Iraqi city that has kicked out the occupiers.' Processions of cars and trucks drove through the city's streets, hooting their horns as people leaned out of the windows shouting that the British had departed. Shots were fired into the sky in celebration. From the minarets the muezzins sounded their satisfaction.

Labouchere and his men never did find evidence of weapons being trafficked across the Iran–Iraq border. Despite it being a given in some quarters that Iran was smuggling equipment into Iraq, it was in fact rare for there to be proof of this. There were intelligence reports that it was happening and off-the-record briefings about sources who claimed suitcases filled with cash were being delivered to Shia militias. Only once, however, did I hear that the British had caught militiamen taking a consignment of roadside bombs across the Shatt al-Arab.

Lack of proof did not mean it was not happening. The length and porosity of the border between Iraq and Iran, the disdain shown for it by nomadic Bedouin, and the number of vehicles using the official crossings all meant equipment could easily have been brought in without anyone knowing. The evidence, however, did not appear to be there, which mattered in the context of the accusations being made against Iran and the reprisals threatened. Faulty intelligence had already caused one war.

Labouchere told the *Washington Post* in October 2006: 'One hears word of mouth, but one has to see it with one's own eyes. There are serious consequences, aren't there?'

The British wanted to pull out of Basra city in the spring of 2006 but the Americans vetoed it because at that time they were pouring troops into Iraq to try to bring order to Baghdad. Relations between the two allies became so tense that the Americans threatened to send a brigade of their own soldiers to Basra to replace the British if they left. This was politically unacceptable for Downing Street, determined as it was to portray the withdrawal as a demonstration that the job of stabilising the area had been completed rather than a sign of defeat.

British troops stayed for another five months as the political wrangling was resolved. This period saw some of the fiercest fighting since the 2003 invasion. The Shia militias were energised by their fury at what had happened to the Golden Mosque in Samarra and the knowledge that the battle for control of post-British Basra had begun.

During those months twenty-five British soldiers were killed and a further 58 wounded.

On 2 September 2007, the 550 remaining British soldiers in Basra finally withdrew, without fanfare and by night to limit the risk of ambush. They joined the troops at the base by the international airport, the last non-logistical British camp in Iraq. A British force would stay, it was announced, to assist the Iraqi authorities when requested, to guard the road between Kuwait and Baghdad that acted as a key American supply route, and to continue the training of the local army and police forces. Downing Street said, however, that the number of British troops stationed in Iraq would be reduced to a couple of thousand by the middle of 2008, few of whom would actively patrol. For Britain, the war in Iraq was essentially over. It is the war in Afghanistan that is now its main focus.

The retreat from Basra prompted an assessment of what had been achieved there. A senior British officer in Iraq told the press that his troops could have continued killing militiamen but there would have been no point. The rebuilding of the south had not proceeded as imagined so there was no longer anything to be gained by prolonging the fighting. The British government acknowledged that considerable problems remained but said Iraqi politicians, not British troops, were best suited to handle them. People never like having foreign soldiers on their streets, it was argued, however fair-minded they might be. The Army's departure was portrayed as an essential prerequisite for the return of normality because it would remove a major source of resentment.

The weeks immediately following the British departure saw more assassinations, gunfights and bombings. With no foreign correspondents in Basra, and the local authorities sometimes hesitant to report bloodshed, the full extent of what happened in the city is not known. A number of incidents were, however, made public and it is widely accepted that, in the 24 days following the British withdrawal, the deputy head of police was attacked by snipers and the head of military intelligence struck by a roadside bomb; the official responsible for the city's finances was killed and his body burned; the imam of a mosque in Mahtta was shot outside his home; a representative of Grand Ayatollah Sistani, the most senior Shia cleric in Iraq, was ambushed by gunmen, the third of his representatives to be killed in Basra in just over a month; pictures of Grand Ayatollah Ruhollah Khomeini, the leader of the 1979 Iranian Revolution, appeared on lampposts; rockets were fired into the al-Zahraa district, though miraculously no one was killed; a lieutenant colonel in the Department of Important Crimes was shot in the shoulder; a car bomb was detonated outside the Iranian consulate; the bodies of three women with gunshot wounds were delivered to the morgue; a bomb left outside a mosque exploded as worshippers left evening prayers; a suicide bomber blew himself up at a police station; and a police captain was shot in the head as he left the city's police headquarters.

11. Mission Accomplished

The judge ordered the courtroom's door opened and an old man in a baggy suit, a copy of the Koran clutched in his hand, appeared in its entrance. He blinked and appeared momentarily confused as he took in the scene around him, before shuffling forward, seeming to limp with his right leg. Then, as he passed the reporters watching him, he stopped, pressing his thumb to the tips of his fingers in the Arabic gesture for 'wait'.

I stared at him through the pane of bullet-proof glass that separated us. The person who had ruled Iraq for a quarter of a century, the dictator whose actions had helped instigate the devastation that had blighted his country, was three feet in front of me. As an enthusiast of pulp fiction I had expected something to mark him apart; that his eyes might in some way hold evidence of depravity or his appearance cause a chill to the blood. There was nothing. It was simply another human being who looked every one of his 68-years, haggard and thin, with a greying beard and a muddled look on his familiar face. He was the banality of evil personified.

Then, amazingly, a look of satisfaction crossed Saddam Hussein's features. I have always maintained it was when he spotted CNN's Christiane Amanpour, the most famous

TV reporter of the day, among the group watching him. Upon seeing her Saddam knew he was back where he liked to be: at the centre of the world stage. As he finished his walk to the dock his shoulders straightened and his limp disappeared.

It was the first day of his trial on charges of war crimes and genocide, and the first time Saddam had been seen in public since he went into hiding in April 2003 when the invading American forces took control of Baghdad. For months US troops had combed Iraq searching for any trace of him, but the only public indication that Saddam was alive was the occasional release of an audio tape in which he would exhort Iraqis to resist the occupiers. In July his sons, Uday and Qusay, were killed during a three-hour gunfight with American soldiers. Then, in December 2003, the US finally got their man. Acting on information gained under interrogation from one of his former body-guards, six hundred American troops converged on Dwar, a village a few miles outside Saddam's home town of Tikrit. Saddam was discovered at the bottom of a narrow hole located beneath a two-room mud shack, its entrance hidden by a square of Styrofoam covered by dirt and a tatty rug. Despite having a pistol, he surrendered without resistance. For the following two years he had been held at a prison next to Baghdad airport. Hardly anything was known of his time there other than a report in an American newspaper that his guards had enter-tained themselves by making him watch the *South Park* film in which he was portrayed as Satan's mean-spirited gay lover.

Instructed by the lead judge to identify himself, Saddam challenged the authority that had dared to put him on trial. 'Who are you? What does this court want?' he demanded. 'I don't answer to this so-called court and I reserve my constitutional right as the president of the country of Iraq. I don't acknowledge the entity that authorises you, nor the aggression, because everything based on falsehood is falsehood.'

Four times he was asked his name; four times he refused to give it. He tried to make a statement to the court and the judge answered that he should 'relax' and promised he would have his chance to speak later.

'You know me,' Saddam replied. 'You are an Iraqi and you know that I don't get tried.'

His fellow defendants – Barzan, who once headed Iraq's barbaric intelligence service; Taha Yassin Ramadan, his former vice-president; Awad Hamed al-Banbar, a former head judge; and four local Ba'athist officials from Dujail – were temporarily enthused by his ardour. When they were led into the court they had appeared as shocked as their former leader and sat hunched in their chairs, refusing to look around. They too now came to life. Barzan demanded that they all be allowed the dignity of wearing their tribal headdresses, which to their considerable satisfaction the court permitted.

During a recess Saddam pointed out the cheap ankle-length robes his fellow defendants were wearing and they laughed. The group resembled nothing but old acquaintances catching up on the latest news. Saddam's lawyers came over and paid their respects. 'President', they called him and he preened with pleasure.

As the court rose at the end of the session, the security guards came forward to take Saddam from the room. Shaking off the arm of one of his guards, he berated them for daring to touch him and refused to move until they stepped back. They did so. He strode out.

The trial started to unravel almost immediately as once again Western expectations stumbled against Iraqi realities. The days after that first session saw the murder of two defence lawyers. A third would be killed before the closing statements. Several others fled the country and would only return for the specific sessions that could not be avoided. Scheduled witnesses failed to turn up because they feared for their safety. To get to the court many had been told to go to the nearest US military base from which they would then be helicoptered to the Green Zone. Unsurprisingly a number decided it was probably best not to be spotted wandering into an American camp.

The judges found their position becoming increasingly politicised as the ruling Shia politicians sought to appease their supporters by demanding a guilty verdict be delivered quickly. As Saddam used his time in the dock to grandstand and make political speeches, the growing criticism of the chief judge's running of the courtroom led him to resign in January.

Crisis turned to farce as the man named to replace him had to step down within days after it emerged that he was a former member of the Ba'ath Party. Judge Raouf Abdul-Rahman was appointed in his place. The prosecution claimed he could not be impartial as he was born in Halabja, the Kurdish town where Saddam's use of chemical weapons killed five thousand people. Their complaints were ignored but proved justifiable. Chief Judge Abdul-Rahman faced defendants whose actions and tactics would have provoked any court, but his frequent loss of temper and erratic rulings to defence requests only added to an impression of bias. He would not tolerate the slightest indication of dissent. Often there was the discomforting spectacle of the court continuing with none of the defendants or any of their original lawyers present. They had either boycotted proceedings or been thrown out for refusing to accept an instruction from the bench.

By the early months of 2006, Saddam's trial had become one of the best demonstrations of artifice in Baghdad. This was a period when visiting the Green Zone, where the court was located, was like entering a scenario sprung from Kafka. Soldiers were still sunning themselves on the tended lawns outside the Baghdad convention centre, there were still five different kinds of ice cream available in the mess hall and people were still getting into trouble if they drove too fast. Officially nothing catastrophic was happening in Iraq, even amid the violence that followed the attack on the Golden Mosque. I would sit in official briefings and US officials would project onto a white screen their slides listing the number of Iraqi troops trained or insurgents killed as if nothing had changed. There had been a blip in Iraq's reconstruction but it would not last, I was assured. Conditions would stabilise once the Iraqi politicians finally agreed on the composition of a new government.

My e-mail inbox filled with the latest press releases. The US military's messages were the best value. A stray dog had been saved by a marine and now had a good home in the States. Rubbish had been cleaned off the streets of Tikrit. A new power substation had been opened in Karbala. There would be no mention of the latest report by the US special inspector for Iraq reconstruction who had discovered that five electricity substations, built at a cost of $30 million, had been put up in places where they could not be connected to the national grid.

The British ambassador, William Patey, accused a British journalist of being hysterical when he suggested that there might possibly be a civil war going on. Patey's protestations were undermined when a secret assessment he sent to Tony Blair was leaked in which he warned that, given the present situation, even President Bush's 'lowered expectations' of an Iraq that could sustain itself, defend itself and govern itself 'remained in doubt'.

Saddam's courtroom existed in its own bubble. The security surrounding the trial was phenomenal. 'Better than the White House,' the guards liked to say. Before being accredited, I had to be vetted by the FBI. On a trial day I would be bused by coach to the court from a car park beside the complex that housed the US military press office. Upon arriving at it I would be frisked and told to stand in a new high-tech security machine which used ultrasound to see not only everything on my body but also if there was anything non-biological within it. During the trial's first months reporters were not even allowed to take in a notebook and pen, though this rule was relaxed after the State Department officials whose job it was to supervise the media tired of having to supply them.

The court had been built in a Ba'athist former HQ located within the area of Baghdad now walled off to form the Green Zone. It boasted the lavish design that typified the former regime's taste in interior decoration. Pillars held up the entrance hall, chandeliers hung from the ceiling and the floors were made of black-grained marble.

I would be searched again before I could enter the courtroom, required to stand in another ultrasound machine with my hands beside my head until a metallic voice confirmed that I was clean. Then it was up half a dozen steps and into the press box. This was a small room built behind a window of bullet-proof glass to ensure that if a weapon somehow had been smuggled in it still could not be used on those in the court. Notices were pinned to the seats at the front warning that anyone sitting in them would be broadcast on the trial's public television feed. The Iraqi journalists were studious in avoiding them in case they were spotted, hunted down and killed.

A red curtain covered the window that separated us from the court and it would be drawn back when the session started to reveal the chamber itself. It was the size of a conference room in a modern office development. A giant Iraqi flag covered a green screen on the far wall. The judicial bench was beneath it, opposite the press box, and had been raised so that the five judges assigned to pass judgement on the case could peer down on those in the dock. The prosecution lawyers sat at desks to our left, the defence in seats to our right. In the centre of the court was a metal pen in which the defendants were placed. Each had their own microphone on a stand.

Until the day's session began you never knew how many defendants and lawyers would be present because they staged frequent walk-outs in protest at the judges' handling of proceedings. Saddam's half-brother and co-defendant, Barzan al-Tikriti, had taken on occasion to wearing to court nothing more than his underwear as a symbol of his disdain.

In Iraq it was being widely viewed as a show trial. Most Sunnis had concluded it to be another attack on their community by the authorities. Most Shia and Kurds simply wanted a guilty verdict, and wanted it as soon as possible. The courtroom feed broadcast by a local television station was largely ignored in favour of the Lebanese soaps and old Egyptian comedies that could be found on the other channels. Even some of the US officials present at the court gave the impression of wishing it was over. The young man from the State Department assigned to press liaison had initially been excited, talking about a demonstration of justice. Now, having witnessed what that actually meant, he only wanted to talk about the trip to South-east Asia he was planning in order to recover from his involvement. He was resigning, his commitment to government service broken, and it was the subject of clean hostels in Ko Pha Ngan, not legal procedure, that he was now interested in.

It was sometimes difficult to remember the excitement there had been when the proceedings had begun the previous October. The trial had been a huge event not only for the Iraqis but for the whole American project in Iraq. With no weapons of mass destruction found, and the prospect of Iraq emerging as a beacon of democracy in the Middle East clearly floundering, it was potentially the Bush administration's last chance to demonstrate that something worthwhile had come out of its Iraq war.

The US had determined the shape that court proceedings would take. The White House had little time for international institutions and had decided it wanted Saddam tried in Iraq, by Iraqis. Western experts were provided to train the Iraqi prosecution. The judges and leading counsel were taken to Britain and to the States to observe how Western courts worked. Millions of US taxpayers' dollars were spent on building the court itself and providing the security that surrounded it.

The trial was intended, American officials made clear, not only to judge Saddam but also to create a comprehensive record of his crimes. This, it was hoped, would leave no doubt for posterity that the US had done the right thing in removing him.

It was therefore odd that they chose the Dujail case with which to charge him. It had not previously registered on the index of Saddam's crimes, dwarfed by the magnitude of his assaults on the Kurds in the north and the Shia in the south in which tens of thousands of people had died. Indeed when the case was first announced many Western commentators had never even heard of Dujail. Yet it was to be what happened there – in an impoverished town surrounded by fruit orchards to the north-east of Baghdad – that finally sent Saddam to the gallows. I suspect he was as surprised about that as the rest of us.

The case hinged on the events of 8 July 1982, when Saddam had been on an official visit to Dujail. As his motorcade pulled close to the village it was ambushed in an apparent assassination attempt. The attack failed and retribution was swift. Hundreds of men, women and children were rounded up by the security forces. According to the prosecution many were tortured and their orchards razed to the ground. It was said that 148 people were executed, a number of them minors, after a summary trial.

The Americans indicated that Dujail had been selected because the evidence against Saddam was so clear-cut that it would leave no doubt as to his guilt. This was important because understandably they were concerned that they might win in the courtroom but lose in the wider arena of international opinion. Documentation was said to exist that would directly link the murders to Saddam himself.

There was, however, another reason why the Dujail case was chosen. The assassination attempt had been carried out by the Da'wa Party, a small fundamentalist Shia political organisation that was among Iraq's oldest dissident groups. It was a body that had never achieved mass appeal but had close historic links to SCIRI. As a result it had considerable influence after the January 2005 elections, in which SCIRI did so well, even though Da'wa itself only won a few seats in parliament.

Though close to SCIRI, the Da'wa Party was not part of it and this ensured Da'wa's senior figures were more acceptable as potential holders of high office. They were less directly linked to Tehran or tainted by the excesses of SCIRI's Badr Brigade and consequently were seen as suitable compromise candidates. The party's leader, Ibrahim al-Jaafari, became prime minister. It was an appointment backed by the secularists, who hoped he would be less fundamentalist than SCIRI's leaders, and by SCIRI, which knew Jaafari would be supportive of many of its policies. Jaafari's appointment proved to be bad news for Iraq as it placed a politician with limited popular support at the helm, thereby depriving him of the political capital needed to control his cabinet. It proved decisive, however, in determining Saddam's fate. Da'wa wanted retribution for the killing of its followers at Dujail. For them this was not some footnote to Saddam's brutality but a pivotal moment in their party's history.

Desire for revenge was driving the legal process. It was an emotion that was as powerful among Iraq's political leaders as among those in the warring gangs in the souks of Amarah, or the gunmen shouting anti-American vitriol in the backstreets of Ramadi.

In the run-up to the start of the trial, it had dominated the local press and international news headlines. President Bush went on record to say that Saddam would now finally face the 'justice he had denied the people' he once ruled. A man whose whim had been law, a dictator who seized power by force and ruled through fear, a psychopath who watched videos of his victims being tortured and would at times enthusiastically administer the coup de grâce himself, was to be reduced to a lowly figure in the dock. Almost everyone in Iraq tuned in to watch the first session. It was another of those rare moments in Iraq when there was a glimmer of excitement and hope.

I was lucky enough to be selected in the lottery used to determine the press pool for each day as one of the correspondents who would witness the proceedings first hand. At the entrance to the courthouse there was a queue waiting to get in. The anti-mortar screens intended for the spot had not yet been completed and the guards who frisked us were consequently nervous. Everyone else seemed to be in a playful mood. Ahmed Chalabi, the Iraqi exile who more than anyone had persuaded the US to invade, was particularly jovial. 'A historic day,' he said, smiling broadly as he led in a delegation of Iraq's new rulers, many of whom Saddam had persecuted and so were now eager to see his humiliation.

When everyone had taken their places in the public gallery, the chief judge summoned the defendants one at a time. It was then Saddam had appeared looking haggard and bemused. When he had stepped into the courtroom, those in the press box had stood up and moved forward to get a clearer look. A young Iraqi radio reporter pressed his clenched fists against the glass partition. Catching sight of Saddam he fell to his seat as if overcome by exhaustion. 'At last,' he said.

In retrospect the events of the first session were a warning of what was to follow. It was not only the pugilistic approach Saddam took as he challenged the legitimacy of proceedings, nor the breakdown of the translation service that illustrated the lack of readiness of the court. It was also the indication that the rules of due process were already being bent to quickly bring about the ruling that many Iraqis, including the new government, dearly wanted to see.

The defence petitioned that it had received files relating to the case so late that it had not been possible to read them properly. At the time this was dismissed as an attempt to further delay the trial's start. It was, however, a failing by the prosecution which was repeated again and again during the coming months. The defence constantly learned of documents only when they were submitted to the court, resulting in claims of trial by ambush. At one point, as the prosecution tried to cope with its failure to produce witnesses, it opted to provide 23 witness statements, with none of those who had made them available for cross-examination. The administrative chaos was such that the court routinely failed to find documentation or requests that the defence lawyers submitted. In the end the chief judge had to admit that he had no idea how many motions the defence had even filed.

Human Rights Watch, one of only two charities that regularly attended the hearings, warned that the proceedings were becoming 'fundamentally flawed'. Despite the fact that the group had spent much of the previous decade gathering evidence to demonstrate the extent of Saddam's crimes, when the verdict arrived they could only conclude that it was 'unsound'.

The court had become a circus with Saddam as its ring-master. The flaws in the trial only gave validity to his outbursts in which he would rant against its illegitimacy, jabbing his finger at the bench with his face contorted in rage. 'This is not a court, this is a game,' he shouted during a session in February, and few watching could disagree.

When, in March, Saddam was given the opportunity to take the stand for his formal defence he did not use it to defend himself but instead to address the subject of the sectarian tit-for-tat killings gripping the country.

'What pains me most is what I heard recently about something that aims to harm our people,' he said, refer-ring to the violence after the Golden Mosque bombing. 'Let the people resist the invaders and their supporters rather than kill each other.'

It was a statement that caused the chief judge, Abdul-Rahman, to lose self-control. 'No more political speeches. We are a criminal court, a judicial court, we don't have anything to do with political issues or anything like this. Testify,' he shouted as he repeatedly cut out Saddam's microphone to prevent him from being heard.

'Political issues are what brought you and me here,' Saddam argued.

Abdul-Rahman, now red in the face with fury, told him he was 'being tried in a criminal case concerning the killing of innocents, not because of your conflict with America'.

Saddam was clearly enjoying himself. 'What about the innocent people dying in Baghdad?' he asked. 'I am talking to the Iraqi people.'

The sound and video feeds were cut, darkening the screens of anyone watching the proceedings on television, and the curtains drawn over the window in the press box.

With Iraq's new masters and their American assistants rarely acknowledging the scale of the slaughter now occurring, it was almost a relief to hear someone, even the man nicknamed the 'Butcher of Baghdad', speak of it on a national stage. Saddam was on trial for ordering the killing of 148 people. That number of people was now dying in Iraq every few days.

The truly astonishing aspect of the trial was that the prosecution failed to make its case. In legal history there can have been few defendants as guilty as Saddam Hussein. On the evidence actually put before the court, however, he should probably have been acquitted.

There were gaps in evidence and unreliable witnesses, many of whom had been children when the events under examination took place. At no point did any of the 21 witnesses who turned up say they had seen Saddam commit a crime. When the much-heralded documentation, which it had been indicated would remove any doubt of guilt, was finally unveiled it primarily showed that he had signed the death warrants.

The prosecution never established the chain of command which linked Saddam to the actions of his underlings. It never demonstrated the legal and practical authority of the numerous security organisations and political institutions involved in the events of Dujail, nor how they were organised or run. It was never shown how information was passed between them and up to Saddam himself. Never was it addressed how his position as president impacted on the behaviour of the Revolutionary

A month later Saddam was dead. A day after the execution, his final moments became public when a film taken on a mobile phone began to circulate. It was not the message for posterity that the trial had been intended to provide. Saddam's death resembled a lynching.

In a former military intelligence building that had been converted into an Iraqi prison, he could be seen on the video standing on an elevated platform made from rusty metal bars. Saddam was wearing an overcoat to warm himself against the December chill. He looked surprisingly calm and composed. Around him a baying crowd of Iraqi police officers, soldiers and government officials, all of whom had been specially selected to witness the moment, were shouting abuse. He smirked at them before starting to pray. An official called for calm. He was ignored, ridiculed for trying to impose order.

'Damn you,' a voice shouted at Saddam. A rallying cry went up hailing the greatness of Moqtada al-Sadr, the voices becoming a tumult of noise as they lauded Sadr's name and pledged their loyalty to him.

The transfer of power from one authority to another was being demonstrated in its most brutal form. Saddam would have understood this. He would almost certainly have done the same himself.

'Quicken the Mahdi's appearance and a curse on his enemy,' the mob cried. 'And support his son Moqtada, Moqtada, Moqtada.'

The trap door opened, Saddam fell and his neck snapped. His body was left to hang for eight minutes.

12. Exodus

While in Baghdad I read books on the Blitz. How unrecognisable London had been. The way the shattered glass in shop windows was replaced by wooden facings featuring brightly coloured pictures of the wares on offer inside. Or how almost all the statues were taken down and put into storage, the fountains in Trafalgar Square replaced by red brick air-raid shelters. Trees were painted white to guide pedestrians during blackouts. To protect people on buses from flying glass the windows were covered with the green baize normally used to line snooker tables. Passengers sat in a gloom. Those who had been on them said it felt like being in someone's drawing room at night, causing strangers to strike up conversations when they would never before have considered talking to each other.

Having grown up on stories of Londoners pulling together to withstand the German attacks, I was shocked to discover that there had been another, if less prominent, reality. Alongside the heroism, sacrifice and camaraderie of many, there was criminality and violence by some. Thieving was widespread and homes stripped of their carpets while their owners hid in bomb shelters. The books told of firemen emerging from burning houses carrying mink coats and teenage gangs taking advantage of the blackout to conduct muggings. Apparently pick-pockets were common in the tube stations where people sheltered from the air raids.

During the first eight weeks of the Blitz there were 390 reported cases of looting. So bad did the problem become that people began to demand that those caught be hanged amid claims that it was not such a problem in Germany because the Nazis were executing looters. Murderers took advantage of the numbers already being killed, which prevented the police properly investigating deaths while also ensuring bodies were buried quickly and with little examination. One, Gordon Cummings, preyed on women, earning himself the nickname the 'Blackout Killer'. He was caught after he was disturbed trying to strangle a woman near Piccadilly Circus and left behind his gas mask when he fled. He was traced through its issue number and hanged at Wandsworth Prison. A man killed his wife and dumped her in a bombed-out building, only for an alert police officer to question why the bomb blast had not left her body more mutilated.

In the five years of the Second World War, I discovered, the number of murders rose by 22 per cent, woundings by 44 per cent and cases of grievous bodily harm by 65 per cent. Criminal gangs, particularly in the East End, used the chaos to tighten their grip, taking out their rivals and strong-arming the locals with the basest of threats.

On the night of 8 March 1941 the Café de Paris, a nightclub in the West End, was hit as it hosted a young and glamorous crowd. The first bomb exploded above the stage, where 'Snakehips' Johnson was leading his West Indian band, and the second in the middle of the dance floor. It was one of the single worst losses of life in the early stages of the German bombardment. The confined space magnified the blast, ripping off legs and heads and exploding lungs. What most disgusted one of the first police constables on the scene, however, was that while the Londoners in the emergency services were trying to help the injured, others slipped in off the street and ransacked the corpses, even cutting the fingers off the dead to get at their rings.

In Iraq it was during the nights that I had to work the hardest not to think about what was going on in the city that surrounded me. I was not alone in this. By the final months of 2006 everyone around the Hamra was trying to keep themselves busy once the curfew hour came and we were stuck for another twelve hours in the compound. Some sought the self-control of the gym but the favourite escape for most was a few drinks. That was my preference as it usually involved the opportunity for some company.

Human contact was by that time precious for everyone: the locals trapped in their homes night after night, month after month by the violence outside; the US soldiers isolated by their fear in their bases with their blast walls and rolls of razor wire; and us – the press corps – hiding like mice in our holes from the killers who sought to abduct us. Sometimes I thought this isolation could in itself be the main cause of all that was happening, that people were able to behave so brutally because they were being deprived of the chance to remind themselves that others could be as human as they were.

Friday night was my favourite time. A few of us would gather on the roof of my hotel and, for one evening at least, forget where we were and pretend that everything was normal. I never knew who would turn up. There would be reporters of course, but also a cluster from the security companies, the ex-Special Forces men who would recount far-fetched stories of Picassos stolen from the walls of Saddam Hussein's abandoned palaces and smuggled back to Britain rolled inside gun barrels. Sometimes there might be a smattering of Iraqi translators and, on rare occasions, an aid worker or a diplomat or two.

There would inevitably be some braggart telling how he had happily driven to the outskirts of Dora and occasionally a fresh arrival ascertaining how dangerous it was by asking the basic questions. Most of the time, however, it was chat along the same lines as you found back home. It was who knew who, who had done what and who had been where. The war was usually a no-no, at least until later in the night when people had drunk more. When I look back, those evenings stand out in my memory as strongly as any of the bombs or the bodies. Which is good news for me, I suppose.

At some point there might be gunfire out in the darkness. The sound was so familiar by then it could usually be ignored. Occasionally, however, a flare would drop from the helicopters crossing overhead, presumably to help some American patrol feeling its way along the streets around us. It demanded attention. Baghdad was by then a city for which electricity was a rare gift. The nights were often as black as those you find at sea, the only illumination being islands of light fed by private generators. The sudden brightness of a flare was always so shocking and beautiful, like a one-rocket firework display, that you could do nothing but stare at it. The haze of the mauve phosphorescence would mark out the tail of the chopper and catch the line of the M-60 poking out of the side hatch before it would finally and thankfully splutter and fade.

In Jordan's capital, Amman, one of the largest shopping centres is called the Mecca Mall. It is a giant place on four floors. Gap, Benetton, Nike and RadioShack have concessions. McDonald's and Burger King feed the hungry. There is a cinema that shows the latest Hollywood films, though they are specially edited to remove even a glimpse of a naked breast.

In 2006 the Jordanians started calling it the 'Baghdad Mall' due to the number of Iraqi refugees who were by then spending their days staring at the goods it offered. They were easy to spot. It reminded me of how out of place the East Germans had looked when they first walked into West Berlin in 1989. The Iraqi clothes looked ill-fitting and unfashionable, the women over-made-up, the men's suits archaic compared to the Westernised and rich Jordanian mall-goers in their Reebok trainers and denim jeans.

By then more than one and a half million Iraqis had fled abroad since the start of the war, the vast majority to Syria and Jordan. In 2007 the number was to pass two million, maybe even three. Nobody knew for certain, though it was unquestionably one of the largest exoduses of refugees in the world.

Their Jordanian hosts had at first been generous, accepting the arrival of their Arab cousins and pleased to help them spend the life savings that they had brought with them. Their generosity waned after the bombing of the Golden Mosque caused the number crossing the border to turn into a flood. The number of coaches arriving in

Jordan rose to forty or fifty a day and the Jordanians questioned whether they could cope with such an influx.

The government started turning back Iraqi males under 35 who were travelling alone. Residency permits were often limited to 72 hours, with those caught exceeding them put on planes back to Baghdad. Rents rose and work was scarce for the new arrivals. After an Iraqi woman was found guilty of being a member of the group responsible for the bombing of three of Amman's most luxurious hotels, Iraqis started to be viewed not only as victims but also as potential threats to stability. It was why Iraqis went in such numbers to the Mecca Mall. With few jobs and increasingly hostile locals, it offered the best way – often the only way – to fill the day.

When I visited the mall in August 2006 I saw a group of Iraqi exiles at a table, taking their time over their coffees. There were three doctors and a university academic. This was not unusual. It was the middle classes who had the means and inclination to get out of Iraq, thereby depriving the country of the very people the Americans had expected to rebuild it.

Perhaps inevitably their conversation focused on what was happening back home. The academic had read that the head of Arabic Studies at Baghdad's Mustansiriyah University had been shot 32 times when his car was ambushed on the way to work. The president of Anbar University in Ramadi had apparently been bundled into the boot of his car as he stepped out of his home. The doctors had heard that in Mosul nine medical workers had been killed in a single day. Doctors and nurses had gone on strike to get the local authority to provide hospitals with enough armed guards.

The most vocal of the group was Omar, a paediatric doctor who, because he had trained in Hamburg, had managed to gain a six-month visa. He was convinced it was no accident that the best educated of the Iraqi people were often targeted by armed groups.

'They want to get rid of independent thinkers,' he said, his baggy brown leather jacket zipped up tight against the air conditioning. 'They want it so that the people no longer have the ability to disagree with their way of thought. They want no one left to challenge them intellectually so they can turn Iraq into a place where the level of thinking is that of the Middle Ages.'

I said nothing, listening to what he had to say. 'You do not believe me?' he exclaimed. 'Examine how many academics and teachers have been killed. The figures do not lie.'

I looked it up. Some 182 university professors had been killed since the war started, while another 85 were recorded as having been kidnapped or having survived assassination attempts. In the preceding four months, 331 school teachers had been murdered.

That was one refugee story. Dhia al-Safi told us another. Such stories were everywhere that year as the sectarian cleansing took hold. Dhia was 23 and had been a Shia who lived in a Sunni area where he worked in a nearby shop. One night there was a knock on his front door and four Sunni Arabs waiting outside. 'Why are you still here, Shia?' they demanded. 'All the rest of you people have gone. You have until morning.'

Dhia, his mother and four brothers did not flee abroad. They piled their most important possessions into their car, drove to the house of a friend who promised to protect them for the night, and then, as the sun rose, drove to north-west Baghdad where Dhia had heard the Sadrists were setting up refugee camps.

That was where Ahmed found him: in Iraq's refugee city at Shu'lah, a place that had not existed at the start of 2006 but which by May, when Dhia and his family arrived there, was home to a thousand people. There was no electricity or water supply. Dysentery was spreading. Storms had knocked down tents. Men and women stood around the few available oil stoves cooking meagre supplies of rice and beans.

'Damn the Sunnis,' Dhia said. 'We used to live like brothers. Now we are reduced to this – living like animals in the dirt. My family has lost everything: our home, our furniture, everything.'

There was a queue outside the Sadr office at the camp's entrance. Dhia joined the end of it. He had been told that the Mahdi Army was securing new homes for refugees, houses in Shia areas that had previously been lived in by Sunnis. He wanted to know if there might be one available for him and his family.

Would he not feel any guilt moving into a building whose owners had been forced out as he had from his home? He shrugged his shoulders. 'The Sunnis are dogs,' he said.

Due to the level of violence in Baghdad it was now not merely districts outside the capital that I could reach only by asking to spend time with a US unit but many neighbourhoods within it. Conditions in the city had deteriorated to the extent that the daily body counts had become predictable, at times barely newsworthy. I would discuss with my employers how many dead Iraqis were needed to get the latest outrage into the paper. Gradually the number of dead required to make it a story rose from 40 to 60, to 75, then to almost 100, and even that it could be a push unless their deaths had been particularly audacious or heart-wrenching.

In May 2006 I got permission to join American troops stationed in an old Iraqi defence ministry building on the edge of Adhamiya, a Sunni neighbourhood in the north of Baghdad. It was one of the smallest FOBs I had been to: fifty or so American troops cramped into the only wing of the building that had not been destroyed during the aerial bombardment that had heralded the start of the war. The soldiers slept on beds placed in former offices and the main conference room had been turned into a makeshift kitchen. The place smelt of sweat and dirty bodies.

I had wanted to stay with these soldiers because I had heard reports that sectarian tensions were particularly bad there. Adhamiya was close to the Shia stronghold of Sadr City so its edge marked one of the city's new battle lines. My intention was to discover if what I was being told about the number of people being killed was reflected in the experience of the soldiers.

The officer in charge of the unit, Lieutenant Colonel Paul Finken, invited me to the daily briefing at which he and his half-dozen officers stationed at the site catalogued the problems of the day. There was little standing on ceremony and the atmosphere was informal. Colonel Finken's subordinates sat in their chairs as he ran his fingers along a map on a wall, sketching out in situation reports the scale of the US military's failure.

'What's the Iraqi army doing?' he asked at one point. 'We informed them two weeks ago about that target and it still hasn't been acted upon.'

'Our understanding is that it's still going up the Iraqi chain of command,' came the response. 'It's caught in the beast, sir, and who knows when it will get out of there and to the men on the ground.'

Finken wanted to know why his officers had not bypassed official procedure and gone straight to a local company commander, Colonel Hussain, who had proved particularly efficient in combating the extremists. The reason was that Hussain had been sacked. The Iraqi general leading the division had deemed him a trouble maker after he complained to the Americans that another Iraqi officer was taking air conditioners from his men's outposts to put in his home.

'Great,' Finken said. 'That was the only unit in the whole division that I could rely on.'

There was a mutter of frustration from the American beside me. 'Sometimes I understand all that's happening here. Sometimes though I don't even understand how the Iraqis found Kuwait when they invaded it. This Iraqi army can barely find a mosque two streets away.'

In the car park outside a line of Humvees was waiting to ferry Colonel Finken to a liaison meeting with his counterparts in an FOB situated on the other side of Sadr City. The soldiers in them had been ready to go for an hour. They were used to that though. Everybody in the US military knew the principle of being told to hurry up and wait.

After the briefing finished I joined them while we waited for Finken to appear. In the third vehicle a Puerto Rican was at the wheel and a 21-year-old from Kentucky was checking the Humvee's machine gun.

'When I talk to my mother on the phone I'm honest,' the Puerto Rican told me. 'I tell her, "I don't want to be here".'

'Last night we were getting shot at and I turned to him' – he pointed at the soldier with the machine gun – 'and I was saying, "I am scared, I am scared". "No shit you're scared," he says. "There're bullets going over our heads. Get used to it." He's right. There's shooting everywhere at the moment. If it's not at us it's at each other. Crazy.'

'That's right,' the machine gunner shouted down. 'Sunni, Shia: they're all shooting at each other and as crazy as each other. How can a people hate each other so much? That's what happens when you allow people to marry their first cousins. Stupid Hajjis.'

He smirked. 'Sorry sir, forgot we're not allowed to call them Hajjis any more. Got an order on it from High Command back in December. Has to be Iraqi Nationals or Third World Nationals now. Good to know they're focusing on the big things up there.'

'What I don't get,' said a sergeant in the next vehicle, 'is why they're so drawn to Baghdad anyway that they fight so dirty over it. That is what we're tryin' to figure out. Place is a shithole.'

Street kids threw stones at us as we drove through Sadr City. We took a route along the neighbourhood's main avenue as the Americans had concluded that the Shia militias were less likely to put roadside bombs in the middle of their own haven.

The American camp by Sadr City was in another former government building that had been requisitioned by the US military. FOB Hope, it was called, and rarely had anywhere been more inappropriately named. Those based there were right on the fault line of the sectarian war, truly under the shadow, stuck by a canal at the point where the Shia in Sadr City met the Sunnis to the south and east. They had been told they were coming to Iraq to rebuild a country. Instead they found themselves reduced to the role of corpse collectors, seventeen having been found in a shallow grave the night before my visit.

Every soldier stationed there seemed to have his story about the sectarian violence. That evening they told me some of them:

There was a car comin' down the road, sir, and I'd a bad spider-sense about that car so we stopped it. They had blood all over their hands and blood all over their clothes. One was drenched in it. They claimed they were butchers, which I suppose was kind of true. We tested their hands with a spray we've got which tells you if they've been handlin' explosives or firin' any kind of weapon. Surprise, surprise, they had. Only time in my life I could've killed someone in cold blood.

We were on a routine visit to a police checkpoint and you could see from it a body lying on the street. His ankles were lying right there in the road. I said to them: 'Are you going to get on and move that body?' – and they shrugged and did nothing. I went over and lifted him up. He was face down and there were cuts all over his back and his kneecaps shot. As I turned him over I saw his face. There were holes all over it where they got at him with a drill. They had really gone to town on that one.

It was near the cigarette factory. We spotted people moving. Something weird was going on. We drove up real fast and there were civilians, around six of them. They all disappeared on foot but they left the civilian they had been dealing with. He was an older gentleman who delivered vegetables for a living. He'd been snatched from his vehicle. They had taken him from his truck. He was blindfolded and his hands were bound and they'd beaten him pretty badly. But he was still alive, which obviously was good.'

The problem is you've got eighteen-year-old soldiers who have not seen this before. They still think all is good in the world. They learn quickly here it isn't.

You can't understand them, sir. Don't try to. If you try and put logic to what they're doin' you'll find yourself going wrong. You are putting military labels to mass murder. It's not logical, not reasonable. Puttin' a gun against someone else's head and shootin' them, it's psychopathic. Call it what it is – psychopathic.

One captain, a studious-looking young man with metal-framed glasses and the closest of crew cuts, kept trying to catch my attention. His name was Troy Wayman and he said he had something he wanted to show me so we went to his cubicle. He picked an envelope off his desk and shook out a pile of cartridge shells. He pointed at the bottom of them and there was a blue paint mark on every one.

'That means that this is police-issue ammunition,' he said. 'There's a blue mark on every bullet given to the police and red on every bullet given to the Iraqi army. I've been collecting these from around the bodies I've been picking up. You understand what this means? It means it's the police doing this. The people we're supposed to have trained are behind it.'

Or it might indicate that the police were selling on their ammunition to supplement their meagre wages, I thought, or it was being stolen, or who knew what. In Iraq, the more you tried to search for explanations or proof the further away certainty became. It was nearly always the same, however desperate this soldier might have been to find his answers.

'I'd a good friend out here,' Wayman said. 'The night before he died we were playing computer games together. Here in this base. It's important that some day people feel proud of what he died for.'

In late summer I was back with the Americans in Adhamiya. The situation had altered. US troops were no longer willing to be mere corpse collectors but were seeking to seize the initiative. Soldiers were pouring into Baghdad in a desperate attempt to restore order. Leave was cancelled and soldiers brought in from elsewhere in the country. A unit that had already got as far as a military base in Alaska on its way back to the States was told to turn round and return to Iraq, its tour having suddenly been extended.

Talk of troop cuts and passing responsibility for security to the Iraqi authorities was forgotten. Where six months earlier the US had been handing over its smaller bases across the capital to the local Iraqi army division or police force, they were now taking them back.

The Americans had little choice. The situation in Baghdad had become really bad, a city of seven million people reduced to barbarism. The new Iraqi government had finally been sworn in but it pursued similar policies to those enacted the previous year. Nouri al-Maliki, a Shia politician who fled Iraq in 1980 after being sentenced to death by Saddam for his political activities, was appointed prime minister. He was a senior member of Da'wa, the religious party led by the post's previous holder, Ibrahim al-Jaafari, and so shared the same ideological and political beliefs as his predecessor. By August 2006 3,500 people were being killed across the country each month. Or rather that was the number known to have been killed, the real total could only be guessed at. The defence ministry issued instructions that Iraqis should not allow anyone from the Iraqi police or army into their homes at night unless they were accompanied by a US soldier in case they were agents of the sectarian killing. A thousand police officers were sacked for either aiding or failing to prevent the violence. Schools reported class sizes dwindling as parents became too frightened to let their children out of their sight. Militiamen brazenly stood at petrol stations demanding payment from anyone wanting to fill up their cars. Even when the Americans managed to kill the leader of al-Qa'eda in Iraq, Abu Musab al-Zarqawi, in an air strike in June it made no difference to the carnage. Iraq's al-Qa'eda branch simply appointed a new leader and continued its bombing campaign. By then the organisation was only playing a bit part in the violence anyway. It was the sectarian violence it had helped spawn that was destroying the American project in Iraq.

The US military faced defeat as conditions spiralled towards anarchy. A new operation, called 'Together Forward', was announced to re-establish order, resulting in the extra soldiers being sent to Baghdad. Tens of thousands of US and Iraqi troops were to fan out across the worst-affected areas of the capital. Their commanding officer, Peter Chiarelli, had no hesitation in making clear the operation's importance, despite the implicit acceptance in this of the failures that had gone before. It was time, he said, to 'take back Baghdad'.

In the city's most violent southern and western parts neighbourhoods were sealed off by blast walls and concertina wire. US and Iraqi troops set up controls to determine who could go in and out, and they conducted house-to-house searches within the cordons to look for weapons and extremist publications. Around 15,000 buildings were searched in Dora alone. Gardens were dug up, cushions pulled apart, and bags and boxes emptied and their contents painstakingly examined.

This radical shift in thinking that had led to the US troops being sent onto the streets in such numbers, a change that had been adopted in haste as the old expectations were torn up when Baghdad exploded, was based on what the Americans called the 'ink spot' theory. Instead of the tactics adopted in America's earlier Iraq operations, which emphasised the need to 'locate and kill' the enemy, the idea now was to provide security for specific areas to win the confidence of the people living there. Once mastered, these secure zones could then spread as an ink spot spreads when dropped into a bucket of water. It was a proper counter-insurgency proposal, even if it was being implemented three years too late.

The theory had been developed the previous year by an academic called Andrew Krepinevich, an expert on counter-insurgency in Vietnam who was heavily influenced by what the British had done to defeat the Communist insurgency in Malaysia. He had warned that the previous obsession with the number of insurgents killed had resulted in tactics which alienated the local population and destroyed homes and livelihoods. His approach was one that prioritised gaining people's support rather than terrifying them. It was what the British had originally tried to do in Iraq's south until the forces stationed there had realised they did not have enough troops to maintain law and order, let alone try to rebuild the region.

Adhamiya was one of the first areas the American troops went into as part of their new operation. Iraqi and US forces were stationed on main junctions. All but seven of the roads that led into it were closed off and their entrances manned with fortified checkpoints. Military–civil-relations teams supervised the removal of thirty thousand cubic metres of rubbish from its streets. Promises were being made of new electricity substations and medical clinics.

In September, the American officer responsible for Adhamiya, Colonel Thomas Vail, took me on a tour of the neighbourhood. He was clearly proud of what his men had achieved. 'See,' he said as he climbed out of his Humvee and stood at a road junction. 'We can walk around here freely now.'

The Sunnis who approached him, it has to be said, did appear delighted that at last someone had stopped the Shia militias from coming into their area at night and threatening them. They were chatting and waving like mad at the Americans, which was unexpected in a place that had been so hostile to the US invasion before the bombing of the Golden Mosque that it had gained the nickname 'Little Fallujah'.

Vail described to me the steps he was taking to safe-guard the local people and the planned rebuilding projects which would gain their trust. 'This is about deeds not just words,' he said. 'We have to deliver this time.'

He did not mention the other conclusions that Krepinevich had come to about what would be required if the United States was to succeed in Iraq: that it would need at least a ten-year commitment by US forces, billions of dollars, more troops to protect the secure zones and, in the short term, a jump in the number of American casual-ties. These conclusions were not being advertised much to the American public either.

Vail's men knew the real score, however, which was why many of them were among the most cynical about the new approach. They could only see in it an acceptance that they were to be in Iraq for years to come. While Vail strode around the streets shaking the hands of the locals and pledging new electricity and water supplies, many of his troops had the air of those who had already been there far too long. Which they had. The two Americans who talked most candidly to me on that visit, First Sergeant Hendrix and Sergeant Briskey, were both on their fourth tour. It was a lot of time to spend fighting a war that you were not winning.

'When I was here last time we were trying to make things good in this country and the Sunnis wouldn't let us and kept on attacking us and killed some of my good friends,' Hendrix said. 'Now the Sunnis are begging us for help from Shia death squads. Well tough luck. I couldn't really care what happens to them. It's their own damn fault.'

That summer the Americans failed yet again to deliver what they had promised. Adhamiya and the other areas cleared were specks in a city of 78 square miles and outside the cordons the killing continued. In fact, in some parts of Baghdad, the killing increased as the gunmen moved out of their sanctuaries ahead of the US operation and continued their bloody sport where it was still safe to do so.

The reason for their failure was that, even with the additional troops made available, the American military did not have enough men to police a project like Operation Together Forward on a city-wide scale. They tried to increase the size of their secure areas but the perimeters did not hold. The militias began passing through and the US troops were too busy searching houses to monitor the behaviour of the Iraqi security forces who were supposed to be preserving security behind them. By the end of the second month of the American operation its commanders were forced to admit the most it had achieved was a 'slight downtick' in the mortality rate. By the end of the year that downtick was back up and rising.

Fresh solutions were sought. Partition, the likelihood of a military coup and military withdrawal were the ideas being bandied around at that time. All seemed a nightmare to me, likely only to herald fresh horrors. Partition would result in tens of thousands of people having to move from their homes, and in Baghdad – where even after the sectarian cleansing of recent months many areas still remained mixed – it was going to be very bloody, much worse than Beirut in the 1970s. The Iraqi army hardly looked like a body committed to democracy and public welfare. And if there was a US withdrawal who was going to fill the gap? It would probably be either the driller killers of the Shia religious militias or the Sunni insurgent groups who had been radicalised by the violence and anarchy into believing ever more extreme doctrines of Islamic fundamentalism. There was no option available that did not seem to guarantee mass bloodshed.

Yet the Americans did not withdraw and nor did they allow partition or a military coup. Britain and almost everyone else might have been getting out of Iraq as fast as they could but the Americans did not give up the fight or adopt some form of softly-softly approach. Instead they ratcheted up the stakes even further. By 2007 the US was pouring troops into Baghdad, taking soldiers from reserve units based across the world. The 'surge', they called it. This was intended to do properly what had failed to be achieved the previous summer and make sure there were enough feet on the ground this time to put the Americans ink spots into effect.

I have read conflicting reports about what these extra men have achieved and only time will make clear the extent of its success. I am no longer in Iraq so I cannot say with any certainty if the 'surge' is working or not. Many commentators cite Vietnam-style hubris as responsible for the move to increase troop numbers, recalling how in that conflict America kept throwing in more men without achieving anything but more pain. The drop in killings reported may simply be because the sectarian cleansing has been so successful there simply are not that many people living close by to murder any more. Or it may merely be because the Iraqis have become tired of the killing and needed time to regroup. Moreover any drop is relative. There are still hundreds of people a month being killed in Baghdad.

When I first learned that the Americans were planning to commit more troops to Iraq, however, I was exultant.

No one else was going to try to stop that slaughter, nor had such a responsibility to do so. The American soldiers on the ground were not going to like it but maybe, just maybe, a little more time would somehow produce a miracle or take the edge off some of the hatred. Back in London, I would watch in slack-jawed bewilderment when I saw pundits on TV pontificate about how the 'surge' was a mistake and that it was time to stop the war by bringing the troops home. By that point no one had the power to stop what was happening in Iraq. If the Americans had packed up and pulled out at that moment Iraq would, I believe, have experienced sectarian bloodletting that not only involved Kalashnikovs and night-time intimidation but helicopters, artillery, overt intervention from all the vested parties that border that country, and dozens of Srebrenicas.

13. Revelation

I once saw an article on the publication of government papers that detailed what was expected to happen to 1950s Britain in the event of a nuclear war. Four days, the authorities had given it, before social cohesion broke down and savagery ruled. It had taken longer, and it had been a different kind of holocaust, but Iraq had descended to a similar level. It was no wonder so many Iraqis believed the end of the world was coming.

This was a time of endings. Lives and individual stories were being brought to a close. Though the violence and suffering continued and the Americans had yet to announce plans for their 'surge', the final months of 2006 marked their own conclusion. The war was never going to come out as those who started it had believed. Nor was life ever going to go back to how it was under Saddam, let alone the way it had been in the time before him, despite many Iraqis wishing that it could do so. It was what Baghdad had become by the final part of that year, what it had descended into and what its people had proved able to do to each other, that would now mould its future.

Iraqis did not know where they would be able to live, for how long, doing what, with whom and under what kind of rule. Hospitals did not work. Shops shut shortly after midday to limit the risk to their owners. Unemployment was at 50 per cent. Inflation had reached triple figures. There was still almost no electricity. Diesel prices had tripled so that even those with generators could often no longer afford to run them. Tap water was polluted. The mobile phone network went down every few minutes. Phone lines were being stolen and sold for scrap.

Workers in a business down the street from my hotel were abducted en masse. Thieves attacked a bank in a road nearby, leaving a trail of bodies. A reporter from a British Sunday newspaper had to be flown out after a plot was uncovered to kill her because of a story she had written about Sunni extremist groups.

The Iraqi translator for the *Chicago Tribune*, a really good guy, one of the nicest you could ever meet, was due to be married. He was driving to his own wedding, with his sister in the front seat beside him, when a stray bullet came through the window. His sister's brains ended up on the present she had been holding on her lap to give to him after the ceremony.

I began to lose touch with people. Contacts would disappear and I would have no idea if they had fled abroad or were dead. We tried to track down Haidar, my translator in Basra. No one knew where he and his new wife had gone. It was said that informers in the city had started identifying the translators working for Western firms so that they could be killed as collaborators. Haidar had apparently fled Basra because it was too dangerous for him to stay.

My hotel complex had become its own fortress. The blast walls in places stood two deep, watchtowers had been built at the entrances and additional rows of ramps and bollards put down to slow any approaching cars in case they carried suicide bombers. Within the complex additional barriers and gates were put up so that if one part of it was breached a defence could be manned to stop the entire area being overrun.

Never, in my time there, had as little been known about what was going on in Baghdad. There were only about a dozen newspaper reporters left at the Hamra where once you could barely find a room, it was so busy. All were too exhausted to socialise, other than around a bottle. Conversation focused on how much longer people thought they could stand it. Insomnia was rampant. Often I would not go out of the hotel for two or three days at a time and then only briefly. It used to be the twenty-minute rule guiding how long to spend in one place. Now after five minutes I was jumpy. Increasingly I did as many interviews as I could via the telephone, though that was only possible during the periods when the phone system was actually working.

Those journalists still in the Hamra complex were nearly all from the States. There were only two Britons, myself and a woman who worked for the *Chicago Tribune* called Liz Sly. She was a reporter who had seen almost every conflict since Beirut in the 1970s and as a result seemed remarkably unfazed by what had happened to Baghdad. She knew this was what happened when wars went wrong. *The Times* was still there, its bureau manned by an American, Ned Parker, but the *Guardian*, the *Independent* and the *Financial Times* were gone except for the occasional visit. I tried to extend the breaks I was allowed away from Iraq and sought to limit my stays in Baghdad to the minimum possible.

Unexpectedly, it was events outside Iraq that determined what happened to me next. There had been changes at the *Telegraph*, which, located where I was, I had not been following with suitable attention. New owners had taken over and new ownership inevitably meant new people. These new people brought new attitudes and policies. Not all of these were bad but the change they brought to the paper's foreign desk was unwelcome news for me, Ahmed, Abu Omar, Marwan and Sajad.

I knew it was going to be a problem from the moment I received the phone call which broke the news. The erudite and experienced journalist who had been my boss was sacked and in his place was installed one of the neo-conservative cheerleaders who had so applauded the rush to war. He wrote a biography of Saddam Hussein in which he explained why he knew weapons of mass destruction would be discovered and described allegations that supposedly linked Saddam Hussein to the events of 11 September 2001 that had subsequently been discredited. He had not been to Iraq since the situation began to deteriorate as the Americans lost control and so had not seen what it had become. This put me in a very difficult situation. It was impossible to provide articles about the Iraq he wanted because it did not exist.

Stories I filed began to be changed back in London to provide conclusions different from those I had come to. He sat on the end of the phone dictating to me how he wanted a story celebrating the American achievements in Iraq to read. There was pressure to find stories implicating Iran's involvement in the conflict, though no evidence existed that was as clear as the conclusions he seemed to require. One time I used the word 'war' in the introductory paragraph of an article. I was told that the war in Iraq had been declared over soon after Baghdad was liberated and that the word had to be cut from the piece.

There comes a time when you have to accept that you are out of step, that an organisation that you thought you knew now marches to a different tune. So it was with me then. You could not witness what I had in Baghdad and comfortably switch agendas. It would have been a betrayal so at the end of November 2006 I resigned.

The changes at the *Daily Telegraph* were not the only reason I stopped working in Iraq, however, as there was another, more personal, reason. There is only so long that anyone can be exposed to the extremes of what we can do to each other without starting to question what it is to be human. There was no good answer to that question in Iraq and I could no longer face that every day. Moreover by that time I had someone waiting for me back in Britain who provided a much better answer to the challenge of what humans can be. My relationship with the girl I had met in London had deepened during my visits away from Baghdad and become serious. Iraq may not have had a future but I did. This was why I knew that I was lucky. It was also why it was time to leave before that luck ran out.

It was a phone call that made this clear and my decision final. It was the moment when I perhaps learnt more about the true meaning of brutality than I ever did through seeing ruined buildings or scorched bodies for this time the people I cared about were at the receiving end.

It was September and we were in our office in the former Australian embassy building trying to set up inter-views for the coming weeks. Although the overwhelming heat had abated, the weather was still hot and we were reliant on the fan in the corner to keep the air moving. It was a pleasant office and it had become our new haven. There was a Gustav Klimt poster on the wall that had been left by an Australian official and a hubbly-bubbly pipe that my Iraqi staff enjoyed puffing on. A stove in the next-door room enabled us all to be fuelled by a diet of sweet black tea.

My team and I had been together a long time by then. We had developed total trust in each other, it was the only way that you could go out onto Baghdad's streets and not doubt that you would come back. If my security guard, Marwan, told us he considered a road dangerous we turned back without question. If we were in an interview and Ahmed had a feeling that the atmosphere was souring we left immediately. Each day we had spent in Baghdad we had trusted our safety in our behaviour and actions. Together we had drilled and trained, watched events unfold and done what we could to record it. We were proud of our work, and proud that we had done it together.

That day in September Ahmed's mobile phone rang. He picked it up, started talking and I could see immediately that something was very wrong. He was told his brother-in-law, the brother of his wife who was also married to one of Ahmed and Marwan's sisters, had been kidnapped. He had been taken from his car in broad daylight in an area being cleansed by Shia. He had apparently been surrounded by gunmen, who identified him as a Sunni, and took him as their captive.

The two families had always been close. Ahmed and his siblings had played with his wife and her brothers and sisters while growing up and they had courted as adults. It was not unusual for Iraqi families to be so intertwined, but it was a custom that magnified the pain when something awful happened.

We all knew immediately that it was a situation that normally ended with the victim joining the corpses found around Baghdad each morning. What none of us had anticipated was the taunting. The kidnappers had found Ahmed's name in the contact book on their victim's mobile phone and decided to have some fun. It had been one of the militiamen who had just phoned Ahmed, it was his brother-in-law's kidnapper to whom he had been speaking.

'Hello my friend,' the voice at the end of the line had said. 'It is so good to speak to you.'

'Who is this?' Ahmed asked. 'What is going on?'

They explained what they had done but told him not to worry. 'He is fine. He is happy. In fact he often tells us how good you are, that your family are all good people. How he misses his family. How he wishes to see you one more time. But do not worry, you will be able to see him again. You will be able to hold him in your arms.'

Then there was a pause. 'You will be able to hold him in your arms when you collect his body from the morgue.'

That went on a lot during the coming days. The militiamen would tell Ahmed that he need not be concerned as of course his dear relation would be able to see his family again, or he would have been able to if they had not just gouged out his eyes.

During the following weeks Ahmed and Marwan did what they could to find their relation. They paid money to tribal leaders who said it could speed up his return. They searched rubbish dumps for his body. They made visits to the morgue. They even hired a fortune teller to see if she could tell them if he was dead or alive.

'You see what we have been reduced to?' Ahmed said. 'Superstitious, ignorant fools.'

Ahmed's wife had a partial breakdown. She spent much of her time in her room crying, struggling to care for her new baby. The abducted man's parents spent their waking hours in near-constant prayer. Neither Ahmed nor Marwan seemed to sleep. At night they would be awake, they said, dwelling on what their relation might be suffering, if his fingers were being dipped in battery acid like others we had heard about, sometimes hoping that he was dead and then rebuking themselves for thinking such a thing.

During all this, pressure was on us from London to find positive stories about what was happening in Iraq.

Then Ahmed broke. A close friend of his was killed by masked men and that was enough for him. 'I cannot take this any more,' he said. 'I cannot take any more bad news and damn surprises. I cannot stay any more in my city. I feel totally isolated from the present and that all the years of my life have been stuck behind me and left behind. My childhood memories, my friends and the good times are like ghosts. Why is all this happening to me and to Iraqis? Why is this happening in my country? What was our fault? When can my real life begin?'

He never found his brother-in-law's corpse. The *Telegraph* closed the Baghdad office following my departure. This was partly a result of the deteriorating security situation and also because the paper had adopted a new business model which involved cutting back on its investment in foreign news to focus on expanding its offerings on the internet. Out of work and with their home city ruined, Ahmed, Marwan and their families abandoned their search and, a week after it was announced the bureau would shut, fled to Syria as refugees. Their relation was almost certainly dead by then anyway, his corpse presumably having joined the bodies plugging the city's sewage system or rotting in the Tigris.

Abu Omar, my driver, hid himself in a district of Baghdad where almost everyone was Sunni like he was. He began to work part time as a driver for the oil company that employed his sister, Asmaa, and this ensured he could still pay the bills. As for Sajad, the driver of our second car, he did not have many choices because he had so many dependants. He went back to being a taxi driver and from dawn to dusk drove the streets of Baghdad looking for customers. He had two IDs, one identifying him as Shia and the other as Sunni, and trusted he would get it right when stopped at a checkpoint. The last I heard he had judged it correctly so far.

On my final day in Baghdad my team drove me to the airport early in the morning. I had spent the previous evening saying my last goodbyes. It had not taken long, so few reporters were left. Most of what I had I threw away or passed on to my Iraqi team. In the end everything I took with me fitted into two bags, my own physical reminders of a seminal event in my life.

The sun was only just up when we left the Hamra complex for the last time. It was one of those soft Iraqi days when enough sand was being blown up into the air to give the sunlight a dirty glow. There were few people on the road. By then Iraqis had to queue for five hours for a tank of petrol and so everyone was conserving fuel for important journeys. Pedestrians mostly avoided going out until later when, it was calculated, there would be enough people around to avoid becoming too distinctive a target.

Unusually, we sped through the streets. Few shops were open and the throng on the pavements was notable by its absence. One old man was out, setting up a vegetable stall at a road junction. He had a box of cabbages and another of tomatoes already on display and he was staring at them with pride. I saw a couple of stray dogs, a cart being pulled down a side road, a truck or two, a dozen cars, but otherwise nothing. There was little noise and less movement, a city without a pulse.

As we drove over the Tigris, two American Apache helicopters swung low over the water, beautiful in the elegance of their technology, like science fiction apparitions from an unimaginable world. They flew up above us, the noise momentarily deafening, and then disappeared into the yellow gloom.

At the airport it was bedlam. A tumultuous mass of people were seeking salvation. Baghdad airport was never an easy place to get out of with its security checks and archaic technology but on this occasion it was worse than I had ever seen it before. There was not even time to properly say my goodbyes because the throng pushed around me and the cars lining up at the checkpoint pressed for those ahead to move on. All there could be was a shake of hands as I grabbed my bags, a quick promise to never forget what we had done together, an inadequate expression of thanks to the people who had kept me alive, and then I was jostled forward by the crowd, on through the checkpoint, while they, my Iraqi friends and colleagues, began their drive along those empty streets back into their city.

There must have been at least five hundred people already at the airport, maybe twice that by lunchtime and another thousand by mid-afternoon when I finally flew out. All had only one thought: escape. They were lined up outside the terminal building trying to get onto one of the few commercial airliners still willing to fly into Baghdad. There were whole families with their most precious belongings packed into multi-coloured bags. Children ran through the crowd as the adults argued with the guards at the terminal's security gates to let them in. Black 4x4s pulled up with their tinted windows to release contingents of Western, shaven-headed military security guards who were intent on getting home. They pushed their way through the masses, ignoring the cries of outrage as they forced their way to the front, airport security stepping aside to let them pass with a half-smile and a nod.

I had suspected what it was going to be like and had with me fistfuls of dollars, at least seven hundred dollars-worth, to ease my progress. It still took me almost six hours, forcing notes into the hands of any who could help me, and being as ruthless and selfish as everyone else in holding my position in the queue. In the end I latched onto a youth who said he knew of a spare ticket to Istanbul, which coincidentally was a good place for me to be heading at that point. He led me through a side entrance and we passed security guards who waved me on. At the check-in desk I pushed over my pile of remaining dollars, everything I had, took the ticket and ran to the coach that ferried passengers to the plane.

There was not one spare seat on the flight. An Iraqi woman seated beside me was praying. When we took off she cried with relief. I was sitting by the window and looked down. The runway fell away and slowly the American military vehicles that surrounded it disappeared. The barracks merged into each other and the city began to spread out around them. There was the expanse of ordered streets with their rows of houses. There were the imperial buildings of the Green Zone with their Ba'athist desire for dominance. There were the mosques, office blocks and highways, all of them the landmarks for a host of interrupted lives. The curve of the Tigris opened up before me, the river snaking its way across that land as it had done for centuries before the Americans came and would for centuries after they left. There was a fishing boat, the wake falling behind it as it pushed itself out beyond the edges of the city. It was going with the tide and even from that distance I could see it was making good progress, heading south to cast the nets that it was hoped would come up filled with fish to take home to sell. That would be a successful day. One worth living. Then we banked again, up into the cloud cover, and it all disappeared from sight.

Epilogue

It was a year before I returned to the Middle East. The intervening period had been spent getting my life back on track. I bought a house in east London. Boxes that had spent years in storage were retrieved and unpacked. My girlfriend moved in and we started decorating. Walls were painted, cupboards built and floors laid. The house became a home. Roots were being put down at last.

I stayed in regular contact with Ahmed. He was having a difficult time coming to terms with life as a refugee in Damascus. His wife was still in a bad way, unable to accept what had happened to her brother and the demise of the life she had grown up with in Iraq. Their daughter became ill and had to have an operation, a treatment that used up a significant chunk of their savings.

The Syrian government, mindful that it already had a significant unemployment problem and therefore keen to dissuade Iraqis from seeking sanctuary within its borders, made it hard for refugees to find work. Companies were encouraged to hire a Syrian over an Iraqi with the same skills. As a result Ahmed was only earning £150 a month as a functionary at a translation agency. It was not enough even to pay the rent on the apartment he had found. After Christmas I became really worried about him. His normal good nature seemed engulfed by pessimism and he began to talk as if it would have been better to have died in Baghdad than to live like a beggar outside his homeland.

In the spring of 2007, however, he came up with a plan that he put into effect with his old gusto. He had originally dreamed of moving to London but discovered that Britain was doing little to help Iraq's refugees, even those with links to British companies. Then he contacted PEN International, a charity established to defend freedom of expression which was one of the few organisations working at the time to provide assistance to Iraq's journalists and translators, and it informed him of a US programme which allowed endangered media workers to settle in America. As PEN guided him through the application process, Ahmed put his networking skills into effect, queuing for hours outside the US embassy in Damascus, knocking on doors and bombarding those responsible for the programme with e-mails. American reporters whom he had met in the Middle East but who were now back in the States were browbeaten into applying pressure at their end. I organised a sponsored event in London to raise money for his family so that they could afford to stay in Syria while their application was processed. Everyone I approached, pleased to be able to help at least one family caught up in the mess of Iraq, was notably generous.

Summer 2007 turned into autumn and Ahmed still did not know if his application was going to be approved. There were interviews, background checks, medical examinations, and then a long period during which he heard nothing.

'The Americans are very useless as we know from Iraq,' he wrote to me, 'so I am not very worried by how long it is taking for them to give me an answer. I am glad, in fact, about the delay. Until we know their decision there is a chance for happiness, a chance for my children to have lives that will not have the sorrow of my own. If we know that they say "no" then that chance has gone. Then what will we have to live for?'

In December 2007 I flew to Damascus for a visit. He met me at the airport and I was surprised by how emotional I was to see him. I had been able to forget those years in Iraq but during the intervening months my life had moved on. I was focusing on the future and embracing normality. Seeing Ahmed was a reminder of my time in Baghdad.

On my second day in Damascus we drove to his apartment in the city's Harasta district. It was a run-down area where a constant trickle of water flowed down the street outside his front door. There were no lights on his building's communal landings, and once inside his flat there was a strong smell of damp. On the walls of the main room Ahmed had put up colourful posters of Thailand. He liked them, he said, as the landscapes were very green and therefore pleasant to a person from a desert country like himself. The main reason they were there, however, was to cover the mould growing through the paintwork.

Ahmed was the first to admit that he was not doing as badly as many of the Iraqis in Damascus. On my first night in Syria we had gone to Jaramana, the district where Iraq's Sunni and Christian refugees had primarily congregated. The Shia had mostly gone to a different area, Sayyida Zaynab, the sectarian division having remained even among those in exile.

Jaramana was eerily reminiscent of Baghdad with the people wearing the same clothes, the roads lined by the same style of apartment blocks and the shops selling the same food, their owners knowing what would appeal to their new Iraqi clientele. It lacked Baghdad's war damage but it was nevertheless still clearly poor. Many of the thousands of Iraqis living there were dependent on money sent from relatives who had succeeded in escaping to the West and that left little to spend on fripperies. Rubbish had accumulated by the kerbside and the overhead electrical wires were frayed. When there was a surge in the power supply they crackled and emitted a stream of sparks. I met some of Ahmed's friends, fellow members of the new Iraqi diaspora, and as we sat drinking coffee the conversation focused on how it might be possible for them to start afresh. They spoke of people-smugglers who could get them to Australia in the back of containers, or an aid programme that allowed Iraqi Christians to settle in France if they could prove they were Roman Catholics rather than Coptic Christians. Each scheme was outlined and its chance of success carefully weighed.

Some of those I met that evening were considering going back to Baghdad as the latest news implied that the situation there had improved, that the nadir might have been reached. Economic growth was reported and the value of the Iraqi dinar was rising on the back of the high price of oil. The Americans were saying that areas of Baghdad and central Iraq previously classed as 'lost' had been wrested back from the extremists. The daily death rate was falling and the worst of the sectarian cleansing appeared over. As a result morale had also apparently improved among US troops.

It was a turnaround primarily achieved by the American 'surge', though it was not the only reason. Moqtada al-Sadr announced a ceasefire in August, which had stopped his Mahdi Army's sectarian killings, and a new phenomenon had emerged called the 'Sunni Awakening'. Sunni tribes had formed an alliance to stop al-Qa'eda and the other extremist Sunni groups from enforcing Islamic fundamentalism on their homeland. It had begun in Anbar, the former insurgent stronghold province in Sunni western Iraq, and then spread to Baghdad. Al-Qa'eda and its supporters were now primarily limited to Diyala province, where most of the fighting in Iraq was now focused. On witnessing the Sunni fighters' achievements, the American military offered them help. It was accepted and the US armed them, providing the weaponry needed if they were to continue taking on and beating the religious fanatics. Consequently, Iraq's Sunnis had been able to not only fight their own extremists but also resist the Shia militias. Parity had been reached and with it came a form of stability.

The fighters of the Sunni Awakening were mostly the very same Sunni militants who had fought so determinedly against the foreign invaders during the first years of the war. Many were tacit supporters of Saddam. Mutual self-interest now allied them to America. Once again in Iraq your enemy's enemy had proved to be your unlikely friend.

Ahmed introduced me to a former army captain from Baghdad who had fled Iraq after his son was killed. He had recently revisited his native city. He said there was still little electricity or other basic services and described how the city remained shut at night because most people continued to be too scared to go outside after dark. During the day, he said, the worst of the random slaughter seemed to have abated. People were not being dragged from their cars and killed in such numbers although it was still wise not to travel too far from areas dominated by your sectarian brothers.

'How safe is Baghdad now?' I asked him. 'Maybe 30 per cent,' he answered. Would he go back? 'Not if I do not have to. It is a tense calm. We do not know what it is that will happen. In Iraq there is still so much mistrust. To regain confidence will take a long time.'

The latest official figures showed that more than six hundred people were killed in Baghdad during November and, in Diyala province, families were still being forced from their homes. America's arming of the Awakening may have meant that the Sunnis could hold their own with the Shia militias and al-Qa'eda extremists but it also ensured that the Sunni fighters were now as strong as other groups in the country, there being no pretence that the US-supplied weapons were ever going to be handed back. Around 69,000 Sunnis had been trained and armed by America and no one knew what this force would do next. Iraq's prime minister, Nouri al-Maliki, was refusing to allow it to be amalgamated into the army, seemingly worried about what this might do to his Shia-dominated force. Moreover the Mahdi Army, though quiet, remained at large and SCIRI's Badr Brigade continued to dominate the upper ranks of the police force. The Shia were still pre-eminent in the south, as the Sunni were in the west and the Kurds in the north. All three groups had the weaponry and experience to fight each other if conditions deteriorated again. The future of Iraq remained uncertain.

During my time in Baghdad I had never been able to spend time with Ahmed's family at his home. Dora, the neighbourhood in which he had lived, was always among the most dangerous in the city. Neither he nor I wanted to endanger his family by organising a visit in case I was spotted and his association with foreigners consequently known. However, I had heard many things about his family and felt part of the drama that had surrounded his wife's pregnancy, their struggle for survival, and the grief that had come when those they loved had become Iraq's victims. Now we could finally meet, talk, share a joke and enjoy a meal. Such things are so easily taken for granted but, as I realised that day, they are very precious.

Ahmed's six-year-old daughter, Labibah, and son, Mohammad, were dressed in their smartest clothes, her hair held in bunches by two clips in the shape of orange ladybirds and he in a brown corduroy waistcoat. They were standing by the door when I walked in and had been told to hold out their hands so I could shake them. Ahmed's wife, Raha, stood behind her children. She was not what I had expected. In the photographs I had seen she was always dressed in a headscarf, but now she was bare-headed, her brown hair with blonde highlights held back in a bun, and dressed in a bright pink tracksuit. She wore pale lipstick and her eyes were heavily made up with eye-liner. Gold-plated earrings decorated her face. Attractive, vivacious and smiling, she was the antithesis of the stern black-clad Islamic figures that too often dominate the West's popular image of the Arab Muslim woman.

She had worked hard to prepare the meal. The dishes were so numerous that they covered the fold-up table erected in the main room. There were starters of marinated apricots and dips. Chicken and rice was the main course, supplemented by salads and a selection of breads and sauces. There were a considerable number of us present for lunch: not only Ahmed and his wife, their daughter and toddler son, but also the wife of his brother Marwan, my former security guard, and their four children, as well as the new wife of their oldest son, Othman. Marwan himself was not present, having gone on a fact-finding trip to Baghdad to see for himself what conditions were like.

While we ate the conversation first dwelt on news of what had happened to those we had known in Iraq: those who had died, those who had survived, and those who had fled abroad. Iyad Allawi, the Iraqi politician who had told me before the second national elections back in December 2005 that he would have to relocate abroad if the Shia religious parties again won at the ballot box, had proved true to his word. He apparently now lived mostly in London and Dubai, returning to Iraq when urgent business required his presence. Haider, the translator who had worked for me in Basra, had been seen in Damascus. He was apparently well, if impoverished, and his wife was pregnant with their first child.

I heard for the first time what happened in the days after I left Baghdad and how Ahmed and Marwan's families had all managed to escape alive. It had been a closer-run thing than I had previously realised. The day before they were to leave, Marwan's oldest son, Othman, had been kidnapped by Shia militiamen. He was seen being pushed into a car and driven away. Ahmed had known the Mahdi Army commander in the area where Othman had been abducted. By coincidence, he had been in the same class as him at school, a time when they were friends. Ahmed went to his former schoolmate's house and pleaded for mercy. It had been granted. Othman was released, his face battered and his body bruised, but alive.

Othman sat across the table from me while we ate our meal in Damascus. There was no outward sign of what he had experienced. He looked like most other young Arab men of his age: his hair cut fashionably short and dressed in a blue fitted T-shirt and loose jeans. I asked if he dwelled on what had happened. He still thought about it every day, he said, and at night woke from nightmares in which he was still being held captive.

The day after Othman's release both families had driven to the border. 'For three hours I could not utter any word,' Ahmed said. 'I felt completely isolated from the world. Everything I had known I was leaving behind. I had no idea what to do when we arrived, just that I had to get out of my country quick.'

There was a pause in the conversation as they all remembered that time, Ahmed thumbing the prayer beads he held in his right hand. Then those memories were put aside and happier moments brought to mind. This was not a day for regrets, it was a day of celebration.

Two days earlier the American embassy had been in touch with the news that Ahmed and his family's lives were going to be taking a new direction once again. The application for resettlement in the US had been approved. In a week they would be on a plane flying across the world to their new home in Atlanta. It was a phenomenal thing: a decision that would change their lives forever, and its impact – the hope it brought – had already begun to cast its spell.

Ahmed and his wife had a seemingly endless list of questions about what life would be like in the States. As I answered I tried to imagine how they would find America. Lives previously lived in Iraq, and then for the last year as refugees in Damascus, an Arab city not that dissimilar to Baghdad, were now to be transported to the US with its shopping malls, commercialism and secular schools. Ultimately it would be a life of commuting along the freeway for Ahmed, navigating the aisles of Wal-Mart for Raha, and high school and prom nights for their children. I tried to imagine it and failed. I could not possibly conceive what it would be like for them or how they would react to it.

Nor, as they made clear, could they. They did not care, however, because for the first time since civil war had come to Baghdad they had something that they had previously feared might be lost forever. They had a future.

They were nevertheless well aware of the irony of their situation. The country that had destroyed their previous lives was the one now offering them sanctuary. Ahmed joked that he would now become as 'useless' as the US administrators who had tried to reinvent Iraq. Raha was nervous that there might be anti-Iraqi feeling in Atlanta due to the fact that her countrymen were killing American soldiers. I assured her that it was far more likely that most people they came across would feel guilt at what had happened to them and their country. I hoped that my prediction would prove to be true.

It was a wonderful afternoon. Ahmed's daughter, Labibah, insisted on proudly demonstrating how she could already count to ten in English. His son, Mohammad, took control of the camera and consequently we ended up with lots of pictures of our feet. Photographs were produced showing the day of Othman's wedding, which had been held shortly after they arrived in Damascus. I was shocked to see how tired and beaten Ahmed and his wife looked. At the time, Ahmed pointed out, they had not known how they could afford to survive in Damascus and were terrified of the consequences of what moving back to Baghdad would entail. 'That period is over now,' he said.

When it was time to leave, his family formed a line to say their farewells. Each wished me good fortune in the future. Then Ahmed drove me back to my hotel. I felt emotional again as I said goodbye to that figure in his brown stripy shirt and oversized blue jeans who was off to start his new adventure, not knowing what he faced, only what he had already endured.

'We had interesting times, eh,' he said, holding both my hands in his, 'but we are alive and our families live. It is a stupid crazy world but what can you do about it? Go in peace, my friend. Stay safe.'

He climbed back in the car, a battered yellow Ford Fiesta, and then wound down the window and leaned out.

'I always say that at least some good things came out of all that badness and one was that we became friends. We showed that you do not have to be so bad, stupid crazy fucking world, that there is some goodness in it. Come and see me in America. Come and see what it is that I become. Let us hope we live for a long time and be happy.'

The next morning I arrived back at Heathrow and took the Piccadilly line across London. It was Sunday and the journey was a quiet one, the people in my carriage hidden behind their newspapers, many of whose front pages were dominated by news of the celebrity romance of a couple who had met on a reality TV programme staged in the Australian jungle.

I walked across the park to get from the tube stop to my house. It was a beautiful December day, the sky a pale wintry blue. Leaves had fallen from the trees and gathered in clumps by the side of paths. I stopped for a while and sat on a bench watching families enjoying the crisp air. Two young men were practising their golf swing by the edge of a municipal football pitch, trying to see who could chip the ball against a tree thirty yards away. A squirrel tentatively made its way forward and looked at me quizzically, hoping for food.

My house was near the park's northern entrance. I put the key in the door, opened it and shouted a 'hello', searching for my girlfriend, Kate. She was in our spare room. I knew that while I was in Syria she had been planning to cut pictures from children's books to make a multi-coloured frieze on one of its walls. I walked upstairs to see how she had got on. She was sitting on a white leather sofa that I had once picked up in a yard sale for $10 when living in Los Angeles. I knew she hated the ugliness of that sofa. She was using it now though, scissors and paper in her hands as she tried to make the room as cosy and as special as possible, the baby bump showing underneath her black wraparound dress.

Kate looked up as I walked in. 'Can you help me put the cot together? The instructions are in the box. And your mum rang. We're going to go there for dinner a week on Saturday. We should probably take our presents over so we'd better hurry up doing our Christmas shopping.'

Then she laughed. 'Welcome home,' she said.

Postscript

At present there are two sources most commonly cited for estimates of the number of Iraqis who have died in the war. The most often used is the Iraq Body Count, an international non-governmental body which notes every mention of Iraqi civilian deaths in the English-language press, including any Arab media that has been translated into English. Iraqi soldiers, suicide bombers, those termed insurgents, or anyone else killed while engaged in what is commonly regarded as war-related activity, are excluded from the count. A running total is then displayed on its website.

Its organisers, mostly academics in Britain and the US, are the first to acknowledge the weakness of this methodology. 'It is likely,' they admit, 'that many, if not most, civilian casualties will go unreported by the media. That is the sad nature of war.'

This is unquestionably true. Areas that are least under US or Iraqi government control, such as Anbar province, are often the places where most people are being killed and where the world is least likely to hear about it. Baghdad morgue is the only one in Iraq that has released figures for the number of victims of violent death that it receives.

Despite this fundamental flaw the Iraq Body Count's strength as a source is that every one of the deaths it records is a documented one. It is not an extrapolation or conclusion from a statistical model. Compared to other studies, the number of civilian dead it cites is therefore the least likely to have been inflated even if, as a result, it probably provides a minimum figure.

The count's findings are nevertheless depressing. It reported 12,000 civilians were killed in 2003, two-thirds of them in the invasion of Iraq itself. In 2004, 10,500 died, a number which rose to 14,000 in 2005 and 26,000 in 2006. According to Iraq Body Count by the end of 2007 the total number of Iraqi civilians killed since the war began was between 80,129 and 87,279.

The second, and far more controversial, source popularly used is the survey published in the medical journal, *The Lancet*, in October 2006. Unlike the methodology of the Iraq Body Count, which is a passive study dependent on the reporting of casualties, its authors sought to estimate the number of total deaths caused by the war. This included not only those killed due to the fighting but also due to the lawlessness, declining healthcare and lack of basic services that came with it.

The survey was sponsored by a number of reputable bodies, including the Centre for International Emergency Disaster and Refugee Studies, and used a team, led by Les Roberts, experienced in estimating death tolls in war zones. Its previous findings on the Democratic Republic of the Congo, where it concluded 1.7 million people had died, have been used as evidence by the United Nations Security Council and the US State Department.

The survey adopted the same methodology as it had in the Congo. It drew its conclusions from a study conducted between May and July 2006 in which 1,849 households were visited in 47 selected areas across the country. Every household approached was asked to present death certificates or documentation as evidence for any family members said to have died since the end of 2001. In the vast majority of cases such proof was provided. From this the pre- and post-invasion mortality rates were calculated and this figure then extrapolated across the Iraqi population as a whole.

The Lancet survey concluded that it could say with 95 per cent confidence that between 392,979 and 942,636 Iraqis had died because of the war, giving a mean of 654,965, or 2.5 per cent of the entire population. Of those killed violently, 56 per cent died from gunshot wounds and 14 per cent due to car bombs and other explosions. Coalition forces were found responsible for 31 per cent of those who had died violently since the invasion.

These findings have been extensively criticised, not least because they were considerably higher than any other study, including those by the United Nations and the Iraqi Ministry of Health. Critics have questioned if the survey areas chosen were representative enough and the numbers questioned large enough. It was also queried how the study's conclusion that Iraq's pre-invasion mortality rate was less than Australia's could be credible, although its authors did subsequently argue that this was due to the relative youth of Iraq's overall population which meant proportionally there were fewer elderly people.

Les Roberts, the survey's head, defended the methodology saying it was 'tried and tested' and the 'best estimate of mortality we have'. It had, he said, been used by the US government in both Kosovo and Afghanistan. A number of epidemiologists and demographers did come out in his support, although just as many have challenged his findings.

When President Bush learned of the study he dismissed it, as did the Iraqi and UK governments. In late 2005 Bush estimated the number of Iraqis that had died at around thirty thousand. He argued that the 'six hundred thousand or whatever they guessed at' was 'just not credible'. When asked what he believed the correct number was, he did not respond with an exact figure but instead said that 'a lot of innocent people have lost their lives'.

In that, at least, he is correct. Although nobody knows for certain how many people have died because of the Iraq war, we do know unquestionably that there have been 'a lot' of them.

DONATION

Part of the profits from the sales of Red Zone will go to International PEN, the world writers' organization, which has been working to support and resettle Iraqi writers, translators and interpreters who have been threatened as a result of their work. A significant number of Iraqi writers and their families have been given asylum by the US government as a direct result of PEN'S support, among them Ahmed Ali.

With 145 centres in 104 countries, as well as consultative status at UNESCO and the United Nations, International PEN seeks to promote literature, defend freedom of expression and enable people worldwide to develop a love of reading and writing.

International PEN is a registered UK charity and welcomes support of its important work worldwide. Please send donations to:

International PEN, Brownlow House, 50 – 51 High Holborn, London WC1V 6ER; Tel (+44) 020 74050338.

ALSO FROM REPORTAGE

ARE WE THERE YET?
Travels with my frontline family
Rosie Whitehouse

This is a travel story with a difference. It's about what it's like to be married to a war reporter and to have one for a dad. It's about being five-years-old and wondering why Daddy's boots are covered with mud from a mass grave and who was in it. It's about criss-crossing frontlines in the family saloon car and telling the kids that they better not be rude to the man with a Kalashnikov.

Part of the profits from *Are We There Yet?* Go to the Rory Peck Trust

Paperback £8.99